The Economics of International Investment

The Economics of International Investment

Edited by

V.N. Balasubramanyam and David Sapsford
Department of Economics, University of Lancaster, UK

Edward Elgar

Published by
Edward Elgar Publishing Limited
Gower House
Croft Road
Aldershot
Hants GU11 3HR
England

Edward Elgar Publishing Company
Old Post Road
Brookfield
Vermont 05036
USA

British Library Cataloguing in Publication Data

Economics of International Investment
I. Balasubramanyam, V.N. II. Sapsford,
David
332.673

Library of Congress Cataloguing in Publication Data

The Economics of international investment / edited by V.N.
Balasubramanyam and David Sapsford.
p. cm.
Papers from the 17th Annual Conference of the UK International
Economics Study Group, held Sept. 11–13, 1992, at the University of Nottingham
Includes bibliographical references and index.
1. Investments. Foreign—Congresses. 2. International business
enterprises—Finance—Congresses. I. Balasubramanyam, V.N.
II. Sapsford, David. III. International Economics Study Group.
Conference (17th : 1992 : University of Nottingham)
HG4538.E32 1994
332.6'73—dc20 93–42474
CIP

ISBN 1 85278 889 5

Printed and bound in Great Britain by
Hartnolls Limited, Bodmin, Cornwall

Contents

Figures

Tables

Contributors

V.N. Balasubramanyam, Professor of Development Economics, Lancaster University.

M. Casson, Professor of Economics, University of Reading.

R.E. Caves, George Gund Professor of Economics and Business Administration, Harvard University.

J.B. Donges, Professor of Political Economy, University of Cologne.

Maxwell J. Fry, Tokai Professor of International Finance, University of Birmingham.

D. Greenaway, Professor of Economics, University of Nottingham.

H. Katrak, Reader in Economics, University of Surrey.

D.F. Lomax, Group Economic Advisor, National Westminster Bank, Plc.

T.C. Mills, Professor of Applied Economics, University of Hull.

C. Milner, Professor of Economics, University of Nottingham.

E. Pentecost, Lecturer in Economics, Loughborough University.

D. Sapsford, Professor of Economics, Lancaster University.

P.N. Snowden, Senior Lecturer in Economics, Lancaster University.

J. Wieners, Research Associate, University of Cologne.

G.E. Wood, Professor of Economics, City University Business School, London.

Discussants

G. Bird, Professor of Economics, University of Surrey.

J. Borkakoti, Principal Lecturer, University of Middlesex.

M. Casson, Professor of Economics, University of Reading.

Deepak Lal, Professor of Economics, University of California at Los Angeles.

P. Mizen, Lecturer in Economics, University of Nottingham.

R. Read, Lecturer in Economics, Lancaster University.

H. Scott, Lecturer in Economics, University of Birmingham.

L.A. Winters, Professor of Economics, University of Birmingham.

M. Wolf, *Financial Times*.

Preface

The chapters in this volume form the proceedings of the 17th Annual Conference of the UK International Economics Study Group held between 11 and 13 September 1992 at the University of Nottingham. The economics of international investment is a topic of wide appeal and analytical diversity and in putting together the programme for the Conference we were particularly concerned to invite a range of contributions which fully reflect this richness and diversity. As convenors of the conference we would like to express our gratitude to the contributors to the Conference – both the authors of the papers and their discussants – for responding so effectively and enthusiastically to our invitation to meet this challenge.

The economics of international investment is a rapidly developing field of enquiry. We hope that this volume will not only provide readers with an overview of the current 'state of the art' but also a useful platform from which future research may be launched.

V.N. Balasubramanyam and David Sapsford
Lancaster, 1993

Acknowledgements

We would like to thank Henry Scott for his help in organizing the Conference, David Greenaway for his support and encouragement and Penny Sallis for cheerfully putting up with our many demands for secretarial help. The IESG expresses its gratitude to the ESRC for financial support.

1. Introduction

V.N. Balasubramanyam and D. Sapsford

There is a copious and controversial literature on international investment. Yet another book on the subject requires justification. The sheer volume and rapid growth of international investment, especially since the early 1980s, provides one justification. Another is the change in the *dramatis personae.* Also the subject has matured in the sense that the concepts, theories and tools of analysis have been refined over the years and now provide an excellent framework for analysing recent issues posed by the growth and altered structure of international investment.

The *London Economist* puts the total value of the stock of all forms of international capital in the world economy at the end of the year 1991 at US $7 trillion. The total stock of foreign direct investment (FDI) alone stood at a prodigious $1.7 trillion at the end of the 1980s, with annual flows exceeding $200 billion throughout the decade. The volume of international production now exceeds the volume of international trade and the rate of growth of foreign direct investment, at 20 per cent per annum, exceeded the rate of growth of world trade, at 5 per cent per annum, during the mid- to late 1980s. The US, once a major net exporter of FDI, is now the leading net importer amongst the developed countries. And Japan, which was only a minor player in the 1960s and 1970s, with a negligible share of total FDI, now accounts for a sizeable 15 per cent of the total stock of FDI, and the annual average rate of growth of Japanese FDI abroad was as high as $22 billion per annum during the 1980s. Much of the FDI flows in recent years have been between the so-called triad – the US, the EC and Japan. Paralleling these developments is the decline in the share of the total flow of FDI going to developing countries, just when their need for such capital has increased for a combination of reasons, including the virtual drying up of bank credit, an aftermath of the debt problem. Another noteworthy feature in this context is the change in attitudes towards FDI and multinational enterprises, which could be described without exaggeration as a *volte-face,* on the part of several developing countries. The Indian government's approval of the establishment in India of McDonald's, the fast food chain, sums it all up.

Also the establishment of the European Single Market, with both its portent of increased barriers to imports into the Community and the promise of an enlarged and increasingly prosperous market with more than 300 million consumers, may have served to divert FDI flows from the developing countries to the Community.

Indeed, the growth of regionalism in Europe, and elsewhere, is likely to have a significant impact on the volume and pattern of FDI flows. The entry of the Eastern European countries into the market for FDI in a major way adds yet another dimension to the research on international investment. A further development of significance is the growth of international investment in the services sector, including banking, insurance and consultancy services. These developments have tossed up a number of issues for research, including the determinants of FDI, the interrelationship between regional groupings such as the EC and FDI and the implications of many of these developments for the theory of the multinational enterprise.

These and other issues constitute the subject matter of this volume, written by recognized experts in the relevant areas. Chapter 2, by David Lomax of the National Westminster Bank, written from the perspective of a businessman, sets the scene for the rest of the book with its exposition of developments in the market for foreign investment since the debt crisis, the role of market forces in shaping the efficient utilization of such investment and the compelling reasons for the international spread of the financial services industry. He also discusses succinctly the regulatory framework governing the operations of banks in the international markets and the impact of the information technology revolution on the banking business. Lomax's contribution, which aroused considerable discussion at the conference, sparked by the comments of Martin Wolf, the discussant on the paper, points to several avenues for further research.

One area of research which appears to have settled down to a steady state equilibrium relates to the *theory* of the multinational enterprise. The early, almost theological, debates on the virtues of, say, the theories grounded in the theory of the firm as opposed to those grounded in macroeconomic theory have now given way to a search for general propositions and empirical tests of the received theories. Mark Casson of Reading University, a leading exponent of the internalization theory, has done more than most to convince the sceptics of the theory of its scientific basis and its generality. Chapter 3 is yet another splendid exposition of the many-faceted nature of the internalization theory. The focus of Casson's discussion is the Scandinavian model of the export and foreign investment decision process of the firm. The Scandinavian thesis is that firms do not enter all available markets in one go but in a sequence, building upon the experience they gain in each market. Casson demonstrates that the Scandinavian thesis, far from rivalling the traditional theory of internalization, neatly complements it and adds to its explanatory power. One frequent criticism of the internalization approach to the explanation of the multinational enterprise it its assumption of rational behaviour on the part of managers, often construed to mean that managers do not make mistakes, and that such an unrealistic assumption robs the theory of realism. Casson argues that the assumption of rationality does not mean infallibility, but just that the mistakes managers make are predictable and the internalization strategy is designed to reduce the incidence of mistakes and not eliminate them. These and other propositions are demonstrated on the basis of an elegant model of the decision-making process of firms.

Homi Katrak provides a splendid example of recent research on foreign direct investment which skilfully utilizes industrial organization theory to analyse the welfare implications of foreign direct investment. Katrak utilizes a simple duopoly model of decision making, developed by Spencer and Brander, to analyse the welfare implications of the R&D activities of multinational enterprises in host countries. He demonstrates the circumstances in which such activity can enhance the welfare of host countries and the policies the host countries ought to pursue in their bid to reap the maximum possible advantages from such R&D. Apart from the many valuable policy lessons it provides, Chapter 4 is to be read for the careful crafting of the model, which progresses from the simple and the uncomplicated to the more realistic situations, with the exposition relying mainly on geometric techniques.

In Chapter 5, Caves and More analyse a much-neglected issue in the international investment literature – intrafirm transfers of intangible assets. As More and Caves note, such transfers, which include technology, goodwill and know-how are crucial to our understanding of the process of expansion and development of the multinational enterprise, as opposed to its origins. Utilizing data from the 1977 and 1982 benchmark surveys of US parent companies and their affiliates, the chapter analyses the variations in royalty payments between host countries and industry sectors received by US multinationals. The results of the exercise support the conjecture that royalty receipts do indicate the revenue-generating potential of intangibles and that royalty flows are not just a measure of transfer pricing practices. Also noteworthy is the finding that inter-industry variations in the growth of intrafirm royalties to some extent depend on differences in technology and other structural characteristics.

Milner and Pentecost investigate the determinants of US investment in the UK, utilizing data for the years 1989 and 1990 for a cross-section of 48 industry groups. The results of the exercise support the hypothesis that US investment tends to be relatively high in capital-intensive industry groups and in industry groups which face little competition from other domestic firms and imports. Market size, including access to the EC markets, however, appears to exercise a stronger influence on the decision of US firms to invest in the UK than does protection. Chapter 6 is to be read not only for its analysis of an issue high on the agenda of UK policy makers keen on attracting foreign investment, but also for its careful design of the statistical model and its ingenuity in quantifying several of the variables identified in the literature on determinants of FDI.

Balasubramanyam and Greenaway's chapter in some ways complements that of Milner and Pentecost. It analyses the determinants of FDI in the wider context of regionalism. Besides providing a succinct review of the interrelationship between FDI and regional integration it seeks to analyse the relative importance of protection afforded by the EC and the potential size of the Single Market in the observed rapid growth of East Asian FDI in the EC. This chapter echoes the conclusions of Milner and Pentecost concerning the importance of market size as opposed to protection as determinants of FDI. A feature of the chapter is its extensive discussion of the policies of the EC towards FDI and the need for policy reform.

Equally pressing is the issue of policy reform and, indeed, policy formulation in the Eastern European countries, with their urgent need for foreign capital and know-how. Donges and Wieners provide a detailed analytical review of the state of play on the issue of FDI in the Eastern European countries. Drawing upon the extensive literature on the costs and benefits of FDI and on the experience of other developing countries, they outline a set of valuable guidelines for policy makers in Eastern Europe. Their warning that FDI is not a panacea for the problem of underdevelopment, their advice that tax and other fiscal incentives for foreign investors should be used sparingly, if at all, and that protection against competition from imports should not be afforded are all timely. Donges and Wieners also warn the East European countries against xenophobic attitudes towards FDI, especially because of the intense competition for such investment from several other countries in the world economy.

In Chapter 9, Terry Mills and Geoff Wood consider an important and widely discussed contemporary issue: the influence which the exchange rate regime exerts upon international trade in general, and international capital flows in particular. This chapter uses current best practice statistical techniques to explore this important question, via an examination of the stochastic properties of five important UK macroeconomic time-series (output, prices, money, short- and long-term interest rates) since the mid-nineteenth century. Given that many of the present-day advocates of fixed exchange rates believe that they have invented the wheel with such policies, Mills and Wood's empirical work covering the experience of almost one and a half centuries is particularly welcome, not least because its findings underline the dangers of ignoring in current debate and policy the lessons of the past (including the gold standard). On the basis of an extremely thorough analysis of the properties of the time-series over almost 150 years, Mills and Wood conclude that the exchange rate regime in place is *not* a source of volatility for the main UK macroeconomic variables and that it does not affect either international trade or international capital movements. This is an extremely important finding which should be studied carefully by current advocates of fixed exchange rates. As Mills and Wood note, the fact that the exchange rate is pegged does not make macroeconomic shocks disappear; it simply causes them to impinge elsewhere in the economy! Policy makers please note.

The concluding chapters of the volume address issues relating to financial capital flows. In Chapter 10, Nick Snowden explores the ways in which privatization schemes may be utilized in order to reduce external debt overhang, whilst also encouraging capital repatriation. The closing chapter of the volume, by Max Fry, examines the apparently perverse (negative) correlation which exists between the saving and investment ratios in Malaysia. Casting his model within the framework of economic liberalization strategies in debtor countries, Nick Snowden explores the ways in which large-scale privatization programmes might be utilized simultaneously to reduce foreign indebtedness and encourage repatriation of flight capital. Using a portfolio approach, he provides a clear statement of the potential benefits arising from such programmes at the macroeconomic level. His analysis suggests that, despite possibly substantial gains, the observed reluctance of some governments to allow shares in privatized enterprises to be exchanged for outstanding debt may not be without foundation. The model set out in this chapter raises doubts about the effectiveness of debt–equity swaps as a means of achieving debt reduction and suggests that they may only be beneficial under the condition that the country in question is already anticipating more or less complete repayment of its external debt.

Max Fry's chapter begins with a review of the existing literature relating to the apparent relationship between savings and investment ratios across countries. The literature here invariably finds the existence of a strong positive correlation between these two ratios. However, as Fry points out, the time-series evidence for Malaysia appears to contradict received wisdom, for it reveals the presence of an inverse and statistically significant correlation. In order to investigate this inverse relationship, Fry estimates separate savings, investment and current account balance functions for Malaysia over the period 1971–91. This analysis pinpoints Malaysia's inverse saving–investment relationship as first appearing with the upsurge in FDI in the early 1980s and detects two main causes for its occurrence. First, the increase in the level of public sector investment which occurred as a consequence of the expansionary fiscal policies of the early 1980s and, second, the government's enthusiasm for, and encouragement of, foreign direct investment. According to Fry, the latter factor exerted, simultaneously, a negative influence on the national savings ratio and a positive influence on the domestic investment ratio.

We noted in the preface that the economics of international investment is an area rich in terms of both the diversity of its subject matter and the analytical approaches adopted. We believe that the contributions in this volume add to this richness.

2. International investment: a business perspective

D.F. Lomax

1 INTRODUCTION

Businessmen lead lives of considerable uncertainty. The definition of economics (making the best use of scarce resources) is extremely apposite to their behaviour. Most companies would be happy to have more capital, more and stronger management, and greater knowledge about their business and about the environment. There is inevitably a fog of uncertainty about changes in the market-place, the nature of the business and the key strategic factors.

Such uncertainty affects all investment decisions. It is likely to be even greater in relation to investment abroad, where distance, different cultural factors and different market conditions are likely to increase the risk. The international dimension of many businesses is fraught with uncertainty, and so needs strong justification. The statistics show that many companies have overcome these inhibitions, and the total of multinational investment is, indeed, massive. The banking industry also has taken part in this international expansion.

2 INTERNATIONAL CAPITAL FLOWS

In one distinct area the banks became involved in international capital flows, to their later regret, through what became the developing country debt crisis. The money the banks lent was a substitute for other capital flows. The countries were mainly credit-worthy through the 1970s, but could not withstand the second oil shock and the recession of the early 1980s. The countries became highly leveraged because of their reliance upon interest-bearing debt rather than on more flexible equity. The banks were being asked to make up for other inadequacies in policy. It was precisely because countries were inefficient, with bad fiscal structures, protected markets and a wide range of controls over international and domestic trade, that they needed to borrow from the banks. It was precisely because they were badly structured that they could not cope with the debt they took on.

The difference in policy structure is shown clearly by figures for 1984–8 regarding growth, inflation and export growth in a group of Latin American countries and in some faster growing Asian countries. Latin American inflation averaged 195.2 per cent per annum, compared with 4.5 per cent in Asia. Latin American growth averaged 2.1 per cent per annum, compared with 6.3 per cent in Asia. Latin American export growth averaged 5.6 per cent per annum, compared with 13.8 per cent in Asia. The contrast could not be starker. One of the clear lessons of the past couple of decades is that the market system works best in achieving worldwide economic growth, among the developing countries as elsewhere.

We saw from the developing country debt crisis the very sharp contrast in performance between Latin American countries, on the one hand, and Asian, on the other. The protectionist, import-substituting economies of Latin America failed abysmally. These countries have now learned the lesson, both from their own experience and from that of South East Asia. There has been a major intellectual revolution in South America. This has been very marked in Chile and Mexico and, in slightly different ways, in Argentina and Brazil. The continent will not be repelling foreign investment as hard as it can, but will be welcoming it. Indeed, its welcome to foreign investment may in some ways be greater than that in South East Asia. In Asia the countries use the markets, but some appear to use a kind of directed state capitalism, building up national champions, with extremely strict control in some cases over inward investment.

The most recent figures show a resurgence of foreign direct investment in Latin America, with a figure of about $14 billion for 1991, compared with only $7 billion as recently as 1989. The trend has been significantly upwards, particularly in Mexico. The changed attitude of the developing world to inward investment is extremely welcome, and very beneficial from their point of view. Many factors and many institutions have contributed to this change of view. The International Finance Corporation (IFC) should not be ignored. It is doing a vast amount of work trying to build up financial service structures in developing countries. Efficient and ethical intermediation is a highly valuable part of the development process. Let us hope that work in that direction continues successfully.

3 INTERNATIONAL REGULATION

The financial services industry is also being brought into the international regulatory net in a way novel to it, but one which has been familiar to other industries for some time. Financial services are for the first time coming under the General Agreement on Tariffs and Trade (GATT) umbrella as part of the Uruguay Round negotiations. The aim of the financial services industry is to achieve full liberalization among the Organization for Economic Cooperation and Development (OECD) countries and to have significant liberalization among the key newly industrializing countries, a policy in which Europe has the strong support of the US. Negotiations are undertaken by the European Commission on behalf of the entire European services industry, including banking. Because of the nature of services, achieving access to the market in another country may require investment, so freedom to invest is one of the crucial elements in the negotiations.

These negotiations are still in progress. We have had strong support from the Commission, and we have close relations with them. Ultimately what emerges will be the best they can achieve, and we are confident that they will do their utmost to obtain a satisfactory outcome. There are potential difficulties: Canada appears to be at present by far the least liberal of the OECD countries; and many newly industrializing countries appear reluctant to make substantial initial steps towards liberalization. A further nuance relates to the North American Free Trade Area. We welcome the United States/Canada Free Trade Area and the formation of NAFTA, which also includes Mexico. We have not yet seen the definitive legal text of the NAFTA agreement, but as we understand the situation some interesting issues of equity and of commerce may well arise.

In Europe, with the passage of the directives relating to banking and the securities industry, any legally established institution in Europe will be able to operate throughout the Community on the basis of an authority from one particular European state. Thus, any bank or securities house legally established in the UK will have the right to operate throughout Europe. It would also have the right effectively to operate in the surrounding countries associated with the Community. Many of those countries have liberal rules anyway, and in any case the rules of the association agreement would almost certainly provide that particular right. Thus, once Citicorp has a subsidiary anywhere in Europe, that subsidiary may expand throughout Europe in the fields for which it was authorized in its European domicile.

In the case of Canada, however, rights in the Canadian market depend, not on the legal establishment of outside banks, but on their ultimate ownership. For example, Canada has at present a quota system on shares of its deposit market. US-*owned* banks (not just banks *legally established* in the US) are outside those quota requirements. But any European bank, whether operating through a subsidiary established legally in the US, or through its parent, would be bound by those quota limitations.

Under NAFTA, Mexico is establishing a similar privileged quota for North American banks and securities houses, but we do not yet know whether this will be based on a similar test of ultimate ownership or of legal domicile. Nor do we know whether there will be a separate allowance for non-North American banks, including Far Eastern and European. Mexico plans to liberalize its financial markets at a controlled pace, which seems reasonable to us. It is quite possible that NAFTA concepts will spread elsewhere in Latin America as other Latin American countries liberalize and join similar free trade areas. It is equally likely, indeed this has been mentioned by the Canadian Prime Minister, that such countries would be pressed to accept similar concepts to those in NAFTA. In other words, the issue of access to markets based on ultimate ownership or of legal domicile could spread throughout Latin America.

As far as Mexico is concerned, the European banks have no intention of trying to swamp the market. All they seek is a foot in the door and a chance of obtaining reasonable access to the market, together with the opportunity of participating in its expansion. Mexico itself has no desire to be swamped by capital from the rest of North America. It is extremely desirous of having capital, including direct investment, from Europe, and it certainly wishes to keep its financial windows open to the rest of the world, including the Far East and Europe. One would therefore hope that a reasoned compromise, a meeting of minds, is possible over this matter. We certainly think that the Canadian-style rules of origins are completely unreasonable, and we should not like to see that concept spread elsewhere.

4 INTERNATIONAL INVESTMENT AND RISK

Looking at business in theoretical terms, the aim should be the maximization of the share price through obtaining the highest possible earnings, taking into account risk. One of the motivations for international investment is the desire to reduce risk through diversification. This may be the result of a conscious decision that excessive concentration in one market is too risky, particularly if that market is thought to be weak. A company could therefore decide to invest in a variety of countries simply to obtain geographic diversification. This could be forced upon a company if it had simply outgrown its own original national market. A variant of this is seen where the company decides to expand its product range, as well as spreading geographically, so as to obtain a greater market diversification. This could imply either a search for income or a search for lower volatility of earning streams.

Of course some investors will ask what the management of a company thinks it is doing behaving in that way: if investors wanted to diversify in North America they would buy there themselves, rather than have a UK company do it for them. Be that as it may, companies do diversify. Boards of directors do see benefit in a more stable earning stream if that can be achieved. As far as banks are concerned, the quality and diversification of the risk portfolio is a crucial aspect of good management. Obtaining a more diversified income stream, providing the underlying quality does not deteriorate, whether through geographic spread or product diversification, thus provides a genuine strengthening of a financial institution. For large institutions, achieving such diversification will almost certainly require some international diversification.

The capital of a bank is the ultimate last resort in case it should hit hard commercial times. A bank is sounder, the more diversified the portfolio which impinges upon a particular base. A bank is thus genuinely stronger if its given capital ratio supports a diversified rather than a more concentrated portfolio. This feature also affects the strategy of a bank in relationship to capital and earnings. Of course, banks wish to maximize their earnings per share, as do other companies. But banks have to maintain a minimum capital ratio in relation to their weighted risk assets, as defined in the relevant Basle agreement. They also wish to have capital above the minimum ratio, partly as a symbol of strength and security. A bank's capital will grow naturally with retained earnings in good years. A bank could always increase its earnings per share by handing back capital to the shareholders and reducing its capital to the minimum ratio.

But for a bank deliberately to weaken its capital would be regarded as unsound, since it would weaken the bank's risk control structure. Thus banks tend to try to maximize the income on their existing capital and on their capital as it grows over time. This mentality, justified by the nature of banking in terms of regulatory requirements and of risk, militates against efforts to reduce the capital employed or to split it.

Alan Greenspan, Chairman of Federal Reserve, has an interesting indicator of the way international trade integrates countries. His example is that the weight to value ratio of traded goods declines steadily over time, and in particular in relation to goods traded in domestic markets. International trade is increasingly in high-value, low-weight (or low-volume) goods and not in bricks or glass, or such items. This trend may be discerned clearly over time.

5 MONEY AS INFORMATION

As far as banking is concerned, money is information, and nothing weighs less or occupies less volume than a message going through telephone wire or up to a satellite. International finance is thus one of the industries most ready for international integration, as indeed we have seen. In areas where controls have come off, such as within Europe through the abolition of exchange controls, the wholesale financial markets became integrated extremely rapidly. Customer pressure enforces common prices, and standards of service and of costs. There may remain some barriers to investment through the regulatory process, but, where markets become integrated, in effect transnational, then companies move readily to operate throughout the market-place. If the competitive strategy of institutions requires defending their own market and also trying to penetrate the markets of their competitors, then it is natural for companies to spread throughout a particular market-place, irrespective of where national boundaries lie.

In Europe this integration applies to the wholesale markets, increasingly to investment management and to venture capital, and also to payments services. In financial services, regulatory factors remain important in determining where economic activity takes place. Both Japanese and US banks may undertake business in Europe which is forbidden in their home markets. In some cases international investment may be linked to cost factors and efficiency of production. In others it may be concerned with access to customers, as with the BA/US Air linkage. Access to resources may be crucial. Providing a service may require investment abroad, such as providing a network for payments, air transport or shipping.

Government intervention is much more important in many markets. The Uruguay Round is bringing financial services under the jurisdiction of trade legislation. This puts greater emphasis on being able to capture political benefits or at least avoid being done down by the regulatory process.

6 WHY INVEST ABROAD?

I have just received some unpublished work based on questions put to a sample of banks about the reasons for investment abroad. Since it has not yet been published I cannot reveal the sources, but it provides a clear indication of some of the factors which affect bank thinking and behaviour on such matters.

Over the past decade there has been an increase in the number of bank subsidiaries and joint ventures in their own country and abroad, including developed countries. But there was a marked difference between US banks, which have if anything been retracting into their own country, and at the opposite extreme Japanese banks, which have been expanding rapidly. The main reason for this has been the capital constraint on US banks, stemming both from losses and from a weak dollar. However, Japanese banks were not constrained by capital ratios until the Basle agreements came into force, and in any case were regarded as adequately endowed.

Looking to the future, there was agreement that banks would have more affiliates in developing countries, but mixed views as to whether the number of affiliates would increase or decrease both at home and in other industrialized countries. Again, the response partly reflects the nationality of the bank concerned. This issue relates to the forces for centralization and decentralization. Major banks divide their business into wholesale and retail sectors. Providing a better service to existing international customers was a strong reason, as regards wholesale business, for moving abroad, whereas it was irrelevant as regards retail business. The other arguments quoted for moving abroad were to obtain market share, strategic positioning (whatever that means), or the only means of providing a particular service. The view was also expressed that going abroad may be necessary to establish the critical mass as an international bank. A bank operating in just one country is not really a heavyweight bank. Is that true? Diversification of profit streams was also implied, as, more relevantly, was the importance of regulatory constraints.

Having opened an affiliate, the question arises as to the circumstances under which it should be closed. The most common reason for doing so was that it was not profitable. It is not always easy to compete in somebody else's home patch. A foreign bank may be less well informed and it certainly lacks much in the way of the size and resources which a domestic bank would have. Another significant reason for closure of an affiliate is that the customers abroad can be reached, given modern telecommunications, directly from the home base. One can avoid the cost of establishing abroad simply by laying in a few dedicated telephone lines. Some banks closed their own affiliates by forming alliances or cooperating with foreign banks. The opening up of Europe through looking towards European monetary union (EMU) and the creation of the Single Market has raised the question of whether alliances or going it alone are the best way of proceeding.

When we look at the importance of information technology there are clear views regarding two key issues. A strong majority think that offices abroad will increasingly report directly to head office, eliminating intermediary reporting relationships. Treasury data may be reported immediately to a home base through modern technology. Banks may have one worldwide information technology (IT) network for their trading business. Communication has great relevance to the issue of control. Since banking is very much a risk business, control of risks, whether credit or market, is crucial. Improved IT makes it possible to do this both more cheaply and effectively through stronger links to the centre.

There is a firm view that cross-border trade will have a role to play as regards wholesale business, although foreign direct investment might prevail. But for retail business only, foreign direct investment is a means of reaching the market-place. Likewise, mainly for the IT reasons, a strong majority think that centralization of control will be the key in dealing with corporate customers worldwide, whereas a corresponding majority think that decentralization will be the key as regards dealing with retail customers. Wholesale business is more technical and culturally neutral, with costs and revenue determining how business is done, but in retail business, cultural aspects and the general feel for the market-place are more important.

A further feature of banking, which is perhaps not strictly linked to investment abroad as such, is that the industry is ripe for deconstruction, disintegration or fragmentation, whichever is the technical term. Many of the services which banks traditionally provide for themselves, like processing, will be contracted out to specialist firms. This will increasingly be done on a multinational basis, with some companies and banks offering those services in many countries. Banks could thus conceivably lose some of their own value added to companies at present operating outside the financial services industry.

7 CONCLUSIONS

In conclusion, the expansion of financial markets has made an international presence almost a matter of course for many financial institutions. Many large institutions have simply outgrown their home market and would find it an extremely artificial constraint if they were to be confined to one country. An area where banks and securities houses have no choice but to confront the issue of multinational competition relates to Europe. The Single European Market programme is making most markets far more competitive. Other major institutions may attack one's home market. Markets may be given the choice of liberalizing or simply losing all their business. The first strategy which most institutions seem to have adopted is to maintain their position in their home market: if that is lost, then all is gone. But the strategy for approaching other markets varies greatly. Some institutions may be able to go it alone, but only the largest and the strongest are likely to be able to do so. Other institutions are forming alliances, to economize on capital and perhaps to allow the partners to concentrate on different markets. Some smaller institutions have formed networks intended to provide a better service for their customers throughout Europe. Other institutions may form alliances for the provisions of particular services, but may take the alliance concept no further.

These differing strategies are responses to the genuine intensification of competition which will enable a service to be provided for the cost of fewer real resources and at the same time will enhance the choice open to customers. We in business are driven by the pressures of the market-place, whose course we perceive dimly. But if our flounderings lead to more efficient use of resources and to better consumer choice then perhaps we have done our bit for progress.

3. Internationalization as a learning process: a model of corporate growth and geographical diversification

M. Casson*

1 INTRODUCTION

Scandinavian literature on the internationalization strategy of the firm emphasizes the incremental and sequential nature of both the export process and the foreign direct investment process (see, for example, Johanson and Vahlne, 1977; Strandskov, 1986). Firms acquire experience of one foreign market before entering the next: they do not enter all major markets at the outset. In this way they benefit from the lessons learnt in the early stages of expansion and avoid making too many big mistakes.

There are two other theories, however – namely internalization and globalization – which seem to imply that, on the contrary, firms will internationalize in a single discrete step involving simultaneous entry into all markets. This conflict between the theories is more apparent than real, however. This chapter shows that the theory of organizational learning implicit in the Scandinavian approach in fact complements these other approaches, by highlighting factors which they omit. A formal model is presented which clarifies these complementarities and so enriches all three areas of theory.

It turns out that this model includes, as a special case, an international analogue of Penrose's (1959) theory of the growth of the firm. This is because it embodies, in addition to Scandinavian insights, one of Penrose's key ideas, namely that it is prohibitively costly for any team of managers to diversify in several directions at once. It touches on an even more fundamental issue, too: the scope of the rational actor model in analysing managerial behaviour. It is widely believed that rational action implies that managers do not make mistakes. It is claimed that, in consequence, behavioural models of learning may provide a better account of managerial behaviour than does the rational action approach.

* I am grateful to John Cantwell, Jeanette Capel and Tony Corley for comments on an earlier draft of this chapter.

This argument ignores the possibility that rational managers will take account of information costs, however. The model presented here shows that, when information is costly, rational managers will make mistakes because the optimal frequency of mistakes is greater than zero. Because the model assumes rationality it can actually predict the kind of mistakes that will be made and the frequency with which they will occur. It shows that the entire internationalization strategy of the firm can be interpreted as a strategy designed to reduce, but not eliminate, the incidence of mistakes in individual market entry strategies. This illustrates one of the main strengths of the rational action approach: it facilitates simple mathematical modelling which not only captures existing insights in parsimonious terms, but deepens these insights and reveals new ones as well.

Section 2 outlines a basic model in which the acquisition of information about a market generates a set-up cost of entry. This set-up cost can only be avoided if the firm has encountered a similar market before. In Section 2 the similarity of foreign markets arises only from coincidence, while in Section 3 it is attributed to a systematic correlation between their characteristics. It is shown that the sequential approach to internationalization hinges on the exploitation of systematic similarities between markets. It is because of such similarity that experience acquired in one market is of potential relevance to another. If foreign markets were all totally different from each other, nothing learnt in one market would have any significance for another.

In the basic model the firm is committed at the outset to entering a given set of foreign markets and the only question concerns the timing of the entry into each. Section 4 allows the firm to choose whether it enters certain markets at all. It is shown that a sequential strategy that defers decisions about the second market until the first has been entered provides an option value which strengthens the case for sequential entry when some markets are only marginally profitable.

Although the basic model explains sequential entry, it is not a pure model of learning by experience. This is because the model assumes that each market is investigated before the local marketing strategy is determined. Under purely experiential learning the market would be entered without systematic investigation and learning would result from responding to mistakes. Section 5 analyses this alternative experiential approach. It is shown that, contrary to common opinion, learning by experience has little direct connection with whether entry is sequential or not. It is shown that the decision to learn by experience depends first and foremost on the confidence of the management, and on the costliness of mistakes, and only peripherally on the issue of sequential entry.

The possibility that firms can make mistakes applies not only to strategy within a given market but to the overall choice of internationalization strategy too. Section 6 considers how the quality of management governs the incidence of mistakes and thereby affects the overall performance of the internationalizing firm.

Section 7 reappraises the relationship between the Scandinavian theory of internationalization and other theories about the multinational firm. Section 8 considers the wider implications and offers some suggestions for further research.

2 SEQUENTIAL VERSUS SIMULTANEOUS INTERNATIONALIZATION

The choice between sequential and simultaneous internationalization is governed by the trade-off between exploiting economies of scope in knowledge (which are maximized by a sequential strategy) and the gains from exploiting profitable market opportunities without delay (which are maximized by a simultaneous strategy).

Dimensions and Structure

The model involves three national markets, indexed $m = 1, 2, 3$. There are two firms, one domiciled in market 1 and the other in market 2. Market 3 is a third-country market in which both firms compete. In the first stage of the analysis only firm 1 is considered and competition with firm 2 is ignored.

Each market can, in principle, be in one of two states, $s_m = 1, 2$. The state of a market is an abstract way of describing the pattern of demand, as governed by local tastes, population, income, relative prices and so on. Each market has the same probability $z (0 \leq z \leq 1)$ of being in state 2, independently of the state of any other market. Since the two states are mutually exclusive and collectively exhaustive, the probability of state 1 is $1 - z$. Marketing strategy involves deciding which of two varieties $x_m = 1, 2$ of a generic product should be launched in each market. Successful entry involves matching product variety to the state of the market. The states are labelled so that in each market, strategy 1 is the best response to state 1, and strategy 2 to state 2. Successful matches achieve the same profits independently of what state prevails.

It is assumed that the process of internationalization must be completed within two periods. This means that there are just three internationalization strategies that need to be considered: for the firm based in country 1 they are (1) enter both foreign markets in period 1; (2) enter market 2 in period 1 and market 3 in period 2; and (3) enter market 3 in period 1 and market 2 in period 2. Strategy 1 is the simultaneous entry strategy and strategies 2 and 3 are two permutations of the sequential one. In addition, there is the null strategy (strategy 0) of staying at home, and also the strategy of deferring simultaneous entry until period 2. The latter strategy does not need to be considered in detail, for with a positive rate of discount (see below), strategy 1 always dominates it when strategy 1 is profitable, whilst strategy 0 dominates it if strategy 1 makes a loss.

Incomplete internationalization strategies, which involve entering one foreign market but not the other, are considered in section 4.

Two Varieties of Uncertainty

There are two varieties of uncertainty in the model, and it is this property which is responsible for some of the model's most distinctive features. The first variety of uncertainty – uncertainty about the state of the market, as described above – can be overcome at a cost. It is this cost that determines how many marketing errors will be made. The second variety of uncertainty pertains to this cost. It is this type of uncertainty which is particularly important for the choice of internationalization strategy. For the cost of determining the state of the market depends on the market type. If the type is familiar, in the sense that it has been encountered before, then the cost is zero, but if the market is unfamiliar then the cost is high. The uncertainty arises because management does not know in advance which market is of which type. The type of a market is an abstract way of describing its institutional framework: in particular, the customs of the society in which it is embedded. There are three types of market: $n = 1, 2, 3$. By convention market 1 is of type 1 and market 2 of type 2.

Psychic Distance

At the time the internationalization strategy is chosen the firm knows only the type of its home market. The type of a foreign market cannot be discovered until it is entered because it is impossible to investigate a market from a distance. Management must therefore take a view beforehand on whether the market will be familiar or not. Management believes that market 2 is likely to be of a different type from market 1 (its home market) with probability q_2. It believes that market 3 will be different from market 1 with probability q_3. These probabilities may be interpreted as subjective assessments of psychic distance, in the sense that they capture the expected degree of unfamiliarity of the foreign market relative to the home one.

The types of the foreign markets, as well as their states, are independent of each other. Thus the probability that market 2 is of type 3, p_2, is independent of whether market 3 is known to be of some particular type. The probability p_2 is defined as a conditional probability, given that market 3 is definitely not of type 1. Similarly the conditional probability that market 3 is of type 2, p_3, is independent of the type of market 2. Multiplying these probabilities together determines the probability that any given market is of any given type. The subjective probabilities of firm 1 are summarized in Table 3.1.

The fact the management is uncertain, not only about the state of each market, but also about its type, reflects the radical uncertainty under which management operates, according to the Scandinavian view. Uncertainty about the state calls for the investigation of unfamiliar markets, whilst uncertainty about the type means that the management is uncertain at the time of entry whether the investigation will be costly or not.

Entry Costs and the Speed of Learning

If the management discovers that it has no previous experience with the type of market it has entered then it must either incur expenditure to discover the state of the market or act upon conjecture about the state; there is no opportunity to withdraw. The irreversibility of entry is crucial in linking the process of learning to the process of entry. It means that a commitment to the market is necessary before learning can occur. Investigation incurs costs but avoids mistakes in the choice of marketing strategy, whereas conjecture avoids these costs but risks mistakes instead. It is assumed to begin with that investigation is always the preferred option; the alternative is analysed in Section 5.

Table 3.1 Probability that a given market is of a given type, as perceived by firm 1 at the commencement of internationalization

	Type			
Market	*1*	*2*	*3*	*Total*
1	1	0	0	1
2	$1-q_2$	$q_2(1-p_2)$	q_2p_2	1
3	$1-q_3$	q_3p_3	$q_3(1-p_3)$	1

Under simultaneous entry it is possible that two unfamiliar markets of the same type could be entered at the same time. But under simultaneous entry no economies of scope are available from the fact that both markets are of the same type (and may even be in the same state). This is because information takes time to communicate – experience can only be used when it has been acquired in a previous period. Only sequential entry affords economies of scope.

Although simultaneous investigation affords no economies of scope, it is possible for simultaneity to exploit economies of scale arising from indivisible resources. The same specialist, for example, may be employed on both investigations, although he could not easily be employed part-time on one investigation in each period. This is essentially a long-run economy that may accrue to a large management team. If the size of the management team is small, however, then short-run diseconomies may outweigh this factor. Simultaneous investigation may overstretch the management team, and it may be difficult to recruit and integrate new managers in sufficient time (Penrose, 1959). If short-run costs outweigh long-run scale economies then simultaneous investigation of two markets will cost more than twice a single investigation undertaken as part of a sequential strategy.

It is assumed that the cost of a single investigation of an unfamiliar market is $c_0 > 0$ and that the net penalty incurred by simultaneous investigation is f, which may be positive or negative depending upon whether short-run or long-run factors dominate. It is assumed that the cost of investigation is the same for all markets, and for both firms, and is independent of the type of the market and the actual state that the market is in. Although knowledge acquired through investigation affords scope economies, it cannot be communicated freely. There is a marginal cost of communication between headquarters and subsidiary $c_1 \geq 0$ and a marginal cost of communication between one subsidiary and another $c_2 \geq c_1$. To capture the public good property of information, it is assumed that communication is cheaper than rediscovery through repeat investigation: $c_1, c_2 < c_0$.

Operating Profitability

A conventional but highly simplified analysis of foreign market sourcing strategy implies that profit in each foreign market varies with both the size of the market, $a_m > 0$, and the timing of entry $t_m = 1, 2$ ($m = 2, 3$). It also depends on whether mistakes are made in marketing strategy, and how quickly they are corrected.

The firm has a monopoly of a generic product demanded by a fixed number of consumers in each market, each of whom purchases one unit at a given reservation price. This price must be discounted by $d_1 \geq 0$, however, if the firm defers its entry to the second period, because the threat of imitation is greater. If the firm offers the wrong variety then a further discount must be offered, but only for one period until it corrects its mistake. If the second variety is offered by mistake when the market is in state 1 then the discount is $d_{21} \geq 0$, while if the first variety is offered in state 2 then the discount is $d_{22} \geq 0$.

The market can be sourced either by local production in a wholly owned plant – the FDI option – or by export from the home country. Transaction costs prohibit licensing or franchising, it is assumed. FDI incurs a recurrent fixed cost of local production, and a constant marginal cost, whilst exporting incurs no fixed costs but higher marginal costs, comprising home production costs, transport costs and tariffs. Given that market size is constant after entry, the sourcing strategy is independent of marketing strategy. The convention is used that market 2 is larger than market 3 by a factor $\Delta a = a_2 - a_3 > 0$. If the average fixed cost of FDI is less than the net savings in production costs, transport costs and tariffs then FDI is preferred to exporting; otherwise exporting is preferred. Thus large, remote and heavily protected markets with cheap labour will be sourced by FDI.

Small neighbouring open markets with expensive labour will be sourced by exports instead.

Under these conditions the minimum cost of sourcing the market is independent of marketing strategy. Thus profit variations are revenue-driven rather than cost-driven. When investigations are carried out, so that no mistakes are made, the profit generated in market m from period t_m onwards is

$$\pi_m = \pi_m{}^* - a_m d_1(t_m - 1) \tag{3.1}$$

where $\pi_m{}^*$ is the maximum profit that can be generated in market m by entry in period l. It is assumed that market 2 is not only the larger foreign market but the more profitable one too, having an advantage $\Delta\pi^* = \pi_2{}^* - \pi_3{}^* > 0$.

With a time preference factor $i > 0$, and each market in a steady state after entry, the present value of the profit stream at the date of entry t_m is

$$v_m = \pi_m / r \tag{3.2}$$

where $r = i/(i + 1)$.

If no investigation is carried out and a mistake is made then, as explained in Section 5, a loss is incurred in the entry period which varies according to the state. This gives a revised valuation of market entry

$$\tilde{v}_m = \begin{cases} v_m - a_m d_{21} & \text{if } x_m = 2, s_m = 1 \\ v_m - a_m d_{22} & \text{if } x_m = 1, s_m = 2 \end{cases} \tag{3.3}$$

Solution of the Model

The owners of each firm are risk-neutral. Management's objective is to maximize expected net present value (ENPV) by selecting the appropriate strategy of internationalization. The ENPV is calculated by identifying the probability of each configuration of market types the firm may encounter, and determining for each strategy the sequence of operating profits and information costs associated with each type. Information costs comprise the investigation costs and communication costs described above. The ENPVs of the three different strategies are then compared, and predictions are derived from the inequalities between them.

The firm has two foreign markets to enter and each market can be of one of three types. This gives the $3 \times 3 = 9$ possible configurations of the foreign market system itemized in the left-hand columns of Table 3.2. The nine configurations fall neatly into four pairs plus a single case. The single case (number 1 in the table) involves no learning because both foreign markets are of the same type as the home one. In the first two pairs, one of the markets is similar to the home market but the other is not. In the first pair, market 2 is similar and in the second pair, market 3. In the third pair both markets are different both from the home market and from each other, whilst in the final pair both markets differ from the home market but are the same as each other. The probabilities of each of the nine configurations are also shown; they are derived by multiplying together appropriate pairs of the elements in Table 3.1. The probability of the four pairs are also shown; they are obtained by simple addition of the probabilities of their constituent elements.

Table 3.2 Derivation of expected information costs associated with each strategy

Permutation Ref	Type of market 2	Type of market 3	Probability: Configurations	Probability: Groups	Strategy 1 Period 1	Strategy 1 Period 2	Strategy 2 Period 1	Strategy 2 Period 2	Strategy 3 Period 1	Strategy 3 Period 2
1	1	1	$(1-q_2)(1-q_3)$		$2c_1$	0	c_1	c_1	c_1	c_1
2	1	2	$(1-q_2)q_3p_3$	$(1-q_2)q_3$	c_0+c_1	0	c_1	c_0	c_0	c_1
3	1	3	$(1-q_2)q_3(1-p_3)$							
4	2	1	$(1-q_3)q_2(1-p_2)$	$(1-q_3)q_2$	c_0+c_1	0	c_0	c_1	c_1	c_0
5	3	1	$(1-q_3)q_2p_2$							
6	2	3	$q_2q_3(1-p_2)(1-p_3)$	$q_2q_3(1-p_2-p_3+2p_2p_3)$	$2c_0+f$	0	c_0	c_0	c_0	c_0
7	3	2	$q_2q_3p_2p_3$							
8	2	2	$q_2q_3(1-p_2)p_3$	$q_2q_3(p_2+p_3-2p_2p_3)$	$2c_0+f$	0	c_0	c_2	c_0	c_2
9	3	3	$q_2q_3p_2(1-p_3)$							

The time paths of investigation and communication costs associated with each strategy are shown in the right-hand portion of Table 3.2. Notice how both investigation costs and communication costs are deferred under the sequential strategies 2 and 3. The most significant point, however, is that investigation costs are halved when both foreign markets turn out to be of the same unfamiliar type (see the bottom two lines of the table). This is because simultaneous investigation does not permit the same flow of knowledge between markets that sequential investigation does. Sequential investigation does, however, incur communication costs between subsidiaries, which may be quite substantial (that is, c_2 may be large) if communication has to be mediated by headquarters.

The present values of investigation costs and communication costs are summarized in Table 3.3. The values of the sequential strategies 2 and 3 differ from the value of the simultaneous strategy 1 in only two respects. The first arises because entry into one of the markets is deferred, so that the information costs associated with the entry are deferred as well. The gain from deferral differs between the two strategies whenever one of the markets is more likely to be different from the home market than is the other. The gain is maximized by entering the market which is most similar to the home market first. The second difference arises from the fact that, when both the foreign markets are similar, but different from the home one, duplication of investigation is avoided under the sequential strategies. This gain is the same for both the strategies. The value of the gain is discounted, however, because it is generated only in the second period.

Where the profit streams are concerned, the simultaneous and sequential strategies again differ in two main respects. The first respect is that deferring entry under the sequential strategies defers the start of one of the profit streams. The implications of deferral are different for the two sequential strategies, just as they were in the case of the information costs. In the context of profits, deferral is a disadvantage of the sequential approach; the disadvantage is minimized by entering the most profitable market first. By the convention established earlier, this is market 2. The second consideration is that the sequential strategies also jeopardize the advantage of pre-emption in the market that is entered last. This is potentially large because it is recurrent – unlike the one-off loss of profit caused by deferral – and therefore needs to be capitalized.

Subtracting the information costs shown in Table 3.3 from the operating profits determines the ENPVs of the three strategies e_1, e_2, e_3. The results are summarized in Table 3.4. To obtain predictions it is useful to express the results in terms of comparisons between alternative strategies. The first line of the table compares the simultaneous strategy with the null strategy of remaining a domestic firm. Since the null strategy yields a null reward, the relevant expression is simply the ENPV of strategy 1. This expression shows that internationalization is more likely to be undertaken the more optimistic is the management that foreign markets will be of a favourable type, as indicated by low values for q_2, q_3 and p_2, and a high value for p_3. It is particularly advantageous that the foreign markets should be of the same type as the home market – that is, q_2 and q_3 are low – so that home market experience can be used to avoid the costs of investigation abroad. It is also advantageous, naturally, that both investigation costs, c_0, and communication costs, c_1, should be low. The former is particularly important when the foreign markets are likely to be different from the home market, and the latter when they are likely to be the same.

Table 3.3 Present values of the information costs associated with each strategy

	Costs		
Strategy	*Period 1*	*Period 2*	*Present value of costs*
1	$(q_2+q_3)c_0 + (2-q_2-q_3)c_1 + q_2q_3f$	0	$(q_2+q_3)c_0 + (2-q_2-q_3)c_1 + q_2q_3f$
2	$q_2c_0 + (1-q_2)c_1$	$q_3(1-q_2b)c_0 + (1-q_3)c_1 + q_2q_3bc_2$	$(q_2+q_3)c_0 + (2-q_2-q_3)c_1 - r(q_3c_0 + (1-q_3)c_1) - (1-r)q_2q_3b(c_0-c_2)$
3	$q_3c_0 + (1-q_3)c_1$	$q_2(1-q_3b)c_0 + (1-q_2)c_1 + q_2q_3bc_2$	$(q_2+q_3)c_0 + (2-q_2-q_3)c_1 - r(q_2c_0 + (1-q_2)c_1) - (1-r)q_2q_3b(c_0-c_2)$

Note: $b = (1-p_2)p_3 + (1-p_3)p_2 = p_2 + p_3 - 2p_2p_3$. The value of b is a maximum when both markets are likely to be in the same state, i.e. $p_2 = 0, p_3 = 1$, or $p_2 = 1, p_3 = 0$ and is a minimum when they are likely to be in different states, i.e. $p_2 = p_3 = 0$ or $p_2 = p_3 = 1$.

Table 3.4 Comparative valuations of internationalization strategies

Strategy	*Comparative strategy*	*ENPV*
1	Null	$e_1 = ((2\pi_3^*+\Delta\pi^*)/r) - (q_2+q_3)c_0 - (2-q_2-q_3)c_1 - q_2q_3f$
2	1	$e_2 - e_1 = -\pi_3^* + r(q_3c_0 + (1-q_3)c_1) - ((1/r)-1)a_3d_1 + (1-r)q_2q_3b(c_0-c_2)$
3	2	$e_3 - e_2 = -(\pi_3^*+\Delta\pi^*) - \Delta ad_1 + r(q_2-q_3)(c_0-c_1)$

Note: $b = (1-p_2)p_3 + (1-p_3)p_2$ (see Table 3.3).

The most important comparison is between strategy 1 and strategy 2, which is shown in the second line of the table. This is the nub of the issue where the choice between simultaneous and sequential internationalization is concerned. The relevant expression contains four components. The first is the loss of profit incurred by deferring entry into market 3. The second is the saving in interest payments achieved by deferring the costs of investigation and communication connected with entry into market 3. The greater the profitability of market 3, and the greater its expected familiarity – as indicated by a low value of q_3 – the more likely is the simultaneous strategy to be preferred. Conversely, low profitability combined with unfamiliarity in market 3 encourages the sequential approach. So too does a high cost of investigation and a high cost of communication, because both these costs are deferred under the sequential strategy.

It is obvious that a large pre-emption advantage, as proxied by a large d_1, will favour simultaneous market entry. The third component in the second line also shows that a large value of d_1 gives considerable weight to the discount factor r. A low discount factor increases the capitalization of the loss of operating profit, and also reduces the value of the savings incurred by postponing information costs. A low discount factor therefore definitely favours the simultaneous strategy.

From the standpoint of this chapter, the most important component in the second line of the table is the last one. This is the gain to sequential entry afforded by the opportunity to free-ride on experience of a foreign market gained in the previous period. The expected value of this gain reflects the probability that both foreign markets are of the same type and that this type is different from that of the home market. If they were similar to the home market then the simultaneous strategy could benefit just as much from previous experience as the sequential one. If they were in different states from each other then, of course, entry into the second foreign market could not benefit from the investigation of the first.

The importance of this final component depends crucially on the relation between the cost of investigation and the cost of communication between different foreign subsidiaries. If the cost of investigation is low, or communication between subsidiaries is difficult, then the advantage of sequential entry is low. Little is lost by replicating the investigation of similar markets in this case. If, on the other hand, investigation of markets is costly, and communication between subsidiaries is good, then the gains to sequential entry may well be high. This is the classic case addressed in the internationalization literature. The practical relevance of this case is considered later on.

The final comparison, in the third line of the table, involves the two alternative sequences represented by strategy 2 and strategy 3. It has already been shown that, so far as operating profit is concerned, it is advantageous to enter the most profitable market first. Because of the convention that market 2 is larger and more profitable, this favours strategy 2. So far as information costs are concerned, strategy 2 is favoured if market 2 is believed to be more similar to the home market than is market 3. This will allow the expected costs of investigation to be deferred, although some of the savings may be lost if the cost of communicating relevant information from market 1 to market 2 is high.

A full solution of the model requires, of course, that all these conditions, represented by the three lines of Table 3.4, should be combined. There are several ways in which interactions can occur, and several different parameters governing them. It must suffice, therefore, to give a simple example of the interaction, and for this purpose it is useful to focus on the cost of investigation, c_0, as the key parameter. Figure 3.1 illustrates a typical configuration of the value functions e_1, e_2, e_3. It represents the case where market 2 is more profitable than market 3 but market 3 is believed to be more familiar. This might be illustrative of firms in early twentieth-century Britain choosing between a near but unfamiliar European market (market 2) and a distant but more familiar empire market (market 3).

$V_1V'_1$ graphs the EPNV of strategy 1, taken from the first line of Table 3.4, against c_0, with the other parameter values held constant. This shows that the value of strategy 1 – simultaneous entry into European and empire markets – declines quite sharply as investigation costs increase. This reflects a fairly high value of q_2: in other words, the belief that the market in Europe will be an unfamiliar one.

$V_2V'_2$ graphs the ENPV of strategy 2, which is obtained by summing the expressions in lines 1 and 2 of Table 3.4. This declines less sharply than $V_1V'_1$ because there is a chance that investigation of the European market may prove useful in entering the empire one. The difference is not very large, however, because, given a high q_2 and a low q_3, the chance is quite small. $V_2V'_2$ intersects $V_1V'_1$ at X_1. To the left of X_1, simultaneous internationalization is preferred to sequential internationalization beginning in the European market, while to the right of X_1 the reverse is the case.

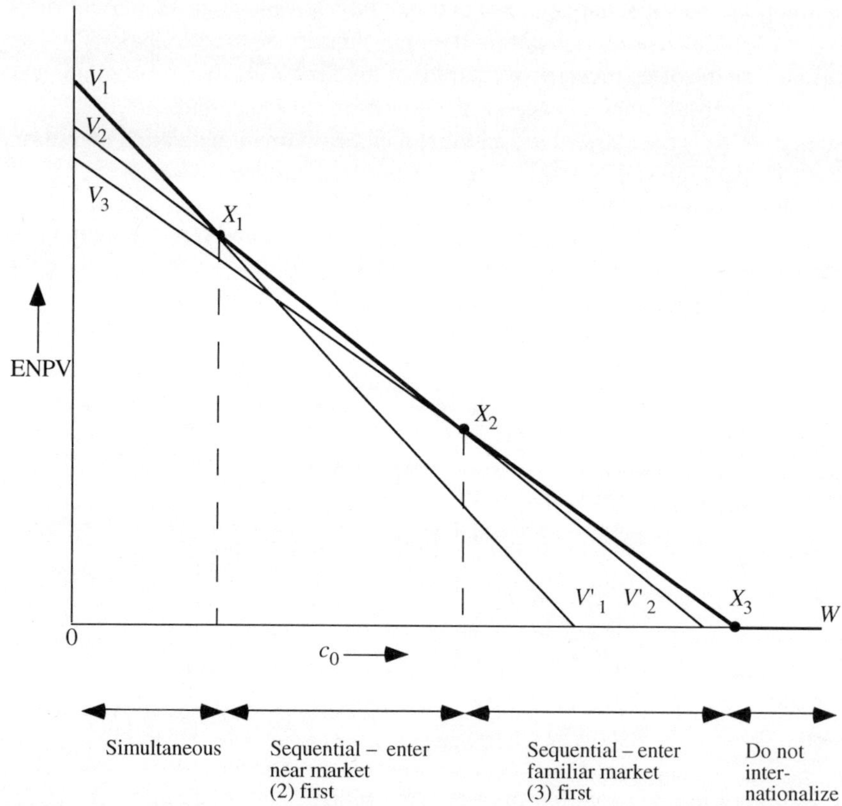

Figure 3.1 Dependence of internationalization strategy on investigation costs – an illustration

Finally, V_3X_3 graphs the EPNV of strategy 3. This is calculated by summing all three lines of the table. The graph is flatter than $V_2V'_2$ because entering the familiar market first defers the investigation costs. Provided that market 3 is fundamentally sound – that is, is not too small – V_3X_3 intersects $V_2V'_2$ at X_2, to the right of X_1. To the left of X_2, entry into the European market is undertaken first, but, to the right of X_2, entry into the empire market comes first. V_3X_3 intersects the horizontal axis at X_3; to the right of X_3, the firm confines itself to the domestic market.

It can be seen that the envelope of maximum ENPV consists of three segments: V_1X_1, where simultaneous entry is preferred; X_1X_2, where the European market is entered first, and X_2X_3 where the empire market is entered first. There is, in fact, a fourth segment too, X_3W, corresponding to the domestic option indicated above.

The principal prediction of this model, conditional on the assumed parameter values, is that as investigation costs decline the firm will switch from purely domestic to international operations by entering the most familiar market first. Only a firm facing modest investigation costs will enter the less familiar market first, and only if it is basically more profitable than the more familiar alternative. A firm must face very low investigation costs if it chooses to enter both markets at the same time. Further predictions can be obtained by performing a similar analysis for other parameters, but because the focus of this chapter is on information costs and learning behaviour these additional predictions are of only peripheral relevance here.

Influence of the Home Country on the Internationalization of the Firm

The model can be used to assess the influence of the home country on the performance of the firm by introducing a second firm domiciled in country 2. This firm will have a different knowledge-base from the first firm because at the time that internationalization commences it will be familiar, not with type 1 markets such as market 1, but with type 2 markets such as market 2. It will also have different subjective beliefs. Its beliefs about market 1 will certainly differ from those of firm 1 because firm 1 knows that market 1 is of type 1 whereas firm 2 does not. Beliefs about market 3 may also differ, with one firm being more optimistic than the other about how familiar that market will be.

The relative performance of the two firms will depend upon whether knowledge gained from one home market is more relevant than knowledge gained in the other home market where entry into the third market is concerned. (By assumption the knowledge gained in each home market is of no value in entering the other firm's home market.) If the third market is of type 1 then firm 1 will be advantaged because firm 2 will have to incur costs of investigation. Conversely, if market 3 is of type 2 then the advantage lies with firm 2, which can draw on home market knowledge while firm 1 cannot. It is only when the third market is of type 3 that the two firms are on a 'level playing field' so far as entry is concerned, since neither has previous knowledge which is relevant in this case.

3 SUBJECTIVE CORRELATION

One of the main results of the preceding model is that the advantages of a sequential approach are greatest when both the foreign markets are of the same type, yet different from the domestic market. An investigation of the first foreign market is very valuable in this case because the experience can be used in the subsequent market entry. But in the model specified above the two foreign markets cannot have a high probability of being similar without the management holding a strong opinion about their exact type. This is because it has been assumed that the subjective probability that market 2 is of some particular type is independent of the type of market 3 and vice versa. In other words, the subjective probabilities cannot allow for a belief that the types of the markets are systematically correlated. This is particularly unfortunate because, as indicated earlier, such a belief is the one most conducive to a sequential strategy.

To introduce the possibility of correlation it is useful to simplify the preceding model by assuming that management is convinced that markets 2 and 3 will be different from market 1. Thus $q_2 = q_3 = 1$. The relevant part of Table 3.1 then collapses to Table 3.5a. Similarly, the only part of Table 3.2 that remains relevant is the last four lines, and these are reproduced, with amendment, in Table 3.5b. This means that the internationalization issue now hinges on whether the two foreign markets are systematically similar or systematically different, or somewhere in between.

Table 3.5 Reduced information sets when both markets 2 and 3 are known to be different from market 1

(a) Reduced form of Table 3.1

Market	*Type* 2	3
2	$1-p_2$	p_2
3	p_3	$1-p_3$

(b) Reduced form of Table 3.2, with modifications

Reference (Table 3.2)	*Type of market* 2	3	*Probability*
6	2	3	$p_{23} = (1-p_2)(1-p_3) - k$
7	3	2	$p_{32} = p_2p_3 - k$
8	2	2	$p_{22} = (1-p_2)p_3 + k$
9	3	3	$p_{33} = p_2(1-p_3) + k$

The four probabilities associated with the four permutations may now be expressed in more general terms than before. Each has been given its own notation, in which the subscripts indicate the respective types of markets 2 and 3: thus p_{22} is the probability that both markets are type 2, p_{32} is the probability that market 2 is type 3 and market 3 is type 2, and so on. The only constraint on these four probabilities is that they are non-negative and sum to one. Comparing the probabilities in Table 3.5a and 3.5b, it is evident that if the types of market were truly independent then each of the entries in Table 3.5b would be the product of two of the elements from Table 3.5a – indeed the relevant products are shown as the first components of the terms in the right-hand column of Table 3.5b. These products must be adjusted if correlation is to be admitted. To determine the relevant adjustment procedure, consider the situation where both markets are type 3. With positive correlation this case is clearly more probable than it would be without correlation, and so it is appropriate to introduce an additive constant *k*. The effect of this adjustment on the other terms may be deduced by noting that the probability that market 2 is of type 2 is, from lines 6 and 8 of Table 3.5b:

$$1 - p_2 = p_{22} + p_{23} \tag{3.4}$$

and that the probability that market 3 is of type 2 is, from lines 7 and 8 of the same table:

$$p_2 = p_{22} + p_{32} \tag{3.5}$$

Combining these equations with the summation condition noted above

$$p_{22} + p_{23} + p_{32} + p_{33} = 1 \tag{3.6}$$

makes it possible to solve for p_{22}, p_{23} and p_{32} as functions of p_2, p_3 and p_{33}. Substituting out the value of p_{33} gives the top three expressions in the right-hand column of Table 3.5b.

It can be seen that the effect of correlation is to increase the probabilities of the situations where the markets are similar and decrease the probabilities of the situations where they are different. This property is also implied by the equation derived from the right-hand column:

$$k = p_{22}p_{23} - p_{23}p_{32} \tag{3.7}$$

The left-hand component of the expression for *k* is the square of the geometric mean of the probabilities of the similar situations and the right-hand component is the corresponding statistic for the different situations. The range of *k* is clearly restricted by the condition that each of the probabilities in the bottom table must lie between zero and one. The simplest way to derive the restriction is to relate k to the correlation coefficient ρ between the types of market. By calculating the variances and covariances of the type variable n across the two markets it may be deduced that

$$k = \rho x \tag{3.8}$$

where

$$x = (p_2 p_3 (1-p_2)(1-p_3))^{1/2} \tag{3.9}$$

Since the correlation coefficient varies between –1 and +1, it follows that k varies between $-x$ and $+x$.

Reworking Tables 3.2 and 3.3 using the modified assumptions gives the ENPVs shown in Table 3.6. As intuition suggests, these ENPVs are obtained from Table 3.4 by substituting $q_2 = q_3 = 1$ and replacing b with $b' = b + 2k$. The replacement affects only line 2 of the table. It indicates that, when subjective correlation is positive, so that the probability that both markets are similar is higher, the potential economies of scope from the initial investigation are greater, and so the profitability of the sequential strategies is increased. Conversely, when the subjective correlation is negative, so that both markets are likely to be different, the economies of scope from the initial investigation are limited and the simultaneous strategy is more likely to be preferred.

Table 3.6 Comparative valuations of strategies when foreign markets are different from the home market but may be systematically similar to or different from each other

Strategy	*Comparative strategy*	*ENPV*
1	Null	$e_1 = ((2\pi_3^* + \Delta\pi^*)/r) - 2c_0 - f$
2	1	$e_2 - e_1 = -\pi_3^* - ((1/r)-1)a_3 d_1 + rc_0 + (1-r)b'(c_0 - c_2)$
3	2	$e_3 - e_2 = -(\pi_3^* + \Delta\pi^*) - \Delta a d_1$

Note: $b' = b + 2k = p_2 + p_3 - 2p_2 p_3 + 2k$.

The replacement does not affect line 3, which means that the relative position of the two sequential strategies is not affected. Thus whichever is preferred on marketing grounds will dominate the other for all values of k. While the subjective probabilities p_2, p_3 affect this choice, because they influence beliefs about market profitability, the subjective correlation does not. Because the choice between sequential strategies is independent of the value of k, the strategic effects of k can be captured by a simple comparison of the simultaneous strategy and the dominant sequential strategy. It is convenient to assume that strategy 2 rather than strategy 3 is dominant, so that the analysis can be based entirely on line 2 of the table.

Figure 3.2 illustrates how subjective similarity between the foreign markets favours the sequential strategy. The upward-sloping schedule VV' indicates the net advantage of the sequential strategy. VV' intersects the horizontal axis at X, to the right of the origin 0. If the states of the two foreign markets were believed to be independent then simultaneous entry would be preferred because 0 is to the left of X. It is only for values of k to the right of X that the sequential strategy is worthwhile. In the case illustrated, therefore, a significant degree of positive correlation between the market states is required before the sequential strategy is worthwhile.

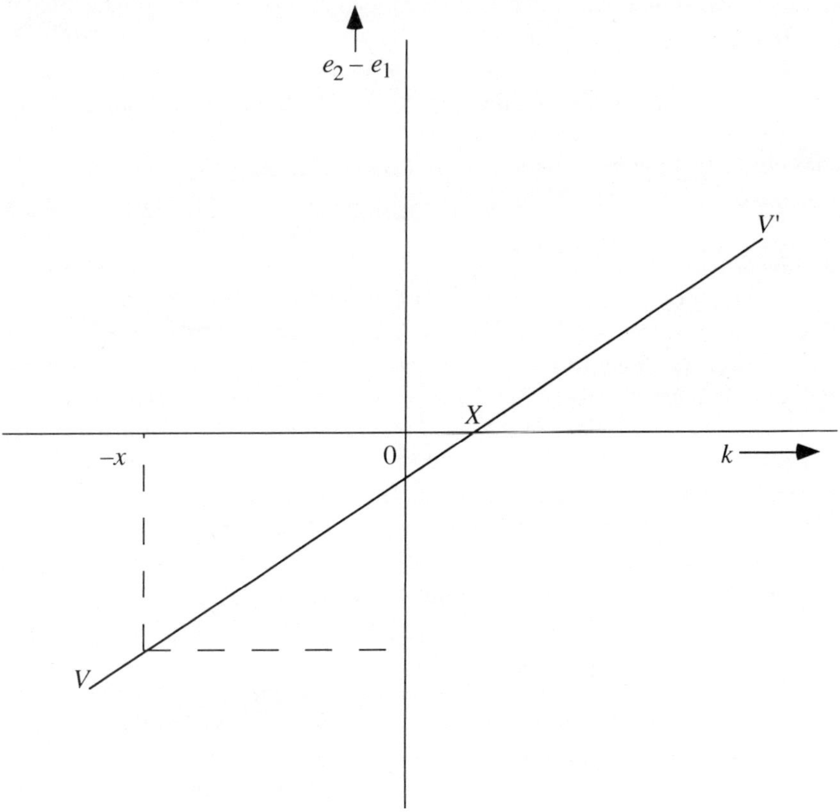

Figure 3.2 Influence of subjective correlation on strategic choice

4 PARTIAL INTERNATIONALIZATION AND THE OPTION VALUE OF A SEQUENTIAL STRATEGY

The strategies considered so far all involve the complete internationalization of the firm. The firm could also decide to internationalize partially by entering just one of the two foreign markets. It could enter this market in either the first period or the second period. If it is profitable to enter, however, then it is always more profitable to enter in the first period rather than the second, since the net gain from entry is only deferred in the second period case. This advantage is reinforced if pre-emptive advantage is taken into account as well. Thus partial internationalization in the first period dominates partial internationalization in the second period, and so it is the only partial internationalization option considered here.

The appraisal of partial internationalization is complicated by the fact that it may be advantageous to defer the choice between a partial strategy and the corresponding complete sequential strategy to the start of the second period. Indeed, since nothing is lost by this approach, it is efficient to defer the decision unless there is some administrative cost of doing so. Complete simultaneous internationalization pre-empts all such decisions about entry, however. Thus sequential strategies can provide an 'option value' that the simultaneous strategy cannot.

Table 3.7 compares the value of each of the complete internationalization strategies (strategies 1–3) with the value of an initial commitment to partial internationalization (strategies 4 and 5). It also compares these with the corresponding deferred decision strategies (strategies 6 and 7). Strategies 4 and 6 involve entering market 2 first and strategies 5 and 7 involve entering market 3 first instead.

Because the calculations of the ENPVs are complicated, it is useful to focus on the special case $b' = 1$. This means that the number of different market types is effectively reduced from three to two. Either type 2 or type 3 is eliminated, or the two types are perfectly correlated across the two foreign markets. In this context perfect correlation implies that, if market 2 appears to be of a given type, then market 3 is known to be of the same type. This simplification is also useful because option values tend to be relatively large in this case.

Deferral of the decision generates value only if it actually changes the decision that is made. This means that the second period decision about a given market must differ from the decision about that market implied by the best alternative strategy. The change in the decision must in turn be imputed to new information. The new information is the type of the first foreign market to be entered. If this is type 1 then it means that the firm will go into the second foreign market familiar only with the domestic type of market. If it is type 2, on the other hand, then the firm will enter the second foreign market already familiar with both types. The expected costs of entry into the second market therefore vary according to what type the second market turns out to be. This information will make a difference only if the second market is just marginally profitable. If the second market is type 1 then the expected entry costs will be too high and entry will not occur – the partial option will be chosen – whereas if it is of type 2 then the cost of entry will be lower and entry will occur – the complete option will be chosen instead.

Table 3.7 Strategies of incomplete internationalization and deferred sequential entry

	Net income		
Strategy	*Period 1*	*Period 2*	*ENPV*
1	$e_{21} + e_{31} - q_2q_3f$	0	$e_{21} + e_{31} - q_2q_3f$
2	e_{21}	e_{32}	$e_{21} + (1-r)e_{32}$
3	e_{31}	e_{22}	$e_{31} + (1-r)e_{22}$
4	e_{21}	0	e_{21}
5	e_{31}	0	e_{31}
6	e_{21}	$q_2e_{32}{}^*$	$e_{21} + (1-r)q_2e_{32}{}^*$
7	e_{31}	$q_3e_{22}{}^*$	$e_{31} + (1-r)q_3e_{22}{}^*$

Notes
$e_{21} = ((\pi_3{}^* + \Delta\pi^*)/r) - q_2c_0 - (1-q_2)c_1$
$e_{22} = ((\pi_3{}^* + \Delta\pi^* - a_2d_1)/r) - q_2(1-q_3)c_0 - (1-q_2)c_1 - q_2q_3c_2$
$e_{31} = (\pi_3{}^*/r) - q_3c_0 - (1-q_3)c_1$
$e_{32} = ((\pi_3{}^* - a_3d_1)/r) - q_3(1-q_2)c_0 - (1-q_3)c_1 - q_2q_3c_2$
$e_{22}{}^* = ((\pi_3{}^* + \Delta\pi^* - a_2d_1)/r) - (1-q_2)c_1 - q_2c_2$
$e_{32}{}^* = ((\pi_3{}^* - a_3d_1)/r) - (1-q_3)c_1 - q_3c_2$

The question is now whether, in the absence of this information about the first market, the second market would be entered in the second period or not. If it would then the complete sequential strategy (2 or 3) is preferred to the corresponding partial strategy (4 or 5) and the option value is the gain from being able to abandon the second foreign market should the first foreign market turn out to be of type 1. Conversely, if the second foreign market would not be entered – 4 or 5 is preferred to 2 or 3 – then the option value consists of being able to enter the second foreign market when the first foreign market turns out to be of type 2. It is this second case that is discussed below.

In the light of this, consider the choice between simultaneous entry and sequential entry using the deferred approach. Suppose to begin with that market 2 is to be entered first, so that the relevant comparisons are between strategies 1, 2, 4 and 6. There is a probability $(1-q_2)$ that market 2 will be of type 1. If

$e_{32} < 0$ (so that strategy 4 is preferred to strategy 2) then the preferred option is not to enter market 3. There is a probability q_2 that it will be of the other type. If $e_{32}^* > 0$ (so that strategy 6 is preferred to strategy 4) then the option will be exercised. It follows that compared to the best alternative strategy (strategy 4) the deferred decision strategy (strategy 6) has an expected option value (after discounting) of $(1-r)q_2e_{32}^*$.

The existence of an option value will affect the attitude to strategy 1 only if strategy 1 is preferred to strategy 4 but not to strategy 6. Since strategy 4 is in turn preferred to strategy 2, sequential internationalizaton will be rejected in the absence of deferred decision making, but accepted with it. The relevant condition is $(1-r)q_2e_{32}^* > e_{31} - q_2q_3f$ (strategy 6 is preferred to strategy 1) and $e_{31} - q_2q_3f > 0$ (strategy 1 is preferred to strategy 4). Compared to simultaneous internationalization, the option value of strategy 6 is

$$\begin{aligned} e'_2 = {} & (q_3c_0 + (1-(1-r)q_2)(1-q_3)c_1 + q_2q_3(f-(1-r)c_2)) \\ & - ((1-(1-r)q_2)(\pi_3^*/r) + (1-r)q_2(a_3d_1/r)) \end{aligned} \tag{3.10.1}$$

The terms in the first main bracket are the cost savings associated with deferring or avoiding entry to market 3 and the terms in the second main bracket are the revenues forgone. The first term in the first bracket is the saving from not entering market 3 at all when it is completely unfamiliar. The second term is the saving in communications with headquarters when market 3, being of type l, is either not entered or, if entered, is entered later than under the simultaneous strategy. The third term is the saving in the costs of simultaneous investigation when both foreign markets are of the same unfamiliar type, less the cost of communication between subsidiaries incurred under these conditions by the sequential strategy. The first term in the second bracket is the loss from deferring the commencement of operating profits from market 3 under the sequential strategy, while the second term captures the loss of any pre-emptive value that immediate entry would provide.

A similar analysis for initial entry into market 3 involves strategies 1, 3, 5 and 7. The option value in this case is

$$\begin{aligned} e'_3 = {} & (q_2c_0 + (1-(1-r)q_3)(1-q_2)c_1 + q_2q_3(f-(1-r)c_2)) \\ & - ((1-(1-r)q_3)(\pi_3^* + \Delta\pi^*/r) + (1-r)q_3(a_2d_1/r)) \end{aligned} \tag{3.10.2}$$

Option values tend to be fairly small components of the overall values of sequential strategies because they only exist where there is a market with limited incentive to pre-empt and very marginal profitability. They are also complicated to calculate. These two factors probably explain why the option value has not so far received much attention in the internationalization literature, even though it is recognized as very important in other aspects of international operations (Capel, 1992).

5 LEARNING BY EXPERIENCE

Errors in Marketing Strategy

The preceding model does not really do full justice to the concept of learning by experience because the choice of marketing strategy is always preceded by an investigation which guarantees the correct decision. An important aspect of learning by experience is learning from mistakes, and so it is appropriate to consider how mistakes arise.

Recall that an inappropriate choice of marketing strategy will cause a loss of profit which depends only on the size of the market and its true state. The costs of error are independent of the type of the market and the period in which it is entered.

In the absence of investigation the expected value of pursuing strategy 1 in market m is (from equation (3.3))

$$v_{m1} = v_m - a_m d_{22} z \qquad (3.11.1)$$

where z was defined earlier as the probability that state 2 prevails. The corresponding expected value of strategy 2 is

$$v_{m2} = v_m - a_m d_{21}(1-z) \qquad (3.11.2)$$

Maximizing the value of the market with respect to the strategy x_m gives

$$x_m = \begin{cases} 1 \text{ if } z \leq z^* \\ 2 \text{ if } z > z^* \end{cases} \qquad (3.12)$$

where

$$z^* = d_{21}/(d_{21}+d_{22}) \qquad (3.13)$$

Note the way in which the critical probability z^* depends on the relative discount factors. The strategy that is the best response to the most likely state is not necessarily the strategy that maximizes expected value. It may pay to act as though the unlikely state prevailed in order to control the risk of heavy losses should that state occur.

The maximum attainable value of the market under experiential learning is

$$v'_m = \begin{cases} v_{m1} & \text{if } z \leq z^* \\ v_{m2} & \text{if } z > z^* \end{cases} \tag{3.14}$$

If $v_m' > v_m - c_0$ then it pays to choose experience over investigation. If $c_0 > c_0^* = d_{21}d_{22}/(d_{21}+d_{22})$ then experience is always preferred. Otherwise the rule is to investigate if $z_1 < z \leq z_2$ and not to investigate if either $z \leq z_1$ or $z > z_2$, where

$$z_1 = c_0/a_m d_{22} \; ; \; z_2 = (a_m d_{21} - c_0)/a_m d_{21} \tag{3.15}$$

Investigation is chosen for moderate values of z_1 and experience for extreme values of z_1, because with extreme values management is confident that mistakes are unlikely to occur.

With an optimal investigation strategy the net value of the market is

$$v_m'' = v_m - h_m \tag{3.16}$$

where h_m is the minimum cost of entry given by

$$h_m = \begin{cases} a_m d_{22} z & \text{if } z \leq z_1 \\ c_0 & \text{if } z_1 < z \leq z_2 \\ a_m d_{21}(1-z) & \text{if } z > z_2 \end{cases} \tag{3.17}$$

The derivation of the minimum cost of entry is illustrated in Figure 3.3. The line *OB* shows how the expected losses associated with implementing strategy 1 increase as the probability of state 2 increases. The slope of this line is greater the larger is the market and the greater the discount associated with a marketing error in state 2. The converse error is illustrated by the line *AA'*, which shows how the expected losses generated by strategy 2 increase as the probability of state 2 decreases. The two lines intersect at *E*, and this determines the critical probability z^*. To the left of *E* strategy 1 is preferred in the absence of investigation, while to the right of *E* strategy 2 is preferred. In the absence of investigation the minimum cost of entry would be indicated by the height of the frontier *OEA'*, which peaks at *E*. But with a modest cost of investigation, indicated by the height of the horizontal line *CC'*, investigation becomes efficient along the chord Z_1Z_2. The cost of entry schedule becomes OZ_1Z_2A' and over the chord Z_1Z_2 investigation rather than experience is preferred.

Since learning by experience will not be chosen if its expected costs exceed those of investigation, the issue is not so much whether high costs of mistakes will affect the firm's internationalization strategy as whether low costs of

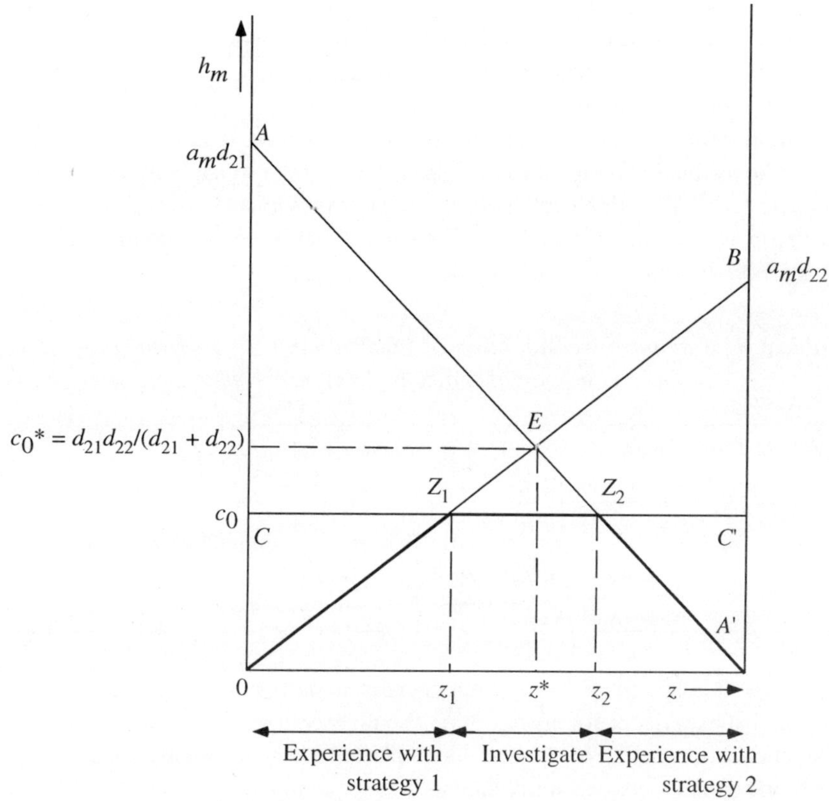

Figure 3.3 Determination of the minimum cost of entry

mistakes will do so instead. Table 3.8 recalculates the ENPVs of the three internationalization strategies given in Table 3.4 by substituting for the fixed cost of investigation c_0 the minimum cost of entry h_m. Unlike c_0, h_m varies according to the size of market a_m, the discount factors d_{21}, d_{22} and the probability z. The appearance of the market-specific factor a_m in the cost of entry means that size of market can now affect internationalization through the cost of entry as well as through its effect on market profitability and the pre-emption gain. The fact that it is only significant when costs of investigation are relatively high means that when costs of investigation are high there will be a greater tendency to enter small markets first. Because mistakes are more costly in large markets than in small ones, it is advantageous to use small markets as 'test' markets in this case.

Two more general points seem to emerge from this discussion. First, the fact that the management of a firm may decide quite rationally, on the basis of subjective beliefs, not to incur investigation costs, provides an interesting perspective on the issue of 'bounded rationality' in the theory of the firm (Simon, 1983; Williamson, 1985), for it shows that management may deliberately choose to opt for a strategy which makes it likely that mistakes will be made. It is more efficient to take a calculated risk of a mistake than to incur a certain cost of investigation merely to avoid a possible mistake. What looks like an error at the level of marketing strategy may represent the consequence of a deliberate decision where the wider choice between experience and investigation is concerned.

Table 3.8 Comparative valuation of internationalization strategies conditional on an optimal choice between experience and investigation

Strategy	*Comparative strategy*	*ENPV*
1	Null	$e_1 = ((2\pi_3{}^*+\Delta\pi^*)/r) - q_2h_2 - q_3h_3 - (2-q_2-q_3)c_1 - q_2q_3f$
2	1	$e_2 - e_1 = -\pi_3{}^* + r(q_3h_3+(1-q_3)c_1) - ((1/r)-1)a_3 + (1-r)q_2q_3b(h_3-c_2)$
3	2	$e_3 - e_2 = -(\pi_3{}^*+\Delta\pi^*) - \Delta ad_1 + r(q_2h_2-q_3h_3) - r(q_2-q_3)c_1$

The second lesson to be drawn is that there is no particular reason why the substitution of experience for investigation should encourage a sequential approach. The choice between investigation and experience is conceptually quite distinct from the choice between simultaneous and sequential entry strategies. If there is any connection it tends to favour a link between experience and simultaneous entry rather than the other way round. Experience tends to be favoured by confident individuals who hold strong beliefs that some particular state will prevail in a given market. Confident beliefs also generate low expected costs of error, which translate into low expected costs of entry which it is normally not worthwhile to defer. This confidence tends to encourage both learning by experience and simultaneous market entry and for this reason variations in confidence across a population of firms will tend to generate a positive association between the two. Confident managers will appear both impulsive and pragmatic, whilst less confident managers will appear both cautious and systematic. This association is very different from the kind of pattern hinted at in the established internationalization literature, where managers are expected to be cautious (that is, sequential) and pragmatic (learning by experience, not investigation) at the same time.

6 QUALITY OF JUDGEMENT AND THE PERFORMANCE OF THE FIRM

While the present model 'rationalizes' marketing errors, however, it does not rationalize errors in the internationalization strategy itself. While management chooses, within the model, whether or not to improve its own subjective estimates of the state of each market, it does not choose whether to improve its estimates about the type of market in order to make a better choice about investigation or about the sequence of market entry. This is because of the focus of the model on the 'hands on' investigations that are carried out after a commitment to market entry has been made.

It would be possible, in principle, to extend the analysis back in time to a period before the management was required to make the internationalization decision. At this stage management could consider investing in information which would improve the quality of the subjective probabilities used to determine the internationalization strategy. Since the cost of additional information would itself be uncertain, however, this would introduce a third variety of uncertainty into the model. Indeed, the process could be continued back even further until a time was reached in which the management had just a few simple theories about how information on various subjects might conceivably relate to this issue, and a small amount of initial information with which to prime the learning process. It would then be possible to impute subsequent successes and failures to the reliability of these early beliefs and their relevance to subsequent situations. With the regression of the quest for information further into the past, the cultural heritage of the management team would emerge as the key to its performance.

In the absence of such ambitious analysis, however, the present model does at least provide a simple basis for relating the accuracy of the subjective beliefs, as inherited from culture and past experience, to the performance of the internationalization strategy. Generally speaking, the more accurate are the beliefs, the better will be the performance of the firm. The relation between accuracy and performance is not a continuous one, though, because, as noted earlier, errors in probabilities translate into errors in strategy only when critical probability thresholds are exceeded. This amplifies the earlier comparison between two firms in which it was just the relevance of the home country marketing experience which affected subsequent performance. It suggests that it is not just the firm's own experience in its home market that is important, but the culture it acquires from its domestic environment too.

To analyse the impact of beliefs upon performance the modeller must, of course specify what the true situation – unknown to the management – really is. Suppose, for example, that each market is of a different type, so that correct beliefs are represented by $q_2 = q_3 = 1$, $p_2 = p_3 = 0$. Suppose also that there is no correlation,

$k = 0$. Under these circumstances a simultaneous strategy is almost certainly preferable to a sequential strategy because, with both foreign markets being different, the sequential approach offers no economies of scope to information.

A very optimistic management might take the view that all the markets were of the same type, so that both foreign markets were exactly like the domestic market: that is, $q_2 = q_3 = 0$. With expected costs of internationalization well below their actual level, the firm could decide to internationalize when in fact the null strategy of remaining a domestic firm might be better. Moreover, being so confident in its beliefs, management may not investigate the states of individual markets either, so that costly errors may be perpetrated in marketing strategy too. Thus the firm will expand into the two foreign markets simultaneously without any investigation, and make losses as a result. Misguided subjective beliefs therefore provide a simple rationalization for impetuous globalization.

At the other extreme, so far as strategy is concerned, is the management that wrongly believes that both foreign markets, though different from the home market, are of the same type, but recognizes that it does not know what state this is. This firm will opt for the cautious strategy of sequential internationalization when in fact simultaneous internationalization with investigation at each stage would definitely be better. This kind of firm is typically commended in the internationalization literature, although, as this example makes clear, its strategy is inefficient in certain circumstances.

7 EVALUATION OF THE SCANDINAVIAN APPROACH

The preceding analysis has immediate relevance to the evaluation of alternative theories of the firm. To begin with, the analysis highlights the importance of subjective beliefs about the similarity and dissimilarity of different markets. It shows that the advantage of a sequential approach to expansion is greatest when foreign markets are believed to be different from the home one, but are likely to be similar to each other. Given that they are indeed similar, the sequential approach maximizes the economies of scope that the first investigation affords. Conversely, the advantage of the simultaneous strategy is greatest when the foreign markets are believed to be similar to the home one and, if different, to be different in their own particular way. This means that experience gained from any particular market will be of little relevance elsewhere.

The strategic management literature advocating globalization (Porter, 1980) clearly adopts this latter view. The markets of different industrialized countries are claimed to be basically similar – at least so far as the preferences of young high-income consumers are concerned – and any variation tends to be imputed to local factors peculiar to each market. Globalization therefore appears in the present model as a specific response to a particular configuration of the international market system (see Table 3.9).

Internalization theory is often alleged to favour a rather similar strategy. This is because of the theory's emphasis on the public good properties of knowledge developed in the domestic market, and the advantage of exploiting these properties internally through expansion of the firm. In fact, however, most authors in this tradition have been very aware of the 'psychic costs' to the firm of entering foreign markets (Buckley and Casson, 1976). Internalization theorists have tended to assume that all markets are different, so that there is always a cost of entry. Because all markets are different, the scope economies of accrued experience of market entry have not been emphasized in the same way as in the Scandinavian literature. The internalization view has supported the simultaneous approach simply because there is little point in deferring entry if the costs cannot be reduced using experience gained in other markets first. Simultaneous entry is also promoted by the fact that, where technological knowledge is concerned, patents expire and trade secrets leak out, so that early entry into all markets is advisable before the potential monopoly rents are dissipated. Internalization theory, in other words, highlights a particular kind of pre-emptive advantage.

Table 3.9 Classification of theoretical approaches to internationalization

	Home and foreign markets	
Foreign markets	*Same*	*Different*
Same	Globalization	Scandinavian
Different	—	Internalization

Note: Because globalization assumes that foreign markets are essentially the same as the home market it follows that differences between foreign markets must be small. But in so far as these small differences are idiosyncratic to each market, the logic of simultaneous internationalization will be more secure.

Where internalization theorists have argued for sequential entry it has generally been in terms of the 'Penrose' effect – that simultaneous internationalization of the firm will overstretch its managerial resources. The Penrose argument is, however, quite distinct from the argument for sequential internationalization based on economies of scope available from the learning process. The two approaches are, in principle, rival explanations of the sequential expansion of the firm, although they can be regarded as complementary and mutually reinforcing within a synthetic view. While this chapter is committed to elaborating the learning approach, it has been useful, from the standpoint of practical application, to have incorporated the Penrose theory within the model as a special case.

The difference between the internalization approach and the globalization approach lies not, therefore, in the recommended internationalization strategy but rather in the perceived profitability of internationalization *per se*. Because internalization theory recognizes psychic costs that globalization theory discounts, it more often favours the null strategy of remaining at home and licensing the technology to other firms overseas. Licensing to foreign firms with local knowledge of market conditions is an important element of internalization theory precisely because the psychic costs of foreign market entry are fully recognized.

It can be seen that, by elimination, the Scandinavian approach focuses on those situations where foreign markets are unlike the home market but very similar to each other. The older Scandinavian literature associated with the Uppsala school emphasizes the need to expand in stages in a manner reminiscent of (but not coincident with) the product cycle model (Vernon, 1979). The more recent literature, on the other hand, emphasizes the importance of speeding up the learning process by improving communication between foreign subsidiaries.

Recall from Section 2 that the net advantage of the sequential approach depends on, amongst other things, the excess of the cost of investigation over the cost of communication between subsidiaries. To encourage subsidiaries to learn from each other, it is desirable not only to improve headquarters–subsidiary communication but to encourage subsidiaries to communicate directly with each other. Organizational learning needs to be decentralized, in other words. This is an important aspect of the thinking underlying the 'heterarchy' or the 'network' firm (Hedlund, 1986; Chesnais, 1988). Whilst the discussion of heterarchies tends to focus on the organizational restructuring of the mature multinational enterprise, the present model emphasizes the more general advantage to the firm of building up the heterarchy in stepwise fashion from the very start of the internationalization process.

As indicated earlier, learning by doing is a satisfactory alternative to systematic investigation if the costs of making a mistake are not too great. To control these costs, firms will tend to make small commitments to begin with, and only increase their commitments once experience has been gained. Thus sequential entry into markets is accompanied by incremental expansion in these markets over time. Because systematic investigation reduces the likelihood of mistakes (in the model above it eliminates it altogether – which is clearly a very extreme case) it supports a greater initial commitment. Thus sequential expansion will be associated with different degrees of initial commitment according to the way that knowledge of markets is acquired. This coincides with the general thrust of the Scandinavian approach.

8 SUMMARY AND CONCLUSIONS

This chapter has modelled the internationalization process of the firm using a few key assumptions which are of a distinctly philosophical nature. It has been argued that the main advantage of the sequential approach to internationalization is that it exploits economies of scope in knowledge. These economies depend on the uniformity of markets of a similar type, which allows firms to learn from one market how to diagnose the states of all markets of the same type.

The knowledge to which the economies of scope apply is knowledge of how to diagnose the state of a market, and not knowledge of the state of the market itself. It is, therefore, most appropriately regarded as know-how rather than factual knowledge. The model therefore emphasizes, in line with the Scandinavian approach, that international expansion is a process of know-how acquisition and accumulation, and not just the exploitation of given know-how generated through research and development at home. Since the 'how' in the know-how relates to learning about individual markets, its acquisition pertains to what Lall (1987) describes as 'learning to learn'.

The fact that the economies of scope are confined to a particular type of market emphasizes that know-how is culture-bound, in the sense that what is learnt about how to investigate a society of one type cannot necessarily be applied to a society of a different type. The sequential approach maximizes the exploitation of economies of scope because relevant information takes time to communicate, so that the simultaneous use of information is often less effective than its sequential use. This is quite apart from the fact that the simultaneous processing of different information may overstretch management resources. It is possible to economize on information processing by forgoing investigation and learning from experience instead. The cost of this economy is the mistakes that will be made. But the converse of this is quite interesting – mistakes can also be an economy since they make it possible to avoid investigation costs.

The model developed above has shown that, by introducing into this philosophical framework specific assumptions about market profitability and communication costs, a number of interesting results can be derived. These include the following.

1. When internationalizing the firm using a sequential approach it normally pays to enter the most familiar type of market first. This is because major set-up costs can be deferred until later.
2. Sequential internationalization is favoured when foreign markets have very different location advantages, since the cost of deferring entry into the most 'distant' markets tends to be relatively low.
3. Significant pre-emptive advantages favour simultaneous internationalization.
4. A low rate of discount favours simultaneous internationalization, particularly when the first-mover advantage is also large. This suggests that long-termism promotes rapid international expansion.
5. Sequential internationalization is favoured by a combination of high costs of learning and a low cost of inter-subsidiary communication.

6. Sequential internationalization is favoured by systematic similarities between foreign markets combined with differences between these markets and the domestic one. Such similarities maximize the potential economies of scope available from the learning process.
7. The existence of a highly marginal foreign market favours a sequential strategy in which the decision about entry into this market is deferred.
8 Firms that are domiciled in markets that are very similar to major foreign markets have an advantage over rivals domiciled in idiosyncratic markets because they have a 'head start' where the acquisition of relevant knowledge is concerned.
9. Firms that plan to enter foreign markets that they believe are similar to their home one will be concerned to minimize the cost of headquarters–subsidiary communication, whereas firms that plan to enter unfamiliar foreign markets will be concerned to minimize the costs of subsidiary–subsidiary communication. If it is supposed, additionally, that small home markets are more idiosyncratic than large ones, then it is to be expected that firms domiciled in small home markets will be oriented to decentralized organizational structures designed to reduce the cost of subsidiary–subsidiary communication.
10. Confident managements tend to rely on experience and less confident managements on investigation. It is cheaper to gain experience in small markets than in large markets of the same type, so when investigation is costly firms are more likely to enter small markets first.
11. Confident managements also tend to favour simultaneous internationalization, so that experiential learning and sequential internationalization do not normally go hand in hand.
12. In the absence of investigation, the marketing errors that are made reflect erroneous subjective beliefs, but the relation between the two is a sharply discontinuous one. The location of the discontinuities is governed by the relative magnitude of the losses associated with various kinds of error.
13. The home country is an important influence on internationalization strategy not only because the home market is a specific source of experience (see (8)) but because home culture is a source of beliefs that may influence the learning process both before and after the internationalization decision is made.
14. The performance of the firm is affected by the incidence of strategic errors, not only in marketing, but in internationalization and investigation strategies too. Both premature globalization and overcautious sequential internationalization are common errors that may result from inappropriate beliefs.

Overall this model demonstrates one of the key advantages of the rational actor approach to modelling managerial behaviour, namely that it is a highly productive way of generating new hypotheses. By allowing for information costs, many of the limitations of the more conventional models based on this approach are avoided. Moreover, the fact that the outcome of rational action under costly information reflects subjective beliefs confirms that culture – as a mechanism for the collective formation of beliefs – is an important influence on behaviour. Indeed, the rational action postulate provides a useful mechanism for identifying the behavioural implications of different cultural beliefs.

The rational action postulate by itself, of course, implies nothing – it merely connects the assumptions to the predictions that follow from them. But this allows surprising and contentious hypotheses to be deduced from apparently obvious and innocuous assumptions. Conversely, it allows the hidden assumptions that underlie familiar hypotheses to be revealed. When the hidden assumptions of the Scandinavian approach are revealed, it turns out that they imply far more about behaviour than previous discussion has indicated.

Further insights can be obtained by extending this modelling philosophy into other aspects of international expansion. Nothing has been said in this chapter about alternative strategies for technology generation or inter-firm alliances, for example. The effects of growth and fluctuations in the markets after entry has been completed have also been ignored. The generality of the approach, though, means that all these issues can be tackled within the same framework just by modifying some of the specific assumptions. It is reasonable to suppose that further interesting results will emerge by pursuing an agenda of this kind.

REFERENCES

Buckley, P.J. and M.C. Casson (1976), *The Future of the Multinational Enterprise,* London: Macmillan.

Capel, J. (1992), 'How to service a foreign market under uncertainty: a real option approach', *European Journal of Political Economy*, **8**, 455–75.

Chesnais, F. (1988), 'Technical cooperation agreements between firms', *STI Review No. 4*, Paris: OECD, 51–119.

Hedlund, G. (1986), 'The hypermodern MNC – a heterarchy?', *Human Resource Management*, **25**, (1), 9–35.

Johanson, J. and J-E. Vahlne (1977), 'The internationalisation process of the firm – a model of knowledge development and increasing foreign market commitments', *Journal of International Business Studies*, **8**, (1), 23–32.

Lall, S. (1987), *Learning to Industrialise: The Acquisition of Technological Capability by India,* London: Macmillan.

Penrose, E.T. (1959), *The Theory of the Growth of the Firm,* Oxford: Basil Blackwell.

Porter, M.E. (1980), *Competitive Strategy: Techniques for Analysing Industries and Competitors*, New York: Free Press.

Simon, H.A. (1983), *Reason in Human Affairs*, Oxford: Basil Blackwell.

Strandskov, J. (1986), 'Towards a new approach for studying the internationalisation process of firms', Working paper 4, Copenhagen School of Economics, reprinted in P.J. Buckley and P. Ghauri (eds), *The Internationalisation of the Firm: A Reader*, London: Academic Press (1993), 201–16.

Vernon, R. (1979), 'The product cycle in a new international environment', *Oxford Bulletin of Economics and Statistics*, **41**, 255–67.

Williamson, O.E. (1985), *Economic Institutions of Capitalism*, New York: Free Press.

4. R&D activities of multinational enterprises and host country welfare

H. Katrak

1 INTRODUCTION

Until about three decades ago multinational enterprises (MNEs) used to locate nearly all of their R&D activities in their parent countries and did not assign much of this activity to their overseas subsidiaries. These location decisions appear to have been influenced by certain centralizing and decentralizing forces. As Hirschey and Caves (1981) note, the advantages of centralizing R&D efforts include the economies of scale in R&D and spill-overs between two (or more) projects, while the forces making for decentralization include the costs of transferring technology and the need to tailor some R&D work to the requirements of the overseas markets. The concentration of the R&D activities in the parent companies could be explained by the centralizing forces weighing more heavily than the decentralizing ones.

More recently, however, a large number of MNEs have been conducting a significant proportion of their R&D activities in overseas locations. A number of studies, including Ronstadt (1978), Mansfield *et al.* (1979), Wortman (1990), Cantwell (1989) and Casson (1991), identify three main factors underlying this development. First, the increased scale of production in many of the overseas subsidiaries has required the setting up of local R&D units (RDUs), to help adapt the parent companies' technologies to the host country environment, solve production problems and even develop products for the host country market. Secondly, the increased integration of the MNEs' worldwide operations has induced a division of labour in their R&D efforts such that some aspects of an MNE's global tasks are best performed in the parent country while others are assigned to the overseas subsidiaries. Thirdly, the increasingly specialized nature of technological activities is making it important for an enterprise to have an R&D 'window' in some overseas countries in order to have close communication with the latters' specialized research efforts.

This chapter examines the impact of MNEs' overseas R&D activities on the economic welfare of the host countries. Interest in the question arises because in a number of RDU-importing countries, including Australia, Belgium, Canada and Spain, the scale of the foreign MNEs' R&D activities is quite large relative to that of indigenous enterprises.[1] And even in the case of some other countries, whose own enterprises have overseas R&D operations, foreign-owned RDUs have a significant presence in certain important sectors. This is shown in Stoneman's (1991) data on foreign and domestic funding of business enterprises' R&D expenditures: in the Italian chemical industry nearly one-quarter of those expenditures have recently been funded from abroad, while in the French and UK office machinery and computing industries the corresponding foreign share has been almost one-third.[2] The relatively large presence of foreign-owned RDUs suggests that host countries may enjoy a number of economic benefits but also suffer certain costs.

In analysing the benefits and costs for the host country account will be taken of the following likely possibilities. First, the foreign-owned RDUs may employ some host country factors, such as scientists, engineers and technologists, some (or all) of whom would otherwise have been employed in domestic enterprises' RDUs. The employment of these factors in the foreign-owned RDUs will benefit the host country, but their diversion from domestic enterprises will entail a cost. Secondly, some of the benefits of the foreign enterprises' R&D activities may not be fully appropriated by those enterprises and may spill over to various sections of the host country. Thirdly, the foreign enterprises' R&D activities will affect their costs of production, product quality and so on, and hence the level of their output, prices and profits; these changes may benefit host country consumers and also enhance the governments' tax revenues, but may decrease the output and profits of domestic enterprises. The former two effects, which result directly from the R&D activities, will be called the *direct R&D effects*, while the third will be named the *indirect production effects*.

It is also important to bear in mind three other points. First, we need to distinguish between (a) the effects that arise simply because of an increase in the number of RDUs in a country and (b) those resulting from the foreign ownership of some RDUs. Secondly, in examining the direct R&D effects it is important to take into account certain characteristics of R&D training and evaluation in the host countries. As Stoneman (1991) has noted, in some countries the social costs of training scientists, engineers and technologists (SETs) exceeds the private costs; there is thus a distortion in the R&D manpower market. Moreover, he suggests that, in the UK at least, some enterprises may underestimate even the private benefits of R&D effort. Both these possibilities give rise to concern that the foreign-owned RDUs can obtain local SETs 'too cheaply'. Thirdly, when discussing the indirect production effects we need to recognize that many of the enterprises that undertake R&D are competing with each other and so the welfare effects on the host country may also depend on how the enterprises' R&D efforts affect the competition between them.

It turns out that there is a rather complex list of benefits and costs, the relative importance of which may vary from one host country to another. Consequently, *a priori* analyses alone cannot determine whether host country welfare will be enhanced or reduced. However, such analyses do help provide an operational framework, which may be of use for further empirical research.

The chapter is divided as follows: Section 2 uses a simple model to examine the direct R&D effects and Section 3 extends the analyses by relaxing the assumptions of the simple model. Section 4 considers the indirect production effects. Section 5 summarizes the main findings and discusses some implications. An algebraic Appendix elaborates on some arguments made in Section 3.

2 A SIMPLE MODEL OF THE DIRECT R&D EFFECTS

In analysing the direct R&D effects and subsequent production effects it will be convenient to employ the two-stage duopoly model used by Spencer and Brander (1983). Enterprises have a two-stage decision process: in the first stage each enterprise decides on its optimal level of R&D, given some initial level of output, and then in the second stage they compete and adjust their output levels, given the production costs and product quality achieved in the first stage.

For the present purpose, the duopolists are a host country enterprise and a foreign-owned subsidiary. The initial situation is one where neither enterprise has an RDU. The host enterprise may be using some standardized, off-the-shelf, technologies (or may be licensing know-how from another country), while the subsidiary may be using a technology transferred from its parent company. These technologies will determine the enterprises' initial costs of production which, along with the duopolistic competition, will determine their initial levels of output.

At some point the enterprises set up their RDUs. The R&D effort requires some fixed and variable inputs. The fixed inputs may include tangible items (such as R&D equipment) and also some intangible assets, such as enterprise-specific experience. The variable inputs are assumed to be mainly SETs; for simplicity all these are treated as a single homogeneous factor. An increase in the employment of the SETs will enhance the enterprises' profits, but is assumed to do so at a diminishing rate.[3] Each enterprise will aim for an optimum level of SET inputs, given its initial level of output.

The main point now is that, as long as the supply of SETs is not perfectly elastic, the number that each enterprise can employ will be less than what would have been likely if the rival's RDU had not also been set up. In this sense, the foreign RDU 'decreases' the host enterprise's employment of SETs and hence the latter R&D efforts.[4] In what follows we examine how the subsidiary's R&D activities and the consequent decrease in the host enterprise's R&D may affect the country's welfare. To begin with I make six simplifying assumptions, all of which are relaxed later:

1. Each enterprise correctly predicts the increase in profits resulting from its R&D efforts.
2. Each enterprise can fully appropriate all of the benefits resulting from its R&D, except for the taxes on the increased profits.
3. There is no divergence between the social costs of training SETs and the private costs to the individuals concerned.[5]
4. Each enterprise treats the wage paid to SETs as its marginal costs of employing that factor and equates its gross marginal profits (as defined below) to that wage.
5. There is no 'lumpiness' or indivisibilities in the R&D projects; that is, the R&D efforts can be expanded in very small increments, through marginal increases in the employment of the SETs.
6. All SETs are a uniform homogeneous factor, engaged in a single type of R&D effort.

In Figure 4.1 the schedule *PH* is the host enterprise's marginal profits from the employment of SETs; it shows the effects of a decrease in unit production costs and/or an improvement in product quality, at the initial level of output. The profits are defined as net of the costs of production, but gross of the payments to the SETs and the profits taxes. *PA* is the aggregate of the marginal profit schedules of the foreign and host RDUs. (For diagrammatic simplicity this aggregate schedule has the same intercept as *PH*.) The schedule *ST* is the supply curve the SETs; it reflects the private costs of the training for the SETs.

The effects of the foreign RDU on host country welfare are as follows. If that RDU had not been set up, the host enterprise's employment of SETs would have been ON_1, at the wage OW_1, and so its profits (net of the wages paid to SETs) would have been W_1PE_1. In comparison, if the foreign RDU has also been set up, the SETs' wage rate would have been higher, at OW_2, the total numbers employed would have been higher,[6] at ON_2, but the host enterprise's employment would have been only W_2B. Consequently, the SETs' income would have been increased by $W_1W_2E_2E_1$ and this would have more than offset the reduction in the host enterprise's profits, shown by $W_1W_2BE_1$. In addition, the increase in the subsidiary's profits would yield additional tax revenues: those profits are PE_2B and so, if the tax rate was, say, BC/BE_2, the tax revenues would be PCB. The host country would thus have had a net gain of $E_1E_2B + PCB$.

So the main conclusion from the simple model is that, although the setting up of the foreign RDU reduces the host enterprise's employment of SETs (and its profits), the country as a whole would be better off.[7] The question now is whether this conclusion will hold even if we relax the simplifying assumptions listed above. Before turning to that, however, if is worth noting two aspects of the above results. First, the host country's gain does not arise only because of the increased employment of the SETs; even if the supply of SETs had been perfectly inelastic, the foreign RDU would have enhanced the country's welfare. This is because the SETs' wage rate would have increased to MN_1, and the resulting increase in their income would have more than offset the decrease in the host enterprise's profits. Secondly, the country gains, not because it has a foreign-owned RDU, but because two RDUs are better than one. Each enterprise's RDU employs some fixed inputs which are complementary to the variable input SETs. Consequently, an increase in the number of RDUs increases the marginal returns to the SETs, for each level of their employment. In fact the gain from an additional RDU *per se* would have been $E_1E_2B + PE_2B$; the foreign ownership of the additional RDU reduces this gain, by PE_2C, as only part of its profits accrues to the host country.

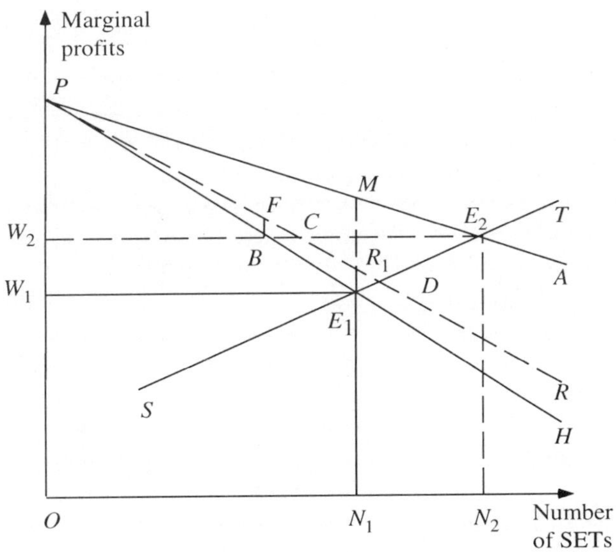

Figure 4.1 Host country welfare effects in the absence of any market distortions

3 SOME EXTENSIONS OF THE SIMPLE MODEL

Let us now allow for the possibility that enterprises cannot correctly predict the profits that will result from an increase in their SET employment. This is likely in view of the uncertainty associated with R&D efforts. Moreover, such uncertainty may be greater in enterprises whose top managers have expertise and experience in fields other than science, engineering and technology.[8]

Suppose first that this problem arises with the host country enterprise, and suppose also that it underestimates the profits that may result from an increase in its SET employment. The effects of this can be examined with the help of Figure 4.1, though we now reinterpret the schedules as follows. Let *PH* be the host enterprise's predicted (marginal) profits, *PR* the actual, *ex post*, profits and, *PA* the aggregate of *PH* and the foreign subsidiary's schedule. (For diagrammatic simplicity I now abstract from profits taxes.)

Now if the host enterprise alone had an RDU, its SET employment would have been as at point E_1, along the underestimated schedule. With that level of employment, the actual profits would have been OPR_1N_1. In comparison, if the foreign subsidiary also had its RDU, the combined level of SET employment would have been as at point E_2, at the wage OW_2, but the number employed in the host enterprise would have been only W_2B. The foreign RDU would thus have increased the SETs' income by $W_1W_2E_2E_1$, but reduced the host enterprise's profits by $W_1W_2BE_1 + BFR_1E_1$. The net welfare effect would consequently have been $BE_1E_2 - BFR_1E_1$ and, as can be seen from the figure, this could be either positive or negative. So in this case, the foreign RDU may either decrease or increase host country welfare. And this outcome is possible even when profits taxes are taken into account.

However, although this argument is of some interest, its empirical validity may be rather limited. This is so for two reasons. First, it assumes that the host enterprise does not learn from past experience. If the enterprise has found that it had underestimated the profits from some past period's R&D efforts, would it not take that experience into account when predicting the profits from its current R&D efforts?[9] Secondly, the argument assumes that the difficulties in predicting the profits lead to an underestimation, rather than overestimation, of those profits. Experimentation with Figure 4.1 shows that, if the host enterprise overestimates its profits, the general conclusions of the simple model will not be affected.[10]

It may also be noted that the above argument has invoked only the host enterprise's uncertainties and predictions. The foreign subsidiary's uncertainties would also affect the level of SET employment, but its RDU would still enhance host country welfare. Specifically, if the subsidiary underestimated (overestimated) its profits, its employment of SETs would be less (more) than otherwise, but nevertheless the SET's income would be increased by that employment and this gain would more than offset the reduction in the host enterprise's profits.

Next let us relax the assumption of full appropriability. The R&D literature has pointed out that enterprises may not be able to fully appropriate the benefits of their product–process innovations; some of their know-how may spill over to other enterprises and there may also be some gains to consumer surplus. Thus the social benefits of an enterprise's R&D efforts may be greater than its private benefits.[11] Would such inappropriability affect the general conclusions of the simple model? We are concerned only with those inappropriables that benefit host country enterprises and/or consumers: benefits to other countries do not feature in our welfare analyses. There are two opposing influences to be taken into account. First, as the foreign RDU causes the host enterprise's employment of SETs to be less than otherwise, the inappropriable benefits of the latter's R&D will also be less than otherwise. On the other hand, the foreign subsidiary's R&D efforts will generate some inappropriables which benefit the host country.

Suppose that the social value of the inappropriable benefits are a constant proportion of an enterprise's gross profits (as defined above). Let β_h and β_f denote these proportions for the host enterprise and foreign subsidiary, respectively. The overall effects of the foreign RDU on the host country would then consist of the gains from the simple model and an 'inappropriables effect'. The latter is defined as $[\beta_f\lambda_f - \beta_h(\lambda_{h1} - \lambda_{h2})]$ where λ_f is the gross profits of the foreign subsidiary and $\beta_f\lambda_f$ is the social value of its inappropriables that benefit the host country, λ_{h1} and λ_{h2} are respectively the gross profits of the host enterprise before and after the foreign RDU is set up and $\beta_h(\lambda_{h1} - \lambda_{h2})$ is the amount by which the host enterprise's inappropriable benefits are decreased by the presence of the foreign RDU.

If the inappropriables effect is positively signed, the foreign RDU will have enhanced host country welfare. Now we know that $(\lambda_f + \lambda_{h2}) > \lambda_{h1}$; this can be seen in Figure 4.1, where $OPE_2N_2 > OPE_1N_1$. So we can say that, if $\beta_f \geq \beta_h$, the inappropriables effect will be greater than zero. Thus the sufficient (though not necessary) condition for an increase in host country welfare is that $\beta_f \geq \beta_h$. If this sufficient condition is met the conclusions of the simple model will continue to be valid.[12] Note also that, although the possibility of a welfare loss cannot be ruled out, the underlying reason is the problem of inappropriability, rather than the foreign ownership of an RDU. The foreign ownership matters only because the enterprise's entire profits do not accrue to the host country.

Up to this point it has been assumed that the private cost of SET employment equals the social costs. However, this need not be the case. From the viewpoint of an individual who has just completed the education and training required for SET employment, the costs may be approximated by the net (that is, after-tax) income that was forgone during the education period, plus the fees (if any) that had to be paid for that education. In Figure 4.1 the private costs of the additional SETs employed because of the foreign RDU are shown by the area $N_1E_1E_2N_2$. But what are the corresponding social costs? These would include (a) the social value of the output that could have been produced by the SETs during their education period and (b) the social costs of that education; the latter, in turn, would include the cost of additional education personnel and/or increased effort on the part of the existing ones, additional equipment, buildings and so on. Thus the social costs may be either less or greater than the private costs.

If the social costs are less than the private costs, the country's gain from the foreign RDU will be greater than in the simple model. The additional gain arises because the wage paid by the subsidiary to the SETs will exceed their incremental social costs. On the other hand, if the social costs are greater than the private costs, the welfare conclusions will be more complex. Figure 4.2 illustrates. Let the area $N_1U_1U_2N_2$ show the social costs of training the additional SETs required by the foreign RDU, while area $N_1E_1E_2N_2$ shows the private costs. The effect of the foreign RDU on host country welfare is then shown by $BE_1E_2 - E_1U_1U_2E_2$, which may be either positive or negative. So if the social costs of SET employment exceed the private costs, the foreign RDU will either enhance or reduce host country welfare.

Here also the possibility of a welfare loss arises because the country has a second RDU, rather than because of the foreign ownership. Thus, even if the second RDU had been home-owned and all of its profits benefited the country, the welfare effect given by $BE_1E_2 + PBE_2 - E_1U_1U_2E_2$ could still have been either negative or positive. The foreign ownership of the second RDU increases the likelihood of a welfare loss, but the underlying cause of the loss is the excess of social over private costs of SET education.

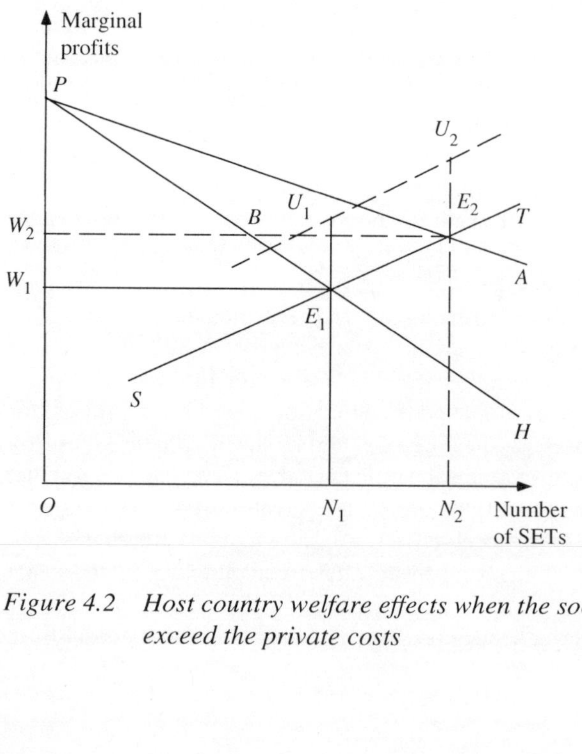

Figure 4.2 Host country welfare effects when the social costs of training exceed the private costs

The fourth assumption of the simple model was that each enterprise treats the wage paid to SETs as its marginal costs of employing those inputs and then equates the wage to its marginal gross profits from that employment. This assumption is now relaxed. As there are only two enterprises employing the SETs, each enterprise will recognize that the increased demand for those personnel may increase the wage that has to be paid to those already employed. The marginal cost of each level of employment will thus be greater than the wage paid. Each enterprise will now equate the marginal gross profits from SET employment to its marginal costs of that employment and so the former will exceed the wage paid. (The wage will continue to be uniform for the two enterprises.)

The effects of this are shown in Figure 4.3. As before, *ST* relates the level of employment to the wage paid, while *PH* and *PA* show the marginal gross profits. For diagrammatic simplicity, the enterprises' marginal cost schedules are not drawn; the factors influencing these costs are examined in the Appendix. Suppose that in the absence of the foreign RDU the host enterprise's optimal level of employment would have been ON_1, with wage OW_1, and so its profits would have been $W_1PH_1E_1$. The triangle E_1H_1K is a social loss due to the enterprise's monopsonistic influence. Suppose also that when the foreign RDU is set up the enterprises' marginal costs are such that the host enterprise's employment decreases to M_2H_2, the subsidiary employs H_2J, the marginal gross profits are OM_2 and the wage OW_2.[13]

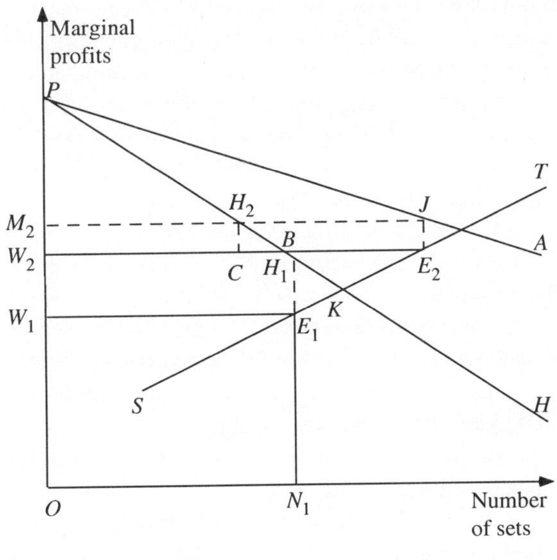

Figure 4.3 Host country welfare effects when the marginal private costs of additional employment exceed the wage rate

The welfare effects of the foreign RDU would then be as follows. The SETs' surplus would have increased by $W_1 W_2 E_2 E_1$, while the host enterprise's profits (net of the payments to the SETs) would have decreased by $W_1 W_2 B H_1 E_1 + C H_2 B$ and so the net outcome of these effects would be $E_1 H_1 K + KBE_2 - CH_2 B$. Clearly, this can be either positive or negative. In addition there will also be the tax revenues collected from the subsidiary. However, even when these revenues are taken into account, the possibility of a negative overall effect cannot be ruled out. Note that in this case the possibility of a welfare loss arises only because of the foreign ownership of an RDU, rather than because of two RDUs *per se*. Thus, if the foreign RDU's profits, which are shown by $H_2 PJ + CH_2 JE_2$, had accrued entirely to the host country, the overall welfare effect of having that RDU would have been $E_1 H_1 K + KBE_2 + BPJE_2$, which is clearly positive. The possibility of a welfare loss therefore arises only because a part of the foreign RDU's profits does not accrue to the host country.

Next let us consider the problem of 'lumpiness' or indivisible inputs. An R&D project may require the use of some indivisible inputs, such as capital equipment, a minimum number of SETs, and so on. Such R&D projects would have to operate at, at least, some minimum scale, or else be shut down. In the present context it is likely that, if the foreign RDU were to draw some SETs away from the host enterprise, the latter might have to close down one or more of its projects. The effect of this on host country welfare will depend on the net change in SET employment.

Figure 4.4 illustrates two possible outcomes. Suppose that in the absence of the foreign RDU the host enterprise would have operated two projects. ON_1 and $N_1 N_2$ are respectively the number of SETs required for the first and second projects, $H_1 N_1$ and $H_2 N_2$ are their gross profits per SET employed and OW_1 is the average cost of the SET employment.[14] Next suppose that the foreign RDU had a project whose SET requirements, say $N_1 N_3$, exceeded those of the host enterprise's second project and whose profits per SET were $F_3 N_3$. The demand for SETs would increase and the wage would increase to OW_3. However, as drawn, the host enterprise's second project would now become unprofitable. Nevertheless, the numbers employed would increase to ON_3 and the wage would increase to OW_2. The increase in the SETs' surplus, $W_1 W_2 E_2 E_1$, would more than offset the decrease in the host enterprise's profits, shown by ($W_1 W_2 BD + DBH_2 E_1$); in addition there would be tax revenues collected from the subsidiary. So here again the foreign RDU would enhance host country welfare.

However, the above case is not the only possibility. Consider an alternative situation where the foreign RDU's requirement of SETs is equal to (or less than) that of the host enterprise's second project, but the former has relatively higher profits per SET employed, shown by $F_2 N_2$. Now if the subsidiary's demand for SETs were to raise the wage above $H_2 N_2$, the host enterprise would have to close down its second project. In this case there would be no increase in SET employment and hence no increase in their surplus. The host enterprise's profits would decrease by DBH_2E_1 and this welfare loss might, or might not, be greater than the tax revenues collected from the subsidiary. So in this case the foreign RDU may either decrease, or increase, host country welfare. This possibility of a welfare loss also arises because of the foreign ownership of an RDU, rather than because of an additional RDU. If all of the profits $DF_1F_2E_1$ had accrued to the host country there would have been an unambiguous increase in welfare.

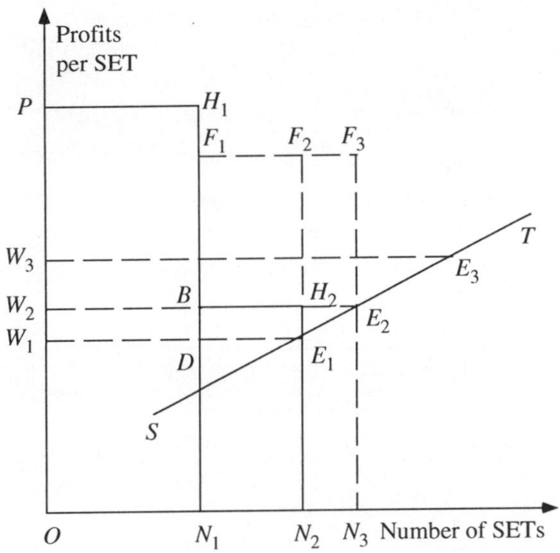

Figure 4.4 Host country effects when R&D projects employ some indivisible inputs

Lastly, let us relax the assumption that all SETs are a uniform homogeneous factor. In fact it is likely that each of the SETs in an RDU (or small groups of them) may be engaged in some specialist R&D tasks, which link up into a team effort. Such specialization raises an interesting possibility. For instance, the host and foreign RDUS may each have a comparative advantage in certain specializations (the latter's advantage being perhaps in areas related to its parent's know-how). The specialists in the two RDUs may be able to exchange information and thereby enhance each other's efficiency. In terms of Figures 4.1, 4.2 and 4.3 there would be an upward shift of the *PH* and *PA* schedules and in Figure 4.4 the profits per SET would increase. Thus specialization amongst SETs and exchange of information makes it likely that, although the foreign RDU may decrease the number of SETs employed in the host enterprise, that loss may be partly (or wholly) offset by an increase in the efficiency of the SETs that remain with the host enterprise.

4 PRODUCTION EFFECTS AND HOST COUNTRY WELFARE

The enterprise's R&D input levels, examined above, will affect their levels of output and these, in turn, may have further effects on host country welfare. In examining these subsequent production effects I will assume the following:

1. the two enterprises produce the same homogeneous products and their R&D efforts have only decreased the costs of production, with no change in product quality;
2. they compete with each other in home and export markets; and
3. the competitive responses of other enterprises are small enough to be ignored.

The last of these assumptions will be relaxed later.

In Figure 4.5 let OC_h and OC_f be respectively the (constant) average costs of the host enterprise and the subsidiary; these costs are consequent to the R&D levels examined in the preceding sections. The subsidiary is assumed to have lower costs; this assumption seems plausible for, as Davies and Lyons (1991) have shown, in the UK at least, foreign subsidiaries have significantly higher levels of productivity than host enterprises in the same industries. Let the initial output levels of the host enterprise and subsidiary be OQ_1 and Q_1T_1, respectively. Their profits will then be shown by the areas $H_1 + H_2 + H_3 + H_4$ and $F_1 + F_2 + F_3$ respectively. (These profits in product space correspond to the gross profits in R&D space shown in the preceding figures).

The initial output levels will now be revised. To illustrate one possible outcome let us suppose that the enterprises engage in Cournot competition. Then, given the changes in their R&D input levels, the output of the host enterprise will decrease to, say, OQ_2, while that of the subsidiary will increase to, say, Q_2T_2. Suppose also that the decrease in the former's output is more than offset by the increase in that of the latter. The product price will then decrease to OP_2.

The welfare effects are then as follows. The profits of the host enterprise decrease by $H_1 + H_2 + H_4$ while those of the foreign subsidiary increase by $H_4 + F_4 + F_5 + F_6 - F_1$. In addition, consumers' surplus increases by $H_1 + H_2 + F_1 + T$; of this, let α be the proportion accruing to host country consumers, where $0 \leq \alpha \leq 1$. Collecting terms and rearranging, we can write the welfare effect as

$$[\alpha(H_1 + H_2 + F_1 + T) + t_h(F_5 + F_6 - F_1) - (H_1 + H_2)] + [t_h(H_4 + F_4) - H_4]$$

where t_h is the host country's rate of profits tax. Clearly the overall sign of this may be either positive or negative. So these production effects, like the direct R&D effects, may either increase or decrease host country welfare.

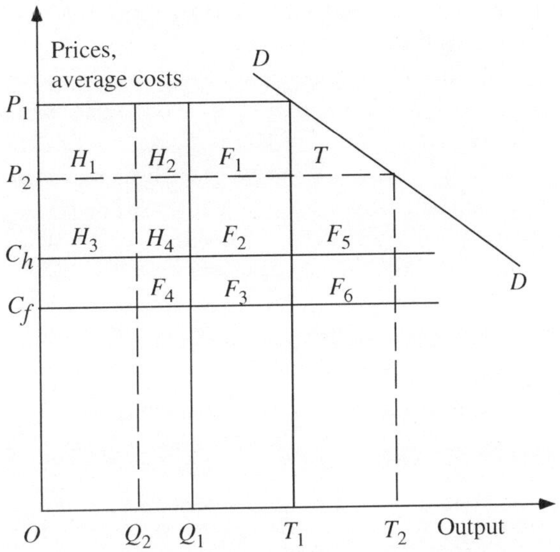

Figure 4.5 Host country welfare effects when enterprises compete in product markets

The expression in the first square bracket above represents an aggregate output effect; that is, the consequence of an increase in the enterprises' combined level of output. The likelihood of this expression being positively signed increases as the export share decreases: specifically, if $\alpha = 1$, this effect must be greater than zero. The expression in the second square bracket represents an output relocation effect; that is, the shift of output from the host enterprise to the subsidiary. The likelihood of this effect being positively signed increases with the subsidiary's cost advantage, relative to that of the host enterprise; specifically, it will be positively signed if $(1 - c_f)/(1 - c_h) > 1/t_h$, where c_f and c_h are respectively the average costs of the subsidiary and the host enterprise.[15] Thus we see that the subsequent production effects are more likely to increase host country welfare the lower is the enterprise's export propensity and the greater is the subsidiary's cost advantage.

Suppose now that the magnitude of the above influences is such as to result in a welfare loss. Would that outcome be because of the foreign ownership of one of the enterprises, or would it be due to the competition between two enterprises? The answer seems to depend on the export propensity. We can see that, if $\alpha = 1$, the overall welfare effect will be negatively signed only because $t_h < 1$; that is, only because part of the foreign enterprise's profits does not accrue to the host country, but if $\alpha < 1$, a welfare loss could arise even if $t_h = 1$. So in the former case the possibility of a welfare loss may be attributed to the foreign ownership of one of the enterprises, but in the latter case the loss could be because of the competition between the enterprises.

The export propensity is of further consequence when we allow for the existence of rival enterprises. An increase in the output of the host enterprise and of the subsidiary is likely to induce a corresponding increase in output of the rival enterprises. The latter would decrease the profits of the host enterprise and the subsidiary, but would benefit the consumers. Now if these enterprises were competing mainly in the host country market, the decrease in profits of the host enterprise and the subsidiary could be partly, or wholly, offset by the gains to host country consumers. On the other hand, if the enterprises were competing mainly in export markets, host country consumers would get little benefit from the responses of rival enterprises.

5 SUMMARY AND IMPLICATIONS

This chapter has examined how the presence of foreign enterprises' RDUs may affect the welfare of host countries. The analysis assumed a simple duopoly scenario, with a host enterprise and a foreign subsidiary, and envisaged an initial R&D stage, when enterprises determine their R&D levels, and a subsequent stage when they revise their output levels.

In the R&D stage, the foreign RDU's presence increased the income of the SETs employed and also the tax revenues collected from the subsidiary, but decreased the profits of the host enterprise. It was shown that under some simplifying assumptions the gain on the former two counts would more than offset the loss on the third count and so the foreign RDU would enhance host country welfare. However, when those simplifying assumptions were relaxed, the outcome was more complex and the country's welfare could either decrease or increase. A welfare loss could have arisen, for instance, if the enterprises' R&D efforts required some minimum number of SETs and/or if the enterprises could not appropriate all of the benefits of the R&D efforts.

The subsequent production effects consisted of a change in the enterprises' combined level of output and a shift in output from the high-cost domestic enterprise to the foreign-owned subsidiary. These changes affected the host consumers' surplus, the host enterprise's profits and the tax revenues collected from the subsidiary. Here, too, the overall welfare effect could be either positive or negative. The possibility of an increase in welfare was greater, the smaller the share of exports in the enterprises' sales (as this enhanced the gains to host consumers resulting from an increase in the enterprises' combined level of output).

The analysis of the chapter has some important policy implications. In so far as foreign RDUs are seen to have some negative as well as positive effects on host country welfare, it would be desirable to consider policies which would reduce the negative effects and enhance the positive ones. In devising those policies it would be desirable to distinguish between those effects that arise because of an increase in the number of RDUs in the host country and those that arise because of the foreign ownership of some RDUs.

There are six measures worth considering, of which the first three deal with effects arising from an increase in the number of RDUs. First, the likelihood of a welfare loss would be reduced if the managers of host enterprises could correctly evaluate the profits from their enterprises' R&D efforts. This might be helped if the manager had received relevant training in a SET area, as well as in finance and business management. Secondly, it is desirable that the host enterprises be able to appropriate most of the benefits of their R&D efforts through improved functioning of institutional arrangements such as the patent system. Thirdly, the likelihood of welfare losses would be reduced by correcting the divergence between the private and social costs of SET education (though if this required raising the fees for such education, there might be objections). Fourthly, in cases where each R&D unit needs to employ some minimum number of SETs, it may be desirable to monitor the foreign RDUs' requirements so as to ensure a net increase in employment of SETs, rather than a mere transfer from the host enterprise. Fifthly, in so far as the foreign and host RDUs each have some comparative advantage in specialized areas, the government could encourage the exchange of information between the enterprises. Finally, in cases where the foreign RDU does lead to a welfare loss, it would be important to consider whether that effect is more than (or less than) offset by any gains from the production activities of the foreign enterprise.

NOTES

1. Empirical evidence of foreign MNEs' R&D activities is reported in Casson (1991), Molera (1983), Patel and Pavitt (1991) and Veugelers and Vanden Houte (1990).
2. These data on foreign and domestic funding may perhaps understate the relative share of foreign-owned RDUs, since some of the latters' activities may have been financed from the MNEs' funds in the host countries.
3. As the SETs are likely to be engaged in cost-reducing and/or quality-improving tasks, and as these activities may be subject to diminishing returns with respect to the numbers employed, we expect that the SETs will increase the profits, but at a diminishing rate.
4. It is being assumed that at least some aspects of an enterprise's current R&D efforts require some know-how that is embodied in its SETs' past experience. So a decrease in the number of SETs employed will reduce the enterprise's R&D efforts and/or the efficiency of those efforts.

5. The factors making for a divergence between the social and private costs of SET training are discussed below.
6. The increase in the SETs' may induce an increase in the numbers employed in the short run (as some individuals who had been trained as SETs but were employed in other occupations now return to SET employment) and also in the long run (as an increased number of individuals would train as SETs). In what follows our interest is mainly with the long-run aspects.
7. These results of the simple model have an obvious similarity with those of Corden's (1974) model of inward foreign investment. In the latter model, foreign capital is complementary to host country labour but competing with host capital and it enhances the income of the complementary factor by more than it decreases the income of the competing factor. Similarly, in the present model the foreign RDU enhances the income of the complementary SETs by more than it reduces the profits of the competing host enterprise.
8. For instance, it is sometimes suggested that the top managers in some of the large enterprises in the UK have experience and expertise in accounting and finance, rather than as SETs.
9. In response to this it may perhaps be argued that past experience may not always be a very helpful guide for predicting profits, because the R&D efforts being currently undertaken may be different (in terms of products and processes) from those undertaken in past periods.
10. The consequences of the host enterprise overestimating the profitability of its R&D efforts can be seen by reinterpreting the *PA* schedule as the aggregate of *PR* and the foreign subsidiary's schedule. The presence of the foreign RDU would increase the SETs' employment from point D to E_2, while the host enterprise's employment would move from point D to C, and so the resulting increase in the SETs' income would exceed the decrease in the host enterprise's profits.
11. Mansfield *et al*'s (1977) study reports empirical evidence that in many US industries the social benefits of innovation exceed the private benefits.
12. The likelihood of this sufficient condition being fulfilled may depend, in part, on the nature of the R&D activities of the host enterprise and the foreign subsidiary. The host enterprise is likely to undertake both basic and developmental research but, as Cantwell (1989) and Ronstadt (1978) have pointed out, the subsidiary may be assigned mainly developmental research, or be restricted to adapting the parent's technologies to the host country environment. Then if, as Mansfield *et al.* (1979) have reported, the difficulty of an enterprise appropriating the benefits of its R&D efforts is greater for basic research than for developmental work, it becomes possible that $\beta_h > \beta_f$. The sufficient (though not necessary) condition may then not be fulfilled.
13. For diagrammatic simplicity it is assumed that the marginal gross profits are equal for the two enterprises. This, however, need not be so. The two enterprises will have a uniform wage but, as equations (4A6) and (4A7) in the Appendix show, the relationship between the uniform wage and each enterprise's marginal costs (and hence its marginal gross profits) will also depend on the enterprise's response to an increase in its rival's employment.
14. Note that, when an R&D project is indivisible, the enterprise's employment of SETs will depend on the average (rather than marginal) cost of SETs for that project and the gross profits per SET.
15. This condition can be seen as follows. As stated in the text, the output relocation effect will be positive if $(H_4 + F_4)/H_4 > 1/t_h$. Translated in terms of the product price and average costs, this condition requires that $(P_2C_f)/(P_2C_h) > 1/t_h$ and then choosing units to set $OP_2 = 1$, the condition becomes $(1 - c_f)/(1 - c_h) > 1/t_h$, where the average costs c_f, and c_h correspond respectively to OC_f and OC_h in Figure 4.5.

REFERENCES

Cantwell, J. (1989), *Technological Innovation and Multinational Corporations,* Oxford: Basil Blackwell.

Casson, M. (ed.) (1991), *Global Research Strategy and International Competitiveness*, Oxford: Basil Blackwell.

Corden, W.M. (1974), *Trade Policy and Economic Welfare*, Oxford: Oxford University Press.

Davies, S.W. and B.R. Lyon (1991), 'Characterising relative performance: the productivity advantage of foreign owned firms in the UK', *Oxford Economic Papers*.

Hirschey, R.C. and R.E. Caves (1981), 'Research and transfer of technology by multinational enterprises', *Oxford Bulletin of Economics and Statistics*.

Mansfield, F. *et al.* (1977), 'Social and private rates of return from industrial innovations', *Quarterly Journal of Economics*.

Mansfield, E. *et al.* (1979), 'Overseas research and development by US based firms', *Economica*.

Molera, J. (1983), Foreign technology in the Spanish economy: an analysis of the recent evolution', *Research Policy*.

Patel, P. and K. Pavitt (1991), 'Large firms in the production of the World's technology: an important case of non-globalisation', *Journal of International Business Studies*.

Ronstadt, R. (1978), 'Research and development abroad by US multinationals', *Journal of International Business Studies*.

Spencer, B.J. and J.A. Brander (1983), 'International R&D rivalry and industrial strategy', *Review of Economic Studies*.

Stoneman, P. (1991), 'Overseas funding for industrial R&D in the United Kingdom', in D. Hague (ed.), *The Management of Science*, London: Macmillan.

Veugelers, R. and P. Vanden Houte (1990), 'Domestic R&D in the presence of multinational enterprises', *International Journal of Industrial Organisation*.

Wortman, M. (1990), 'Multinationals and the internationalisation of R&D: new developments in German companies', *Research Policy*.

APPENDIX

The marginal costs of SET employment for the host enterprise and the foreign subsidiary, denoted by MC_h and MC_f, respectively, are defined as

$$MC_h = (dW/dN_h)N_h + W \tag{4A.1}$$

$$MC_f = (dW/dN_f)N_f + W \tag{4A.2}$$

where W is the uniform wage rate for the SETs and N_h and N_f are respectively the numbers employed by the host enterprise and the subsidiary.

Now, as the wage rate will depend on the aggregate employment, we can write

$$W = w(N_h, N_f) \tag{4A.3}$$

Then, taking the total differential of (4A.3) and dividing throughout by N_h, we have for the host enterprise

$$(dW/dN_h) = (\partial W/\partial N_h) + (\partial W/\partial N_f)(dN_f/dN_h) \tag{4A.4}$$

Similarly dividing the total differential of (4A.3) by N_f we get for the subsidiary

$$(dW/dN_f) = (\partial W/\partial N_f) + (\partial W/\partial N_h)(dN_h/dN_f) \tag{4A.5}$$

The term $(\partial W/\partial N_h)$ is the *ceteris paribus* effect of an increase in the host enterprise's employment on the wage rate and similarly for $(\partial W/\partial N_f)$, (dN_f/dN_h) is the effect of an increase in the host enterprise's employment on the employment in the subsidiary and correspondingly for (dN_h/dN_f).

Substituting (4A.4) into (4A.1) and (4A.5) into (4A.2) we can rewrite the marginal costs as

$$MC_h = [(\partial W/\partial N_h) + (\partial W/\partial N_f)(dN_f/dN_h)]N_h + W \tag{4A.6}$$

for the host enterprise and

$$MC_f = [(\partial W/\partial N_f) + (\partial W/\partial N_h)(dN_h/dN_f)]N_f + W \tag{4A.7}$$

for the subsidiary. Thus the marginal costs for each enterprise depend on the *ceteris paribus* effects and also on each enterprise's response to an increase in the rival's employment.

5. Intrafirm royalties in the process of expansion of US multinational enterprises

R.E. Caves and A. More

Royalty payments received by US multinational enterprises (MNEs) from their overseas subsidiaries reflect the intangible technology and goodwill assets transferred by the parents to those subsidiaries. These transfers, widely recognized as fundamental to the internalization of failure-prone transactions within the MNE, are unobservable and elude the researcher. However, the resulting payments we can observe, and in this chapter we analyse their variation among host countries and among major investing sectors. Despite the central role of transferred intangibles, intrafirm royalty payments have received only a little attention in studies of transfer-pricing behaviour and none for the information that they contain about the (unobserved) transfers of intangibles and their role in the expansion of MNEs.

Some simple facts motivate the investigation. During 1977–82 (the period covered in our statistical analysis) no less than 76.5 per cent of royalty and licence fees received from abroad by US corporations came from their foreign affiliates, only 23.5 per cent from independent parties. Of these foreign affiliates' total royalty payments, 76 per cent flowed to their US parents in 1977, increasing to 83 per cent in 1982. Although only 41 per cent of non-bank foreign affiliates of US non-bank parents made use of their parents' patents and/or trademarks in 1977, this 41 per cent accounted for fully 98.6 per cent of the total value of US direct investment abroad.[1] Analysing product innovations in the five years after their first commercialization, Mansfield (1984, p. 137) found that US firms expect 74 per cent of diffusions overseas to occur through transfers of technology to foreign affiliates, only a minority through exporting the innovative goods (15 per cent), arm's-length licensing (9) and joint ventures (2). The intrafirm transfer of intangibles is clearly the dominant channel.

Given the plethora of quantitative research on MNEs, why have intrafirm royalty payments been neglected? We conjecture that researchers have been put off by distortions present in the data: the reported values lack the underpinning of arm's-length price determination, and multinational firms have an incentive to manipulate transfer prices in order to minimize taxes and evade profit-remittance and other regulations. These sources of noise certainly could destroy the signal value of data on intrafirm royalty payments. Whether the signal is actually inaudible, however, is an empirical question. In this chapter we show that changes in these payments over time in fact support tests of numerous hypotheses about the operation of MNEs, once the principal inducement for transfer-price manipulation is controlled.

1 ANALYTICAL FRAMEWORK: ROYALTIES AND FOREIGN INVESTMENT

Chief among the reasons for investigating the behaviour of intrafirm royalties is what they can reveal about the expansion process of multinational enterprises. Various authors such as Kogut (1983) have complained that research on MNEs focuses on hypotheses about their origin (in incentives to internalize economic activity) at the expense of understanding the process of expansion and adjustment that occurs once they are founded.[2] An observed flow of intrafirm royalty payments bears a complex relationship to this expansion process that we sketch here in qualitative terms.

A US enterprise establishes a foreign subsidiary to manufacture and market abroad products related to those that its parent offers in the US market (and perhaps elsewhere). At the outset the parent provides its subsidiary with various intangible assets–specific technologies, general know-how and experience, and intangibles such as trademarks and designs. If transplanted successfully, each intangible yields a cash flow in excess of the cost of complementary tangible inputs employed by the subsidiary. Further transfers may occur over time as the parent develops or acquires other intangibles that the subsidiary can profitably use, each yielding its own cash flow profile. The intrafirm royalty payments received by US parents in a given year constitute (we assume) a noisy signal of the sum of these cash flows during the year.

Intrafirm royalties thus reflect the flows of services from intangibles, some transferred almost contemporaneously, others emplaced earlier. The intangibles transfers themselves, generally unobserved, similarly occur in a distributed lag after the initial financial investment in the foreign subsidiary and any subsequent enlargement. Little is known about the shapes of these distributed lags: the successive transfers of intangibles following an initial foreign investment, the flows of intrafirm royalties following a transfer of intangibles.[3] Nonetheless, we shall employ a simple set of stock and flow variables that capture at least the rudiments of these distributions.

In preparing to explain variations in intrafirm royalty flows, we face a problem of how best to represent the time structure of these relationships by means of the few data available. We need capability to detect each of the following relationships:

1. A new foreign investment soon yields flows of revenue imputable to intangibles transferred when it was founded.
2. The accumulated stock of foreign investment yields continual opportunities for new intangibles transfers and associated growth of intrafirm royalty payments.
3. At a given time recent additions to the stock of foreign investment might yield better opportunities for the transfer of intangibles and capture of quasi-rents than do more mature foreign investments.[4]

Using data available in the 1977 and 1982 benchmark surveys of US direct investment abroad, we could relate flows of royalty payments in 1982 to stocks of direct investment in place in 1982 and 1977. That formulation would capture the first and third of these relationships. It would not capture the second one, however. For that reason (and certain lesser ones) we chose instead to relate the proportional change in royalty payments over 1977–82 to the contemporaneous change in the stock of foreign investment, the lagged change in that stock (1972–6),[5] and the level of the accumulated stock (as of 1977). From the coefficients obtained in such a model we cannot hope to infer any particular time profile of the transfer of intangibles or the realization of quasi-rents from the transfers, but we should gain some insight into the time structures of these relationships.

With the antecedent foreign investment decisions controlled in this manner, we can test hypotheses about the determinants of changes in intrafirm royalty payments. Those set out in the next section address variations in the revenue productivity of intangibles transfers and/or in the opportunities that multinational firms have to undertake them. Transfer pricing policies will be taken into account. Specifically, we assume that intrafirm royalty payments represent real quasi-rents whose nominal 'prices' might have been modified by the firm in order to minimize its tax bill. The modifications are assumed proportional to the international differences in tax rates that induce them.

We employ the data from the 1977 and 1982 benchmark surveys on revenues received by US parent multinational corporations from their foreign affiliates as royalties and licence fees for the use or sale of intangible property or rights, such as patents, industrial processes, trademarks, copyrights, designs, know-how, formulas, techniques, manufacturing rights and other intangible assets or propriety rights (US Bureau of Economic Analysis, 1985, p. 25). Hypotheses about the determinants of these payments are tested on changes among both industrial sectors in which the parents are based and host countries in which the subsidiaries operate. The 1977 and 1982 benchmark surveys permit us to distinguish 35 industrial sectors and 45 countries.

These two slices through the data allow the testing of both country-specific and sector-specific hypotheses, but with the results subject to bias because of our inability to obtain data on the underlying industry–country cells. Let us consider the consequences of this problem.[6] With royalty flows in a given industry–country cell defined as R_{ic}, with subscripts indicating industry (i) and country (c), the dependent variable becomes $\Delta R_{ic}/R_{ic}$. We expect it to be related to industry-specific (X_i) and country-specific (Z_c) determinants:

$$\Delta R_{ic}/R_{ic} = \alpha X_i + \beta Z_c \tag{5.1}$$

The industry-level and country-level changes that we actually analyse are; $\Delta R_{i.}/R_{i.}$ and $\Delta R_{.c}/R_{.c}$, respectively. The former (for example) can be written as a weighted sum of equation (5.1) for the individual cells:

$$\begin{aligned}\Delta R_{i.}/R_{i.} &= \sum_i (\Delta R_{ic}/R_{ic})\,(R_{ic}/R_{i.}) \\ &= \sum_i s_{ic}(\Delta R_{ic}/R_{ic}) \qquad\qquad \sum_i s_{ic} = 1 \\ &= \alpha \sum_i s_{ic} X_i + \beta \sum_i s_{ic} Z_c\end{aligned} \tag{5.2}$$

When we estimate a regression model on inter-industry differences it will take the form

$$\Delta R_{i.}/R_{i.} = a_o + \Sigma a_i X_i + e \tag{5.3}$$

The term $\beta \sum_i s_{ic} Z_c$ in equation (5.2) becomes an omitted variable. The omission is a potential source of bias and inconsistency in the estimation of the a_i in equation (5.3), as are analogous industry effects in the inter-country analysis. We can make use of conjectures relating to magnitudes and signs of the covariance between X_i and $\sum_i s_{ic} Z_c$ and the coefficient β to assess the distortion. For example, it is clear that the more similar are inter-industry distributions of foreign direct investment among countries, the smaller is the covariance. Also helpful is the degree to which Z_c values are indeed identical among industries (assumed in the preceding argument).

2 OTHER DETERMINANTS OF ROYALTY PAYMENTS

We now set out the other hypotheses about the determinants of (changes in) intrafirm royalty payments and describe how they were represented statistically.

Varying amounts of background discussion of these hypotheses will be provided, some being more familiar and established than others.

The measurement of stocks and flows of US foreign direct investment is straightforward. The variable is defined as US parents' stake in the total assets of their foreign affiliates, whether financed through equity or debt. Its proportional change between 1977 and 1982 is expressed as the logarithm of the 1982 value (for the country or sector in question) minus the logarithm of the 1977 value. The 1977 value is represented simply by the latter logarithmic figure. Data on lagged (1972–6) changes, also expressed as differences in logarithms, are largely compatible with data from the 1977 and 1982 benchmark surveys. These and other exogenous variables are summarized and their sources given in Table 5.1. On the assumption that successful foreign investments involve an initial transfer of intangible assets and possibly subsequent transfers as well, the 1977–82 FDI change and the 1977 FDI stock should take positive coefficients. The effect of the 1972–6 change is uncertain: it depends on the temporal distribution both of intangibles transfers following a given foreign investment and of cash flows from a given transfer of intangibles.

Parents' Stocks of Intangibles

Although transfers of intangibles are not observable, we can control roughly for the stocks of intangibles available for transfer by means of data on the domestic parents' expenditures to augment these stocks: outlays in the US on research and development and on advertising (normalized by US sales).

Little is known about the effect of the domestic stock of goodwill assets on quasi-rents earned by foreign affiliates beyond the findings of numerous studies that advertising intensity is often (but not always) a significant predictor of inter-industry differences in foreign investment activity. For example, Drake and Caves (1992) found that Japanese foreign investment in the US came to be positively and significantly related to industries' advertising intensity in the 1980s, a presumed consequence of the development of goodwill assets and related design and marketing skills within successful Japanese firms.

Regarding research activities and innovations, Mansfield, Romeo and Wagner (1979) found that large US companies would reduce their R&D expenditures substantially if denied the opportunity to exploit their discoveries abroad (through their own subsidiaries, or in any manner). Although process technologies tend to be kept at home and embodied in exports, new product technologies are transferred abroad, more commonly to subsidiaries than through other channels (Mansfield, 1984). Furthermore, newer technologies are more likely to be transferred to a subsidiary (Mansfield and Romeo, 1980; McFetridge, 1987).

Representing the intangible asset stocks that generate intrafirm royalty payments for US parents poses the same problem of stock-flow relations as does foreign investment itself. An ideal measure for explaining the growth of royalties would be lagged gross additions to the parents' stocks, such as normalized total R&D expenditures in the latter 1970s. Because the typical sector's ratios of R&D or sales promotion outlays to total sales vary little from year to year, however, variations among sectors in intangibles stocks and their growth over time are probably summarized well by the ratios of R&D and sales promotion expenditures to sales for a single year – 1977. The 1977–82 change in intrafirm royalties should increase with both ratios. These intangibles can be observed to vary among industries, but not among host countries, so the variables will not appear in the inter-country model.

Productivity of Transferred Intangibles

Royalty payments should increase with the revenue productivity of the intangibles transferred to the host country site, given the intangible stocks available for use and the foreign investments in place to exploit them. We selected three variables to represent variations in this productivity. One of these is simply the growth of gross national product (GNP) in the host country. As a first approximation the revenue productivity of intangible assets should depend on the sizes of the markets in which they are deployed. Those revenue flows should hence grow with GNP.[7] The growth of intrafirm royalty payments is measured in nominal US dollars. The growth of host GNP therefore should be measured so as to incorporate changes in the real bilateral exchange rate between the host's currency and the dollar. The procedure will be explained subsequently.

Given the growth of the host's income, the revenue productivity of intangibles should also increase with the host industrial sector's specific ability to absorb and utilize technology from abroad. This ability might be represented by the host's level of economic development, but we employed a more focused indicator. The 1977 benchmark survey ascertained the number of foreign affiliates reporting that they provided technology to their US parents, allowing us to calculate its ratio to number of affiliates reporting that they utilize technology of their parent. The extent of this reciprocal licensing should reflect the capacity of the host's industrial sector to absorb and use technology from the US parent. Although little direct empirical evidence bears on this conjecture (but see Bertin, 1987), Zejan (1990) found that R&D spending by foreign subsidiaries of Swedish multinationals increases with their parents' R&D expenditures and the size and level of development of the host economy.

Finally, the revenue productivity of transferred intangibles should be related to the costs of transferring technology and other intangibles. Teece (1976) found that costs of transfer to a joint venture are 5 per cent higher than to a wholly owned subsidiary, and those to an independent firm 9 per cent higher. Host countries that restrict the use of wholly owned subsidiaries thereby presumably increase the costs of inbound technology transfers and thus reduce their net revenue productivity. Furthermore, the transfer of proprietary intangibles to incompletely controlled subsidiaries is inhibited by the greater likelihood that it will leak into the possession of other parties with decision rights in the subsidiary. The benchmark survey reports the proportion of subsidiaries in each host country reporting that they are affected by the host's restrictions on the parent's equity holdings. The variable that we measure is the change in this proportion between 1977 and 1982. Its expression as a change rests on the conjecture that royalties generated by foreign subsidiaries adjust fairly fast to such changes in the investment climate.

The growth of host country GNP, reciprocal licensing and changes in equity restrictions measure primarily differences among countries, and the first two will appear only in the inter-country model. The equity restriction variable is available for both countries and sectors and will be used in both models (partly as a check on the problem of omitted-variable bias noted previously). To conclude, we expect the change in royalty payments to increase with the growth of host GNP and extent of reciprocal licensing and to decrease with the change in equity restrictions.

Intrafirm Exports

Our analysis relates the growth of intrafirm royalties to the process of the expansion and development of multinational enterprises, and it should hence embrace the relation between intrafirm royalty payments and intrafirm merchandise trade. Intrafirm trade is estimated to be as much as 35 to 40 per cent of total US foreign trade (Little, 1986, 1987). Questions have been raised about whether its prevalence affects the overall process of adjustment in US international trade and payments.[8]

Intrafirm trade and intrafirm royalty payments may be either substitutes or complements. Intangible assets developed by a US parent can be embodied in US-produced goods for export to foreign markets, or the intangibles can be transferred abroad for embodiment in local production. If this relationship of substitution predominates, changes in intrafirm exports and royalties will be negatively related. Alternatively, intrafirm flows of intangibles and goods may appear complementary in the sense that both grow as new foreign investments expand. Both then serve as organizational responses to the underlying imperfections in arm's-length markets that bring multinational enterprises into being. Local production in the host country embodies intangible assets that cannot be efficiently rented between independent firms. Imports from affiliates are marketed by subsidiaries along with their lines of locally produced items, partly because first-best contracts cannot be written with independent distributors of the imported goods.

Although previous research contains little direct evidence on these relationships, we find a good deal that is relevant but indirect. Mansfield (1984, p. 137) showed that the channel selected by a multinational firm for the diffusion of an innovation depends strongly on the type of innovation: most product innovations are produced and introduced locally by foreign affiliates, while most process innovations are embodied in goods exported by the parent. (Mansfield conjectured that the difference stems from the greater difficulty of maintaining proprietary control over process technology.) If industries' mixtures of innovation types differ, this finding supports the hypothesis that intrafirm royalties and trade are substitutes among sectors.

Nonetheless, a lot of evidence supports the finding that foreign investment and exports are complementary in the development of particular multinational enterprises.[9] Among recent contributions, Pearce (1990) found that for the world's largest multinational enterprises the share of the parent's output exported increases with the proportion of its worldwide sales accounted for by sales (net of resales) of its foreign affiliates. Among sectors, this positive relation seems particularly evident in research-intensive activities (such as electronics) and in industries that produce differentiated lines of products (such as metal manufactures), so that each national market is efficiently offered a product line consisting of items locally produced and others obtained from corporate affiliates. Furthermore, intrafirm trade as a proportion of the parent's total exports increases with the subsidiary's share of the enterprise's worldwide sales and with the parent's R&D/sales ratio; sectors that are positive outliers include product line assemblers (such as measurement and scientific apparatus), while the negative outliers are low-technology and chemical process sectors. Casson and associates (1988) similarly stressed the product line relationship as an aspect of general incentives for vertical integration. Various other research supports the conclusion that the complementarity of foreign investment and exports is evident in high-technology and product line industries; for example, Grubaugh (1987) related the firm's multinational status to a measure of its diversification.

Similar evidence was reported by Blomström, Lipsey and Kulchycky (1988) for US and Swedish multinationals, although with the finding of complementarity somewhat weaker for the US. Complementarity prevailed (but usually without statistical significance) for about five-sixths of their 30 industries. They found substitutability between exports and foreign investment in sales to the foreign affiliates' local markets and not the affiliates' export sales.

More evidence appears in studies of subsidiaries operating in particular host countries. MacCharles (1987) found that foreign subsidiaries in Canada have higher ratios of imports to sales than their domestic competitors for both components and final products. One-half of the subsidiaries' imports take the form of minor products and components (rather than major products). In industries with extensive intraindustry trade vertical integration (measured inversely by the ratio of value of purchased materials to value added) is substantially although not significantly lower for subsidiaries than for domestic firms.[10]

In summary, some evidence suggests that intrafirm royalties and trade behave as substitutes between sectors, but a great deal indicates that intrafirm trade grows in parallel with the expansion of foreign direct investment. The expansion of intrafirm trade thus reflects otherwise unobserved opportunities to expand the activities of foreign subsidiaries, implying a positive relation between changes in intrafirm royalties and intrafirm trade. This complementary relationship is more likely to prevail among countries than among industries, because country differences should generate more variance in general development opportunities for multinational enterprises than should differences in broad industrial sectors. Procedurally we note the hazards of trying to establish substitution or complementarity by means of a single-equation model (see note 9). Furthermore, intrafirm trade would ideally be treated as another endogenous variable, although the available data seem insufficient to permit an instrumental variables approach to intrafirm trade. Thus the exploratory status of our analysis of intrafirm royalty payments applies especially to their relationship to intrafirm trade.

Influence of Taxes on Transfer Pricing

The last exogenous variable is the important control for tax-based incentives for multinational firms to manipulate their transfer prices. The theoretical literature on transfer pricing (see papers by Eden and Diewert in Rugman and Eden, 1985) shows that unconstrained optimization of transfer prices to minimize a multinational's global tax burden leads to corner solutions, with the transfer price set to shift as much reported profit as possible into the lower-tax jurisdiction. This tax-avoidance behaviour may destroy the information content of intrafirm royalty payments, because they seem the easiest transfer prices to manipulate: no way exists to verify them by means of comparable market prices or readily identifiable costs of production.

Nonetheless, tax-induced distortions in transfer prices implicit in intrafirm royalties may be limited, for two reasons. First, Section 482 of the Internal Revenue Code requires that US multinationals' transfer prices approximate arm's-length values constructed by one of a hierarchy of simulation methods. The gross manipulation of transfer prices therefore exposes the firm to the risk of costly legal entanglements. Second, the literature of business administration suggests that firms cannot readily keep two sets of books. Reporting a distribution of profits among affiliates modified to minimize the firm's global tax burden conflicts with its need for efficient monitoring of the revenue productivity of the firm's various activities and incentive-based rewards for managers and employees.

A good deal of empirical evidence bears on these points. We consider first the organizational constraints on transfer pricing, because of their primary importance for preserving the information value of data on intrafirm royalty payments. Yunker (1982), who also surveyed previous evidence on organizational constraints on transfer price manipulation (pp. 34–40), demonstrated the firm's trade-off between tax minimization and effective internal control. She found that firms which rely on financial results for evaluating the performance of their subsidiaries (and managers) tend to use market-oriented transfer prices, while firms that use 'instrumental' transfer prices rely less on performance evaluations. Furthermore, firms assort themselves rationally between these policy combinations: larger firms and firms lodged in more uncertain environments utilize performance evaluation and market-oriented transfer pricing, while firms with high ratios of foreign to total sales tend to employ instrumental transfer pricing.[11] Clinical research by Eccles (1985) elaborated on the integration of transfer pricing with business strategy, organization and performance evaluation, and practitioner-oriented writings such as Abdallah (1989) offer advice consistent with these findings.

Only sporadic evidence is available on the actual distortion of transfer prices (for example, Bernard and Weiner, 1992) but more is known about indirect consequences. Hines and Rice (1990), Grubert and Mutti (1991) and Harris *et al.* (1991) found that, with local profit opportunities controlled, the majority-owned affiliates of US multinationals report significantly higher after-tax profit rates in low-tax jurisdictions (also see Kopits, 1976). Grubert and Mutti also showed that foreign investment is attracted to low-tax jurisdictions, and Hines and Rice established that countries regarded as tax havens more than doubled their combined share of the US-owned stock of foreign capital between 1977 and 1982.

How effectively tax authorities police transfer pricing practices is a matter of conjecture. The discussion of Hines and Rice (1990) suggests that the monitoring is at least somewhat effective.

Because transfer prices presumably can be adjusted quickly, the change in intrafirm royalty payments during 1977–82 should be related to changes in the relevant tax differential over that same period. The specific variable employed is the change in the difference between the host country's and the US corporation income tax rate in 1977 and in 1982.[12] It should exert a positive influence on the reported change in intrafirm royalty payments.

3 STATISTICAL PROCEDURES AND RESULTS

With the general procedure and specific hypotheses set out, we review some properties of the data before turning to the statistical results.

Data Base

Most variables described above were collected from the 1977 and 1982 benchmark surveys (which are in effect censuses) of US parents and their foreign affiliates. We elected to analyze foreign investments in all non-financial sectors (not just manufacturing), omitting the financial sector because of the minimal role played there by intrafirm royalty payments.[13] That is, most data pertain only to non-bank foreign affiliates of non-financial US parents. The sample of 35 industries thus includes 32 in manufacturing (2-digit to 3-digit classes in the Standard Industrial Classification – SIC) plus three others: agriculture, forestry and fishing; mining; and transport, communication and public utilities. We also gathered data on the aggregates of foreign investments by these industries in 45 host countries, including 16 European nations, five other industrial countries and 21 developing countries. Missing values for some exogenous variables caused a few observations to be lost.

Table 5.1 provides definitions and sources of the variables described previously. A few peculiarities need mention. All variables were stated in or measured from nominal US dollar amounts, including the changes in host nation GNP levels, which were taken from a source that converts them to US dollars at the going exchange rate. We initially incorporated the change in the real bilateral exchange rate of each host country as an independent exogenous variable, only to discover that most of its inter-country variance is due to differential rates of inflation that are already controlled by the restatement of host GNP values in US dollars (terms-of-trade changes were apparently unimportant during 1977–82).

To measure goodwill stocks (proxied by sales promotion expenditures) we relied on the Federal Trade Commission's Line of Business data for two advantages that they possess: they cover all sales promotion outlays and not just purchased advertising services; and they pertain to business units of approximately 400 large US enterprises, a population that extensively overlaps the US multinational enterprises covered by the benchmark surveys. Because the Line of Business data cover only the manufacturing sector, we patched the series with data on advertising outlays from the input–output table. As a result of this splice the inter-industry regression models include a dummy variable that allows an intercept shift for the non-manufacturing sectors.[14]

Finally, the differential tax rate change in principle represents the change in the host country's rate relative to the US rate; however, the US rate did not change between 1977 and 1982, so the variable picks up only the foreign change. Average effective tax rates were used rather than marginal rates, because the former affect cash flows and motivate tax avoidance policies.

The regression models that we report were estimated by ordinary least squares with White's procedure employed to ensure heteroskedasticity-consistent variance–covariance matrices. The assumption that the exogenous variables are

Table 5.1 Variables used in the analysis

Variable	*Definition and source*
Advertising/ sales	Media advertising and other selling expenses as percentage of total sales and transfers, Line of Business respondents, 1977. *Source*: US Federal Trade Commission (1985), Master Table, cols 6, 9, 10; US Bureau of Economic Analysis (1984), Table 1.
Differential tax rate change	Logarithm of host country average effective tax rate on corporate profits in 1982 *minus* logarithm of host country average effective tax rate on corporate profits in 1977. *Source:* Price Waterhouse (1978, 1983).
Equity restriction change	Logarithm of (number of foreign affiliates reported subject to restrictions in 1982 divided by total number of foreign affiliates, 1982) *minus* logarithm of (number of foreign affiliates reported subject to equity restrictions in 1977 divided by total number of foreign affiliates, 1977). *Source*: US Bureau of Economic Analysis (1985), Tables II.I.3 and II.I.4; US Bureau of Economic Analysis (1981), Tables II.L.1 and II.L.2.
Exports change	Logarithm of value of exports shipped by parents to foreign affiliates in 1982 *minus* logarithm of value of exports shipped by parents to affiliates in 1977. *Source*: US Bureau of Economic Analysis (1985), Tables II.G.7 and II.P.1; US Bureau of Economic Analysis (1981), Tables II.I.7 and II.T.1.
FDI change 1972–6	Logarithm of US parents' claims on assets of foreign affiliates in 1976 *minus* logarithm of claims on assets of foreign affiliates in 1972. *Source*: US Bureau of Economic Analysis (1982), Table 9.
FDI change 1977–82	Logarithm of US parents' claims on assets of foreign affiliates in 1982 *minus* logarithm of claims on assets of foreign affiliates in 1977 *Source*: US Bureau of Economic Analysis (1985), Tables II.S.3 and II.S.4; US Bureau of Economic Analysis (1981), Tables II.W.3 and II.W.4.
FDI 1977	Logarithm of US parents' claims on assets of foreign affiliates in 1977. *Source*: US Bureau of Economic Analysis (1981), Tables II.W.3 and II.W.4.
Host GNP change	Logarithm of gross national product of host country, 1982, converted to US dollars at going exchange rate *minus* logarithm of gross national product of host country, 1977, converted to US dollars at going exchange rate. *Source*: World Bank (1984), Table l; World Bank (1979), Table 1.
Reciprocal licensing	Number of foreign affiliates that used technology of US parents divided by number of affiliates reporting they had supplied technology to their US parents, 1977. *Source*: US Bureau of Economic Analysis (1981), Tables II.J.1 and II.J.2.
R&D/sales	R&D expenses of US parents of foreign affiliates as percentage of parents' sales, 1977. *Source*: US Bureau of Economic Analysis (1981), Tables II.R.1 and II.U.1.
Royalties change	Logarithm of royalties received by US parents from foreign affiliates in 1982 *minus* logarithm of royalties received by US parents from foreign affiliates in 1977. Source: US Bureau of Economic Analysis (1985), Tables II.V.1 and II.V.2; US Bureau of Economic Analysis (1981), Tables II.Z.1 and II.Z.2.

uncorrelated with the error terms in the models is uncomfortable in the case of the exports change, which rests on policy decisions of the multinational parents, as do the changes in intrafirm royalty payments. We could not identify exogenous variables that would support the obvious instrumental variables approach to the problem. Hence our interpretation of the effect of exports on royalty receipts will be confined to the gross difference that appears between its coefficient in the inter-country and inter-industry models.

Some of the exogenous variables apply chiefly to inter-country differences, others to inter-industry differences. Their availability parallels their applicability: the data on parents' intangible assets only on an industry basis, data on tax changes and host GNP changes only in the inter-country model. The benchmark survey, however, reports on both bases the data on not only foreign investment stocks and flows but also changes in equity restrictions, changes in exports and the incidence of reciprocal licensing. These variables are used in both models. We expect foreign investment activity to depend strongly on both industry and country factors, so its dual appearance is of course appropriate. The same holds for intrafirm exports and reciprocal licensing. For equity restrictions, however, inter-industry variance seems only an incidental consequence of dissimilarity in industries' distributions of their foreign investments among countries. The performance of the equity restrictions variable in the inter-industry model is therefore a rough indicator of the extent of industry–country interaction in the determination of royalty payments and the omitted variable bias that might affect the models.

Statistical Results

Tables 5.2 and 5.3 present the results for the country and industry cross-sections, respectively. Of the three variables that control for the level and growth of foreign investment, the lagged change over 1972–6 proved entirely insignificant and without effect on other variables (compare equations 1 and 2 in Table 5.2). The lagged change is not available on an industry basis, but its omission from Table 5.3 thus seems harmless. The 1977 stock takes a stable although not highly significant positive coefficient in each table, and in Table 5.3 the 1977–82 net flow of foreign investment is also a positive influence on the change in royalty payments (significant at 10 per cent in a one-tail test). In Table 5.2, however, the FDI change 1977–82 takes a negative coefficient ($t = -1.4$). The 1977 level and 1977–82 change are uncorrelated among industries but negatively correlated among countries (–0.36). The negative coefficient for the 1977–82 FDI change therefore results from a shifting country composition of the flow of US foreign investment; we watch for other consequences of this relationship for the inter-country models.

Table 5.2 Determinants of differences among host countries in proportional change in intrafirm royalty payments to US parents, 1977–82

Exogenous variable	*Equation 1*	*Equation 2*
FDI change 1972–6	—	0.033
		(0.15)
FDI 1977	0.062	0.058
	(1.91)	(1.37)
FDI change 1977–82	–0.360	–0.364
	(1.44)	(1.43)
Differential tax rate change	1.192	1.204
	(1.88)	(1.84)
Equity restrictions change	–0.192	–0.197
	(1.77)	(1.81)
Exports change	0.449	0.443
	(2.06)	(1.92)
Host GNP change	0.535	0.538
	(1.06)	(1.04)
Reciprocal licensing	0.165	0.171
	(1.16)	(1.17)
Constant	–0.921	–0.935
	(1.85)	(1.91)
$\bar{R}^2$	0.120	0.094
Number of observations	42	42

Although each table shows a significant association between the change in intrafirm exports and in intrafirm royalty payments, it is positive in Table 5.2 and negative in Table 5.3. This result supports the interpretation offered above concerning the development of multinational enterprises. Among industries intrafirm exports and transfers of intangibles seem to be substitutes. Among countries they vary together, reflecting the differential rates of expansion of host countries' populations of subsidiaries and the webs of transactions linking parent and foreign affiliates. The negative inter-country correlation between the 1977 stock and 1977–82 flows of US foreign investment apparently reflects substantially differing rates of development that are not observed among sectors.[15] The inter-country differences in the rates of expansion of foreign investment allow us to distinguish between the structural forces that seem to drive the inter-industry results and the developmental ones apparent in the inter-country model.

Other country-related factors in Table 5.2 take the expected signs, but their coefficients vary in significance. The growth of the hosts' GNP and the incidence of reciprocal licensing are positive influences, as expected, but not significant. Increasing restrictions on equity holdings in subsidiaries significantly (one-tail test) reduce the growth of intrafirm royalty payments. Finally, the control for changes in the difference between host and US effective tax rates is appropriately positive and significant at the 5 per cent level. That result happily supports our key conjecture that intrafirm royalty payment data can reveal substantial information once incentives for transfer pricing distortions are controlled. The finding should not be oversold, however, because we found that the tax difference variable loses its significance if the FDI change of 1977–82 (which takes a perverse negative coefficient) is dropped from the model. That a host's tax reduction might increase its inflow of foreign investment is of course expected, but this relationship suggests that the magnitude (significance) of the influence of changes in tax differences might be overestimated. Finally, the explanatory power, especially of the country model, is poor, leaving ample room for omitted variables that might be correlated with those included in the model.

Table 5.3 Determinants of differences among industries in proportional change in intrafirm royalty payments to US parents, 1977–82

Exogenous variable	*Equation 1*	*Equation 2*	*Equation 3*
FDI 1977	0.095	0.088	0.091
	(1.70)	(1.56)	(1.63)
FDI change 1977–82	0.259	0.253	0.249
	(1.76)	(1.60)	(1.71)
Advertising/sales	0.013	—	—
	(1.56)		
Advertising/sales dummy	–0.048	—	–0.037
	(0.02)		(0.16)
Equity restrictions change	–0.059	–0.005	–0.044
	(0.53)	(0.04)	(0.39)
Exports change	–0.217	–0.251	–0.229
	(2.75)	(3.36)	(2.85)
Reciprocal licensing	–0.056	–0.054	–0.056
	(1.23)	(1.17)	(1.21)
R&D sales	—	0.024	—
		(1.05)	
(R&D + advertising)/sales	—	—	0.011
			(1.49)
Constant	–0.294	–0.161	–0.258
	(0.78)	(0.43)	(0.71)
$\bar{R}^2$	0.173	0.157	0.171
Number of observations	33	33	33

In the inter-industry results (Table 5.3) the roles of US parents' stocks of intangible assets remain to be considered. The three equations reported treat the advertising/sales and R&D/sales variables differently in order to illustrate the effects of the multicollinearity involving them. Consider these zero-order correlations in the inter-industry data:

	R&D/sales 1977	*FDI 1977*	*Royalty payments change*
Advertising/sales 1977	0.380	0.013	0.261
R&D/sales 1977		0.228	0.134
FDI 1977			0.259

The dependent variable (royalty payments change) is more closely associated with advertising than with R&D. However, advertising is uncorrelated with the FDI stock in 1977, while R&D is substantially correlated, and the FDI stock in turn is correlated with royalty payments. Although the FDI stock is not normalized by any measure of industry size, we nonetheless believe that these correlations correctly indicate that the FDI stock has absorbed much of the effect of differences in industries' levels of research intensity but not of their differences in sales promotion.

Now we can compare the three models in Table 5.3. If both advertising and R&D are included (not shown), neither is significant. Advertising by itself is significant only at the 10 per cent level in a one-tail test (equation 1); R&D by itself is not significant and competes for significance with the FDI variable (equation 2). To estimate equation 3 we simply summed the advertising and R&D variables, on the conjecture that they might be regarded as broadly homogeneous stocks of intangibles potentially exportable to foreign subsidiaries. The sum is significant at 10 per cent, like advertising, but this manoeuvre does not improve on the explanatory power of equation 1. These findings are consistent with the interpretation of the zero-order correlations offered previously. It seems clear that FDI 1977, R&D/sales and advertising/sales provide partly overlapping controls for the US parents' stocks of exportable intangibles and the unobserved transfers of them that give rise to intrafirm royalty payments.

4 CONCLUSIONS

This chapter changes focus in two ways from mainline research on the basic operation of multinational enterprises: it emphasizes their processes of expansion and development and not their origins; it treats published data on intrafirm royalty and licensing payments as measures of the revenue productivity of multinationals' intangible assets and not just arbitrary data manipulated for tax advantage. Because US foreign investments in host nations grew at quite diverse rates between 1977 and 1982, inter-country variation in the growth of intrafirm royalties reveals this complementarity with the previous expansion of foreign investment and with the concurrent growth of intrafirm trade, controlling (not very successfully) for factors distinguishing between host countries' potentials for yielding growing streams of revenues from intangibles. At the same time, differences among industries in technology and other basic structural conditions shed some light (obscured by multicollinearity) on the dependence of changes in these revenue streams on US parents' investments in proprietary intangibles through expenditures on research and sales promotion.

NOTES

1. Calculated from *Survey of Current Business*, March issue, 1978–83, Table 1–2; US Bureau of Economic Analysis (1981), Tables I.Z.2 and III.J.10.
2. See Grubaugh (1987) for an attempt to shift the analysis of internalization in response to the criticism. Most research on financial transactions and intrafirm trade of multinationals is of course not vulnerable to the criticism.
3. The one safe empirical conclusion about the cash flows due to transferred intangibles is that the more productive ones are long-lived. This is evident for trademarks from survey evidence on multinationals' operations, and for technology transfers from the long durations observed for inter-firm technology licensing agreements.
4. These categories do not exhaust all possible patterns (the depreciation profiles of quasi-rents to intangibles are not considered, for example). They are intended only to expose the range of relevant stock flow relationships.
5. The data for 1972–6 are incompletely comparable to the benchmark survey data in ways that do not appear to involve significant biases. They rest on a similar respondent base, and they include all foreign affiliates (rather than non-bank affiliates of non-bank parents, which we took from the benchmark surveys).
6. We are grateful to Alan Winters for suggesting this treatment.
7. For descriptive observations from German data supporting this and several other hypotheses, see Deutsche Bundesbank (1992).
8. For example, Lipsey (1991) suggested that US intrafirm trade is more sensitive to variations in the exchange rate than is trade between independent parties, consistent with the flexibility option held by enterprises with facilities in place in different national markets (De Meza and van der Ploeg, 1987). Benvignati (1990) concluded that the factors determining differences among industries in intrafirm US exports are essentially the same as the factors determining arm's-length exports. Her analysis can be criticized, however, because she took no account of the extent of foreign investment, which is a necessary enabling condition for intrafirm trade; the collinearity between the inter-industry determinants of trade and of foreign investment make it unclear how the conclusions would change if this step were taken.
9. For historical and analytical background on this issue, see Caves (1982, pp. 131–47). An important point is that in general equilibrium exporting and foreign investment cannot be complementary for the nation, because both draw on its stock of scarce factors of production. However, no such constraint precludes complementarity for the individual firm or sector. Regarding this literature, Grubert and Mutti (1991) made an important improvement in the procedure for establishing the complementarity between exporting and foreign investment while confirming the earlier substantive findings.

10. He found (p. 93) that in Canada subsidiaries are active exporters less commonly than are their domestic rivals, but the pattern reverses for firms in small-size classes. Affiliation with a multinational enterprise thus appears to mitigate the high fixed costs that otherwise confine exporting to large companies.
11. Similar to Yunker, Lecraw (1985) found that transfer prices not based on market prices are used by the more centralized multinational enterprises and those facing higher perceived risks and greater incidences of profit-invading controls in host countries. Benvignati (1985) examined the transfer pricing methods employed by business units reporting to the Federal Trade Commission Line of Business programme; her evidence suggests that international transfer prices are commonly pegged to market prices for homogeneous goods with well defined market prices, but to cost-based constructed values for heterogeneous and differentiated goods unlikely to have comparable market prices.
12. Previous investigators have commonly found that distortions increase disproportionately with tax rate differences (for example, with the squared difference) but it seems infeasible to carry this hypothesis over into a model based on changes.
13. In 1982 royalty and licence fees paid to financial institutions by their affiliates accounted for only 0.002 per cent of their net receipts from affiliates (US Bureau of Economic Analysis, 1985, Tables I.V.1 and II.V.2).
14. Industry variables not taken from the benchmark surveys had to be converted to the same industrial classification. The data sources all rely on the Standard Industrial Classification of the US Bureau of the Census, so this conversion is straightforward.
15. The growth rates of foreign investment in 1972–6 and in 1977–82 are uncorrelated, –0.04.

REFERENCES

Abdallah, Wagdy M. (1989), *International Transfer Pricing Policies: Decision-Making Guidelines for Multinational Companies*, New York: Quorum Books.

Benvignati, Anita M. (1985), 'An empirical investigation of international transfer pricing by US manufacturing firms', in Alan M. Rugman and Lorraine Eden (eds), *Multinationals and Transfer Pricing*, New York: St Martin's Press, 193–211.

Benvignati, Anita M. (1990), 'Industry determinants and "differences" in U.S. intrafirm and arm's-length exports', *Review of Economics and Statistics,* **72**, August, 481–8.

Bernard, Jean-Thomas and Robert J. Weiner (1992), 'Transfer prices and the excess cost of Canadian oil imports: new evidence on Bertrand vs. Rugman', *Canadian Journal of Economics*, **25**, February, 23–40.

Bertin, Gilles Y. (1987), 'Multinational enterprises: transfer partners and transfer policies', in A.E. Safarian and Gilles Y. Bertin (eds), *Multinationals, Governments and International Technology Transfer*, New York: St Martin's Press, 85–100.

Blomström, Magnus, Robert E. Lipsey and Ksenia Kulchycky (1988), 'U.S. and Swedish direct investment and exports', in Robert E. Baldwin (ed.), *Trade Policy Issues and Empirical Analysis*, Chicago: University of Chicago Press, 259–97.

Casson, Mark and associates (1988), *Multinationals and World Trade*, London: Allen & Unwin.

Caves, Richard E. (1982), *Multinational Enterprise and Economic Analysis*, New York: Cambridge University Press.

De Meza, David and Frederick van der Ploeg (1987), 'Production flexibility as a motive for multinationality', *Journal of Industrial Economics*, **35**, March, 343–51.

Deutsche Bundesbank (1992), 'Patent and license transactions and other exchanges of technological know-how with foreign countries in 1990 and 1991', *Monthly Report of the Deutsche Bundesbank*, **44**, April, 32–49.

Drake, Tracey A. and Richard E. Caves (1992), 'Changing determinants of Japanese foreign investment in the United States', *Journal of the Japanese and International Economies,* **6**, September, 228–46.

Eccles, Robert G. (1985), *The Transfer Pricing Problem: A Theory for Practice,* Lexington, MA: Lexington Books.

Grubaugh, Stephen G. (1987), 'The process of direct foreign investment', *Southern Economic Journal*, **54**, October, 351–60.

Grubert, Harry and John Mutti (1991), 'Taxes, tariffs and transfer pricing in multinational corporate decision making', *Review of Economics and Statistics*, **73**, May, 285–93.

Harris, David, Randall Mørck, Joel B. Slemrod and Bernard Yeung (1991), 'Income shifting in U.S. multinational corporations', National Bureau of Economic Research, Working Paper No. 3924.

Hines, James R., Jr. and Eric M. Rice (1990), 'Fiscal paradise: foreign tax havens and American business', National Bureau of Economic Research, Working Paper No. 3477.

Kogut, Bruce (1983), 'Foreign direct investment as a sequential process', in Charles P. Kindleberger and David B. Audretsch (eds), *The Multinational Corporation in 1980s*, Cambridge, MA: MIT Press, 38–56.

Kopits, George (1976), 'Intrafirm royalties crossing frontiers and transfer pricing behaviour', *Economic Journal*, **86**, December, 791–805.

Lecraw, Donald J. (1985), 'Some evidence on transfer pricing by multinational corporations', in Alan M. Rugman and Lorraine Eden (eds), *Multinationals and Transfer Pricing*, New York: St Martin's Press, 223–39.

Lipsey, Robert E. (1991), 'Foreign direct investment in the U.S. and U.S. trade', National Bureau of Economic Research, Working Paper No. 3623.

Little, Jane Sneddon (1986), 'Intra-firm trade and U.S. protectionism: thoughts based on a small survey', *New England Economic Review*, January–February, 42–51.

Little, Jane Sneddon (1987), 'Intra-firm trade: an update', *New England Economic Review*, May–June, 46–51.

MacCharles, Donald C. (1987), *Trade among Multinationals: Intra-Industry Trade and National Competitiveness*, London: Croom Helm.

Mansfield, Edwin (1984), 'R&D and innovation: some empirical findings', in Zvi Griliches (ed.), *R&D, Patents, and Productivity*, Chicago: University of Chicago Press, 127–48.

Mansfield, Edwin and Anthony Romeo (1980), 'Technology transfer to overseas subsidiaries by U.S.-based firms', *Quarterly Journal of Economics*, **95**, December, 737–50.

Mansfield, Edwin, Anthony Romeo and Samuel Wagner (1979), 'Foreign trade and U.S. research and development', *Review of Economics and Statistics*, **61**, February, 49–57.

McFetridge, Donald G. (1987), 'The timing, mode and terms of technology transfer: some recent findings', in A.E. Safarian and Gilles Y. Bertin (eds), *Multinationals, Governments and International Technology Transfer*, New York: St Martin's Press, 135–50.

Pearce, Robert D. (1990), 'Overseas production and exporting performance: some further investigations', University of Reading, Discussion Papers in International Investment and Business Studies, No. 136.

Price Waterhouse (1978), *Corporate Taxes: A Worldwide Summary*, New York: Price Waterhouse Center for Transnational Taxation.

Price Waterhouse (1983), *Corporate Taxes: A Worldwide Summary*, New York: Price Waterhouse Center for Transnational Taxation.

Rugman, Alan M. and Lorraine Eden (eds) (1985), *Multinationals and Transfer Pricing*, New York: St Martin's Press.

Teece, David J. (1976), *The Multinational Corporation and the Resource Cost of International Technology Transfer*, Cambridge, MA: Ballinger.

US Bureau of Economic Analysis (1981), *U.S. Direct Investment Abroad, 1977*, Washington, DC: Government Printing Office.

US Bureau of Economic Analysis (1982), *Selected Data on U.S. Direct Investment Abroad, 1950–1976*, Washington, DC: Government Printing Office.

US Bureau of Economic Analysis (1984), *The Detailed Input–Output Structure of the U.S. Economy, 1977*, Washington, DC: Government Printing Office.

US Bureau of Economic Analysis (1985), *U.S. Direct Investment Abroad, 1982*, Washington, DC: Government Printing Office.

US Federal Trade Commission (1985), *Annual Line of Business Report, 1977*, Washington, DC: Federal Trade Commission.

World Bank (1979), *World Tables, 1979*, Baltimore: Johns Hopkins University Press.

World Bank (1984), *World Tables, 1984*, Baltimore: Johns Hopkins University Press.

Yunker, Penelope M. (1982), *Transfer Pricing and Performance Evaluation in Multinational Corporations: A Survey Study*, New York: Praeger.

Zejan, Mario C. (1990), 'R&D activities in affiliates of Swedish multinational enterprises', *Scandinavian Journal of Economics*, **92**, (3), 487–500.

6. The determinants of the composition of US foreign direct investment in UK manufacturing

C. Milner and E. Pentecost

1 INTRODUCTION

Since the early 1960s the UK has been a large recipient of US foreign direct investment (FDI). In 1962 US corporations accounted for 64 per cent of the UK's stock of inward FDI in non-oil industrial and commercial companies. This share remained constant through the 1960s, but had fallen back to 56 per cent by the time of the 1974 survey. By contrast a greater share of FDI was now accounted for by Western European countries, probably as a result of the UK joining the EC in January 1973. According to UK data sources the share of US FDI in the UK total has been eroded further during the 1980s, to stand at about 46 per cent at the end of 1987 (see Table 6.1). Despite this diminishing share the US is still the most dominant single source of FDI to the UK, with the next highest source being the EC with a share of about 26 per cent.

In terms of the level of manufacturing FDI, the US is even more dominant. In the late 1960s US firms accounted for nearly 70 per cent of the stock of the UK's inward FDI in manufacturing, a share which remained steady until 1981. Since 1981 this share has declined, to stand at a little over 60 per cent at the end of 1987. The next largest share of manufacturing FDI comes from the EC with just over 14 per cent of the total stock at the end of 1987.

From the source country perspective in 1990, over 35 per cent of all US manufacturing FDI in the EC was in the UK. In fact in the banking and finance categories the proportion of US FDI in the UK is in excess of 50 per cent, which raises the dominance of the UK as 'the' host country for US FDI to over 40 per cent of all European investment. Table 6.2 shows a broad sector breakdown of US FDI in the UK at the end of 1990, compared to the EC. Even at this relatively high level of aggregation there is inter-sectoral variation in both the absolute and relative importance of US FDI. The absolute differences no doubt reflect size and capital-intensity variations across the categories reported, but there are significant sector variations in the UK's share of the EC total (17.6 per cent in the case of machinery, but 32.8 per cent in the case of transport, for example).

On further disaggregation these variations become even more marked. Table 6.3 provides information on each manufacturing industry's share of US FDI in UK manufacturing and the UK's share of total (worldwide) US FDI in the case of each industry. Thus, although there may be cultural and linguistic reasons for the overall dominance of the UK as a destination within the EC for US FDI, there are significant inter-industry variations in the importance of the UK as a location for this inward investment. Clearly, in some cases the UK is a dominant destination for a US industry with relatively little outward FDI (as in optical goods, electric lighting), but there are also cases where the UK is an important destination for significant amounts of US FDI (for example, motor vehicles, photographic equipment, office and computing machines). It is with the explanation of these inter-industry variations that this chapter is concerned. Are there systematic locational and industry characteristics that account for these variations?

Table 6.1 The importance of US FDI in the UK (£ millions) 1987

Source of FDI	*Value*	*%*
US	25 032	46
EC	14 032	26
EFTA	5 545	10
Other developed countries*	7 243	13
ROW	2 755	5
Total	54 607	100

	Manufacturing	*Non-manufacturing*
US	12 115	12 915
	(61%)	(37%)
EC	2 497	11 535
	(13%)	(33%)
EFTA	2 308	3 237
	(12%)	(9%)
Other developed countries*	2 493	4 750
	(13%)	(14%)
ROW	365	2 389
	(2%)	(7%)

* Includes Canada, Australia, New Zealand, South Africa and Japan.

Table 6.2 US stock of FDI in the UK and the EC in 1990 by sector ($ millions)

	UK *(1)*	*Other EC*[1] *(2)*	*(UK/EC)*[2] *(%)*
Petroleum	11 331	7 430	46.5
Manufacturing	20 636	60 628	25.4
Food	*2 083*	*5 951*	*25.9*
Chemicals	*3 521*	*15 568*	*18.4*
Metals	*1 020*	*2 826*	*26.5*
Machinery	*3 141*	*14 708*	*17.6*
Electrical	*1 268*	*3 276*	*27.9*
Transport	*2 864*	*5 871*	*32.8*
Other	*6 739*	*12 427*	*35.2*
Wholesale	2 746	12 674	17.8
Banking	3 575	3 929	47.6
Finance	23 071	17 647	56.7
Services	2 249	3 252	40.9
Other industries	1 375	2 397	36.5
Total	64 983	107 957	37.6

Notes
1 Defined as the 12 (less the UK) throughout.
2 UK share is the largest for all sectors except: Machinery (Germany 24%); Transport (Germany 51%); and Wholesale (Netherlands 19%).

A number of recent papers have been concerned with the factors that motivate inward investment, especially Japanese FDI, in the EC (see, for example, Heitger and Stehn, 1990; Balasubramanyam and Greenaway, 1992; and Thomsen and Nicolaides, 1991). Particular attention has been focused on the possible 'protection-jumping' incentive of increased European integration and of EC enlargement. Emphasis on location-specific advantages that are predominantly fashioned by government policies is not however in line with the more eclectic ownership, location and internalization (OLI) paradigm (see, for example, Hymer, 1976; and Dunning, 1977). Indeed, this tradition would suggest that there may be non-policy determinants of locational advantage. The advantages attached to producing in a foreign locale, such as access to cheaper raw materials or to cheaper labour, are what trade theory would see as influencing comparative advantage and trade in the host country. Thus the protectionist explanation of FDI needs to be investigated alongside a number of other (not necessarily competing) hypotheses. Let us turn to a consideration of the possible determinants of the industry structure of FDI.

Table 6.3 The relative importance of stock of US FDI in UK manufacturing industries (1989/90)

	In US FDI in UK manufacturing (%)	*Of total US worldwide FDI in industry (%)*
FOOD		
1. Grainmilling	5.5	3.3
2. Meat products	0.3	21.8
3. Dairy products	0.0	0.0
4. Other	1.7	6.4
CHEMICALS		
5. Industrial & synthetics	5.3	6.4
6. Drugs	4.5	8.9
7. Soaps, cleaners & toilet goods	2.7	12.2
8. Agricultural	0.0	0.5
9. Paints etc.	0.0	10.9
10. Other	3.7	15.3
PRIMARY AND FABRICATED METALS		
11. Ferrous	0.4	12.3
12. Non-ferrous	0.5	7.0
13. Metal cans & containers	0.9	10.0
14. Cutlery, tools etc.	0.7	9.8
15. Plumbing & heating equipment	0.0	0.0
16. Fabricated structural products	0.2	19.4
17. Screw machine products & bolts	0.1	13.0
18. Metal stamping & forging	0.0	1.0
19. Other fabricated products	1.3	11.1
MACHINERY, NON-ELECTRICAL		
20. Construction & mining	2.7	15.0
21. Office and computing machines	9.0	9.7
22. Engines & turbines	2.3	35.6
23. Metal working machines	0.5	24.6
24. Special industrial machinery & equipment	0.8	18.8
25. General industrial machinery	1.9	28.6
26. Refrigeration & service industry machinery	0.5	11.7
ELECTRIC AND ELECTRONIC EQUIPMENT		
27. Household appliances	0.4	4.0
28. Radio, TV etc.	0.3	4.8
29. Electronic components etc.	3.1	9.8
30. Electric lighting, wiring etc.	0.1	26.3
31. Other electrical machinery	1.5	10.7
TRANSPORT EQUIPMENT		
32. Motor vehicles & equipment	20.2	17.5
33. Other	0.0	0.0

	In US FDI in UK manufacturing (%)	*Of total US worldwide FDI in industry (%)*
OTHER MANUFACTURES		
34. Textile mill products	0.8	12.1
35. Apparel etc.	0.3	14.2
36. Lumber and wood products	0.0	0.6
37. Furniture & fixtures	0.2	13.1
38. Miscellaneous converted paper products	0.2	27.8
39. Paper board products	2.0	6.0
40. Printing & publishing	1.7	28.4
41. Rubber products	0.6	3.8
42. Miscellaneous plastic products	0.9	5.6
43. Scientific & measuring instruments	1.3	15.9
44. Optical goods etc.	0.0	50.0
45. Medical instruments & supplies	0.7	6.8
46. Photographical equipment	9.3	44.9
47. Watches, clocks etc.	0.0	17.6
48. Leather & leather products	0.0	0.0
49. Miscellaneous manufactures	1.0	24.1
UNDISCLOSED	9.1	

2 COMPARATIVE ADVANTAGE AND ALTERNATIVE INDUSTRY-LEVEL DETERMINANTS OF FDI

In the present discussion we take the ownership advantages of (US) firms associated with their home (US) location (such as a technological advantage or local factor abundance in intensive factors) as given.[1] In line with the OLI paradigm, we seek to explain inter-industry variation in the level of outward FDI to a particular destination (UK) in terms of differences in industry characteristics and structure that influence the extent of or scope for locational and internalization advantages in the host (UK) economy. There are a number of explanations of the motivation for FDI that can be found in the literature. Confirmed or not, the different explanations would not constitute a robust test of the OLI paradigm, though it is invariably the case that the different hypotheses could be simultaneously consistent with the paradigm. The ensuing explanations should not necessarily be viewed, therefore, as competing.

Comparative Advantage and Local Resource Endowments

A hypothesis that foreign (US) firms tend to invest in host (UK) industries, even under free trade conditions, where the host (UK) economy has a comparative advantage is more consistent with the view that there is a complementary role between factor and trade flows (Markusen, 1983) than with the Mundellian proposition (Mundell, 1957) that they are substitutes for each other in a Heckscher–Ohlin–Samuelson (H-O-S) context. Given an incentive to internalize, that is where the costs of servicing a distant foreign market through arms'-length trade are sufficiently high, we would hypothesize that foreign (US) firms have a greater incentive to invest (*ceteris paribus*) where internalization provides greater access to specific sources of comparative advantage in the host economy. Baldwin (1979) reports evidence, for instance, of US firms investing abroad in manufacturing in order to take advantage of relative abundance of unskilled labour. If we assumed the UK to be relatively well endowed with unskilled labour,[2] then we would expect (*ceteris paribus*) in the context of the H-O-S world that there would be more inward investment in the UK from the US in those industries where production is relatively (unskilled) labour-intensive.

We might of course wish to remain agnostic as to the model of trade or source of comparative advantage or locational advantage, and argue that FDI will merely tend to be greater the more export-oriented or the better is the trade performance revealed to be in the host industry. Note also that such a hypothesis is consistent with FDI aimed at servicing the host market and/or markets outside the host economy.

Circumventing Trade Barriers

It has been suggested by some commentators (for example, Heitger and Stehn, 1990) that, either in addition to host sources of comparative advantage or as an alternative to these natural sources of advantage, already exporting foreign firms seek access to policy-induced locational advantages when establishing or acquiring production capacity through foreign investment. The benefits that then accrue to the investing firms are access to protected markets and the extraction of any rents generated by trade barriers. These benefits are required, so the argument goes, to compensate for other disadvantages (such as higher information and communications costs) that foreign firms experience in establishing and producing in the host economy relative to local firms. Thus one would hypothesize that, where foreign firms invest to 'jump' trade barriers, more FDI will flow to markets with higher levels of protection, provided that the markets are of equivalent size.

Of course, market size does in practice tend to vary substantially between industries (product ranges); in which case market size and trade barriers may interact positively to affect investment levels. In this regard the market integration/enlargement associated with the EC Single Market programme may provide a greater incentive for inward investment for a constant level of (actual and perceived) protection. But therein lies a difficulty, in empirically testing the 'protection-jumping' hypothesis. Increased EC market integration may have altered perceived or expected protection (the 'Fortress Europe' threat), but changes in perceived protection cannot be systematically measured.[3] Indeed, actual protection levels are difficult to measure systematically in the (simultaneous) presence of tariffs and a range of non-tariff (often hidden administrative) barriers to trade. But there are now more comprehensive data available on actual trade barriers to investigate the protection-jumping motive for FDI.

Size of the 'Local' Market

The above discussion of the natural and policy-induced locational advantages that may motivate foreign investment indicates that we need to control for market size effects. For given locational advantages of that kind in the host economy, one would expect more inward FDI into those industries with the largest 'host' market. In the context of US investment in the UK a critical issue is the delineation of the 'host' or local market. A narrow definition would include the value of sales in the UK. With the completion of the EC Single Market programme, the value of sales for a given industry throughout the EC may be a more appropriate (broad) representation of the host market. Prior to full implementation of the Single Market, with differential degrees of market integration across different markets and given differential costs of transporting in different industries, the size of the relevant 'host' market will lie at varying points for different industries on a spectrum between the 'narrow' and 'broad' market size concepts.

However, even where FDI in the UK is 'bridgehead investment' aimed at providing access to a wider EC market, we would need to identify other non-market size factors which explain the decision to locate the investment within the UK rather than elsewhere in the EC.

Market Structure Influences

The broader the nature of the host market subject to inward investment in the UK, the more competitive it is likely to be (as the number of EC producers in a given product range increases). Increased competitiveness will in turn reduce the opportunity for monopoly profits, and reduce the incentive for inward foreign investment to try to capture these 'abnormal' returns. Therefore the delineation of the market and the competitiveness/concentration of the market should be simultaneously determined. Data constraints force us in this present context to restrict the focus of attention to the competitiveness of the 'narrow'/domestic market. *A priori* one would expect the degree of competitiveness to be influenced by the domestic market structure, the scope for product differentiation and the opportunity for market entry (firm entry or product entry from abroad). Thus FDI motivated by the desire to capture monopoly profits in the host market would tend to be higher in those (differentiable goods) industries which have a relatively concentrated production structure, and which are less subject to foreign competition.

Other Factors and Flow Changes

Clearly there are many other factors that may affect the FDI decision that have not been captured by the above hypotheses. The present focus, however, is on the structure or composition of FDI and we do not have strong prior views about the way factors such as exchange rate movements, taxation policy and other policy incentives will affect the inter-industry structure of the stock of FDI. Indeed, in the short term these non-systematic influences on flows of FDI may be particularly important and difficult to capture. Thus we may wish to hypothesize that the long-term determinants of FDI flows (that is, changes in stocks less revaluation effect) should be in line with the above hypotheses, namely that flows of FDI will be related to changes in comparative advantage, protection, market size and competitiveness. Nonetheless, the lumpiness of investment decisions, the variable length of the gestation period and the erratic nature of policy and other macroeconomic factors on short-term FDI flows are likely to make it difficult to capture systematic structural influences on these flows.

The testing of a flows model of FDI does, however, permit a partial testing of the 'defensive investment hypothesis' proposed by Ray (1977), who finds evidence that the demand for US manufactures was more elastic in host markets than in the domestic (US) market. This was consistent with the view that host markets were in general more competitive than the comparable US market, and that increased competition in host markets provided an incentive for increased (defensive) foreign investment.

Finally, it should be noted that there are a number of commentators on foreign direct investment decisions (for example, Dunning, 1977) who emphasize the influence of less tangible factors such as managerial attitudes and cultural proximity. To some extent the focus on industry rather than firm-specific factors allows us to abstract from such influences.[4]

3 METHODOLOGY AND DATA

The determinants of FDI outlined in the previous section can be represented by the following equation:

$$FDK_j = \alpha_0 + \alpha_1 CA_j + \alpha_2 PROT_j + \alpha_3 COMP_j + \alpha_4 MARK_j + U_j \quad (6.1)$$

where the expected signs of the estimated coefficients are:

$$\alpha_1, \alpha_2, \alpha_3, \alpha_4 > 0$$

and where

$FDKj$ = the stock of US foreign direct investment in UK product group j;
CA_j = index of revealed comparative advantage or trade performance in product group j;
$PROT_j$ = average percentage rate of protection in product group j;
$COMP_j$ = proxy of competitiveness in product group j;
$MARK_j$ = market size (value of sales or production) for product group j.

Some comments on the choice of proxy measures are required. (Details of data definitions and sources are available from the authors on request.)

Foreign Direct Investment

Information on the US direct investment position in the UK is available for all broad sectors of the (host) economy. Given the present focus on the trade–FDI relationship, the disaggregated cross-section analysis here is concerned with manufacturing only. Within manufacturing information is available for varying levels of aggregation of the US Standard Industrial Classification: some individual 3-digit levels and some combinations of 3-digit categories. Availability of data at differing levels of aggregation was also only partial, since disclosure is restricted and varies from year to year. Nonetheless, it was possible to obtain FDI stock information for 49 product categories (j) within manufacturing for 1990 and for 48 categories (excluding construction, mining and materials handling machinery (20)) for 1989. See Table 6.3 for the list of 'industries' involved. (Information on the concordance with the UK SIC that was used in order to match the FDI data with right hand side (RHS) variables (based on UK industrial conditions) in the regression analysis is available from the authors on request.)

The crude change in stocks in the two years or flows in 1990 could be obtained for the smaller sample. Adjustment was required for market revaluation effects that this crude change in stock also incorporates. Valuation change estimations for 1989–90 could be derived for more aggregate sectors within manufacturing, and these were applied in proportion to shares of the stock in 1989 to each category in our sample.

Comparative Advantage and Resource Endowments

The measurement of comparative advantage, especially in a cardinal manner, is of course problematic. For the present purpose we resorted to the use of revealed trade performance measures of comparative advantage. Two alternative proxies were constructed:

$$CA_1 = \text{net trade ratio} = \frac{(X_j - M_j)}{(X_j + M_j)}$$

and

$$CA_2 = \text{export } (X) - \text{sales } (S) \text{ ratio} = \frac{X_j}{S_j}$$

In both cases, as improved export performance is revealed (for given imports), the *CA* index increases within the range $-1 \rightarrow +1$ in the case of CA_1 and $0 \rightarrow +1$ in the case of CA_2.

CA_1 is the more conventional revealed comparative advantage index (based on own trade data only).[5] There were *a priori* grounds, however, for expecting the index to be distorted in the present context by the variable and high levels of aggregation of product groups (imposed by the FDI data); indices for the more aggregated product groups tending to be pulled towards unity by the inclusion of both export-oriented and import-competing activities. By excluding imports, this aggregation effect and the complication of intra-industry trade is abstracted from in the case of export/sales ratio.

Revealed trade or export performance indices can be interpreted without recourse to any model or view as to the source(s) of comparative advantage. However, some possible sources of comparative advantage relative to factor abundance in the host (that is, UK) economy were investigated:

CA_3 (= labour intensity proxy) = wages and salaries as a percentage of gross value added, or

CA_4 (= alternative labour intensity proxy) = number of employees required to generate £1million of gross value added;

CA_5 (= skill intensity proxy) = percentage of total employment accounted for by operatives.

The unavailability of appropriate capital stock data necessitated the use of the suggested labour-intensity proxies. (The expected signs on CA_3, CA_4 and CA_5 are fashioned by the nature of UK relative factor endowments).

Trade Barriers

There are a wide range of actual and potential trade and other policy instruments that can be used to restrict imports and thereby protect local producers. We can separate these analytically into tariff, non-tariff and administrative barriers. Identification and measurement of the rate of protection associated with each type of barrier separately is often difficult. Systematic evidence about the nature of all the barriers combined is virtually non-existent. We have to rely upon the use of measures of tariff protection to proxy the structure of total protection, on the assumption that the alternative instruments are complementary: namely, that the adjustment and political economy pressures for protection provide an incentive for the incidence or use of all the instruments to be positively correlated across economic activities. To the extent that the different types of barrier are substitute instruments of protection, tariff protection will be a biased measure of overall protection.

In the present study two proxies of the rate of protection were employed:

$PROT_1$ = effective rate of (scheduled) tariff protection, and
$PROT_2$ = dummy variable for the incidence of non-tariff barriers.

The first proxy measures the net effect of tariffs on value added in activity j resulting from the taxing effect of tariffs on importable intermediate inputs and the subsidizing effect of tariffs on import-competing final production. Estimates on a UK input–output table industry classification for 1986 were used (using a concordance with the UK SIC) to obtain an overall rate for each 3-digit category comprising our categories (j). Where an average was necessary, a simple arithmetic average was calculated. This was computationally convenient, but it was not in any case evident what the appropriate weighting should be. Weights in production may differ in the case of US- and non-US owned production in each product category in our sample.

The variable $PROT_2$ is a crude method of dealing with the difficulty of providing comprehensive evidence and of dealing with the problem of measuring both their extent (for example, through coverage ratios) and their nominal (and effective) protection equivalence at this highly aggregated level.

Market Structure

The scope for monopoly profits arising out of the structure of the host market is something that can be proxied on a systematic basis through traditional measures of market concentration and import penetration. The measurement of product differentiation and entry barriers is not feasible at this level of aggregation. Thus the proxies of market competitiveness used were as follows:

$COMP_1 =$ (SALES) CONCENTRATION RATIO, or

$$COMP_2 = \frac{COMP_1}{impen_j}$$

where $impen_j$ = import penetration ratio for category j.

The unadjusted concentration ratio ($COMP_1$) measures only the concentration of domestic sales without allowance for competition from imports; the higher the ratio the greater the scope for monopoly profits. By contrast, the alternative adjusted ratio ($COMP_2$) reduces measured concentration as import penetration increases; again, however, a higher adjusted ratio is interpreted as an indicator of reduced competitiveness.

In the case of the regression analysis using FDI flows, information on changes in concentration for a one-year period was not available. In this case changes in competitiveness were proxied by changes in import penetration only.

Market Size

As discussed in Section 2, the exact nature of host 'domestic' market is somewhat unclear in the context of the UK's membership of the EC. Thus alternative possible measures of market size were also investigated:

$MARK_1$ = value of domestic sales, or
$MARK_2$ = value of EC production.

$MARK_1$ is a narrow concept of the market and $MARK_2$ a broader definition. Note, however, that it is production and not sales data that is being used to proxy the EC market for each j category.

In order to investigate the earlier suggestion that market size and trade barriers may interact positively to affect investment levels, a further market size variable was constructed, as follows:

$$MARK_3 = (MARK_{1(2)}) \times (PROT_{1(2)})$$

Estimation

All of the equations were estimated using ordinary least squares for a sample of 48 product/industry categories. All data apply to the year 1989 (and 1990 where changes in variables are used for the 1990 flow model, except for the effective protection estimates ($PROT_1$) which are for 1986, and for the value of EC production ($MARK_2$) which is for 1987).

4 RESULTS

Given the combinations of alternative proxies that are available, a large number of estimations of equation (6.1) is possible. In order to compare the performance of the alternative proxies, however, Table 6.4 summarizes the performance (sign and significance) of the proxies for each variable in equation 6.1.[6] It is in general easy to discriminate between alternative proxies.[7] The net trade ratio measure of revealed comparative advantage (CA_1) and the incidence of non-tariff barriers measure of protection ($PROT_2$) have the wrong sign. Both competitiveness proxies have the right sign, but the unadjusted concentration ratio ($COMP_1$) is insignificant even at the 10 per cent level. In terms of the basic equation (6.1), it is only in the case of the market size proxies that there are consistently correct signs with significance. The domestic market size proxy ($MARK_1$) only achieves significance, however, at the 10 per cent level.

Table 6.4 Summary of performance of alternative proxy variables in explaining the stock of FDI

Comparative advantage variables					
	CA_1	CA_2	CA_3	CA_4	CA_5
sign	–	+	–	–	–
significance[1]		***		*	*
Protection variables					
	$PROT_1$	$PROT_2$			
sign	+	–			
significance[2]					
Competitiveness variables					
	$COMP_1$	$COMP_2$			
sign	+	+			
significance[2]		**			
Market size variables					
	$MARK_1$	$MARK_2$	$MARK_3{}^2$		
sign	+	+	+		
significance[2]	*	**	**		

Notes
1 *** denotes 1%, ** denotes 5%, * denotes 10% levels of significance, respectively.
2 $(PROT_1) \times (MARK_2)$.

Explaining the Stock of FDI

The results provide support for the host comparative advantage, the host non-competitiveness and host market size hypotheses; the signs on CA_2, $COMP_2$ and $MARK_2$ are all positive and significant at least at the 5 per cent level. The sign on $PROT_1$ is positive in accordance with the 'protection-jumping' hypothesis, but this coefficient is not significantly different from zero even at the 10 per cent level. Thus we are able to reject this hypothesis, *when tested with an effective tariff protection measure of protection.* We noted earlier, however, the difficulties of measuring protection in a comprehensive fashion, and especially at this relatively high level of aggregation. We suspect, therefore, that the 'protection-jumping' hypothesis should be tested at the firm/product level, and with more comprehensive information on the nature and impact of tariff, non-tariff and administrative interventions. It remains credible that foreign investors do search for policy-induced rents. Indeed, the results do not reject the view that US FDI is drawn towards manufacturing sectors that are less competitive (that is, more concentrated and less subject to import competition) and where there is greater scope for monopoly rents.

Although there is support for the domestic market size hypothesis (the sign on $MARK_1$ is positive and significant at the 10 per cent level), there is stronger support for the EC market as being the relevant or perceived host market. Significance at the 5 per cent level is achieved for $MARK_2$, and a range of alternative non-nested tests favour the inclusion of this market size variable. A word of caution is in order, however, since $MARK_2$ was a proxy measure of the size of the EC market based on production data.

Finally, the possibility of interaction between market size and the level of protection was explored. The term $MARK_3$ represents $MARK_2$ (EC market size proxy) times $PROT_1$ (estimates of the effective rate of tariff protection based on EC common external tariff). The coefficient on this term is positive and significant at the 5 per cent level. It is difficult, however, to draw strong conclusions from this result since $MARK_2$ and $MARK_3$ are highly collinear.

FDI and UK Resource Endowments

Alternative regressions to explain the stock of FDI were run, in which the measures of revealed comparative advantage or trade performance were replaced by proxies for the factor intensity of host (UK) production.

The expected signs on CA_3, CA_4 and CA_5 in the context of a standard H-O-S model are dependent on the relative factor endowments of the UK economy. In the absence of robust and recent evidence on this,[8] we can either remain agnostic or infer something about factor endowments from evidence on the factor content of trade. The recent work by Webster (1991) on the factor content of UK trade indicates that the UK is relatively well endowed with capital and non-manual skills, in which case, if US FDI in UK manufacturing seeks to take advantage of this relative abundance/cheapness, one would expect more (less) investment in the more capital-(labour-) intensive industries (that is, the sign on labour intensity proxy CA_3 or CA_4 to be negative) and for more investment in the more non-manual skill-intensive industries (that is, the sign on (non-manual) skill intensity proxy CA_5 to be negative).

The summary results in Table 6.4 are in line with these expectations: negative signs in all three cases, but only with significance at the 10 per cent level in the case of CA_4 and CA_5 when included separately in the regressions. (The correlation coefficient between CA_4 and CA_5 in this sample is 0.52.) There is therefore weak support only for the view that FDI seeks to take advantage of host factor endowments, in this present case of US FDI being more intensive in relatively capital- and non-manual skill-intensive activities within UK manufacturing. Further work is required on this issue, however, in order to improve and refine the measurement of the factor content of UK manufacturing.

Explaining the Flow of FDI

As indicated in the previous section, short-term changes in the stock of FDI (even adjusted for market valuation effects) are expected to be affected by a range of factors that are not captured by changes in the variables that have been used to explain FDI stocks. The results in Table 6.5 on the estimated flow model appear not to confirm these expectations; ΔCA_2, $\Delta COMP_2$ and $\Delta MARK$ are all highly significant (1 per cent level and with the expected sign) and the overall explanatory power of the model is higher than for the stock model. Only the $PROT_1$ variable (not $\Delta PROT$, for which data was not available) is insignificant, albeit with the right sign. This result, however, needs to be viewed with caution, as 1990 data on sales (total or domestic only) were not used in the present empirical work. Thus each of the significant variables in equations (1) and (2) in Table 6.5 are proxies of the changes required and may be subject to significant measurement errors.

Nevertheless, the results do encourage further work in this area, since they support the earlier results for the stock model. The flow results suggest that the increases in 'new' FDI are greatest (or the reductions in existing stocks are smallest) the greater the export performance improvement and (domestic) market growth and the smaller the increase in competitiveness on the domestic market. Note also that the model fit with *adj* FDI (90) (that is, with adjustment for market valuation effects) is better than that with FDI (90) (without adjustment) as the dependent variable.

Table 6.5 Estimated flow model, 1990

Independent variables[1]	Expected sign	Dependent variable (1) adj FDK (90)[2]	(2) FDK (90)[2]
CONST		–14.26	22.89
		(–0.32)	(0.64)
ΔCA_2[3]	(+)	2427.3	1780.8
		(2.84)***	(2.83)***
$PROT_1$	(+)	1.28	1.64
		(0.22)	(0.34)
$\Delta COMP_2$[4]	(–)	–4243.0	–3459.2
		(–2.74)***	(–2.88)***
$\Delta MARK_1$[5]	(+)	0.7	0.53
		(4.08)***	(3.98)***
$\bar{R}^2$		0.58	0.52
F-statistic		17.33	13.53
N		48	48

Notes
1 Adjusted White's heteroskedasticity-consistent 't' values in brackets.
2 *** denotes 1%, ** denotes 5% and * denotes 10% levels of significance.
3 Proxied by change in exports relative to sales value for 1989.
4 Proxied by change in imports relative to domestic sales values for 1989.
5 Proxied by increase in imports less increase in exports.

5 SUMMARY CONCLUSIONS

This chapter has investigated a number of possible explanations of the industrial pattern of US FDI in the UK manufacturing sector, using data for the years 1989 and 1990 for a sample of 48 industrial groupings. The cross-sectional regression analysis indicates that inter-industry variations in industrial/market characteristics do systematically influence the extent of or scope for locational and internalization advantages for US investors in the UK economy. Specifically the chapter finds empirical support for the hypothesis that US FDI is higher, *ceteris paribus,* where there is access to sources of UK comparative advantage in general, and specifically where it provides access to local endowments in the case of relatively capital- and non-manual labour (skill)-intensive activities. The results also support a 'restricted competitiveness' hypothesis: US FDI is higher the lower is the scope for competition from other domestic firms and from imports. Finally, FDI is shown to be positively related to the 'host' market size, with the EC being the relevant market. This supports the view that US FDI in the UK is, in part at least, 'bridgehead investment', motivated by access to the wider EC market through (relatively) unrestricted exports. Indeed, market size appears to have a stronger influence on investment decisions by US firms than do external trade barriers, there being weak support only for a separate 'protection-jumping' hypothesis.

All of the above conclusions are subject, however, to the usual caution that applies to empirical work of this nature. The proxy measures used for the explanatory variables and the measurement of FDI itself (especially at variable levels of aggregation) are likely to be subject to measurement error. There are also potential macro or firm-level influences which may have a systematic influence on the pattern of FDI at the industry level, and these are omitted from the present analysis. Nonetheless, the results are sufficiently encouraging to merit further investigations based on refined measures of the explanatory variables. The work may also be extended to investigate a number of other issues: the potential simultaneity between FDI and comparative advantage, the link between 'host' and 'home' country locational advantages, and the impact of relative locational advantages within the EC on the specific country location of US FDI within the EC.

NOTES

1. The types of factors that affect those commodity or industry patterns of ownership advantages in the home market, that is the pattern of comparative advantage in the home market, may well also affect the industry or commodity pattern of outward direct foreign investment. This is a subject that has been investigated, for instance, in the case of the US by Baldwin (1979). The focus here, however, is on the determinants of the industry pattern of ownership advantages in the host economy. There has been systematic empirical work of this kind conducted for direct investment in the US (for example, Ray, 1989; Caves, 1988; Mann, 1989).
2. This assumption is consistent with the H-O-S interpretation of factor content analysis of UK trade. Webster (1991) for instance finds that the UK exported in 1984 relatively capital-intensive goods and services, and to a lesser extent goods intensive in non-manual skills, and imported goods intensive in natural resources and in skilled and semi-skilled labour.
3. Changes in expectations about the influence of policy upon locational advantages may also affect the way the flow of investment is distributed over time, rather than the total amount of investment over a given time period.
4. This is not necessarily the case, however. Where industries are, for instance, differentially distributed across regions, and the regions are of varying attractiveness to foreign investor/management, then these less tangible factors may systematically affect FDI across industries. Measuring and capturing such influences may be very difficult, however.
5. Indices based on relative shares of world trade were often also used as indices of revealed comparative advantage (for example, Balassa (1977)). In the present case the need for trade data on an industry classification basis constrained the analysis to use of own trade data.
6. More detailed results and diagnostics for specific specifications are to be found in Milner and Pentecost (1993).
7. It should be noted that the correlation coefficient between any two independent variables in the regressions summarized in Table 6.5 was always less than (±)0.4 (and usually less than (±)0.2). The assessment of the performance of the variables in terms of signs is not undermined, therefore, by evident multicollinearity problems.
8. There are some estimates of relative factor endowments for a large sample of countries for 1975 in Leamer (1984), which are rather dated now.

REFERENCES

Balassa, B. (1977), '"Revealed" comparative advantage revisited: an analysis of relative export shares of the industrial countries', *Manchester School,* **33**, 99–123.

Balasubramanyam, V.N. and D. Greenaway (1992), 'Economic integration and foreign direct investment: Japanese investment in the EC', *Journal of Common Market Studies*, **30**, 175–93.

Baldwin, R.E. (1979), 'Determinants of trade and foreign investment: further evidence', *Review of Economics and Statistics*, **61**, 40–48.

Caves, R.E. (1988), 'Exchange rate movements and foreign direct investment in the United States', *Harvard Institute of Economic Research*, Discussion Paper 1383.

Dunning, J. (1977), 'Trade, location of economic activity and the MNEs', in B. Ohlin, P. Hesselborn and P. Wijkman (eds), *The International Allocation of Economic Activity*, London: Macmillan.

Heitger, B. and J. Stehn (1990), 'Japanese direct investments in the EC – Response to the internal market 1993?', *Journal of Common Market Studies*, **28**, 1–15.

Hymer, S. (1976), *The International Operation of National Firms*, PhD Dissertation, Cambridge, MA: MIT Press.

Leamer, E.E. (1984), *Sources of International Comparative Advantage: Theory and Evidence*, Cambridge, MA: MIT Press.

Mann, C.L. (1989), 'Determinants of Japanese direct investment in US manufacturing industries', *Board of Governors of the Federal Reserve System*, International Finance Discussion Paper 362.

Markusen, J. (1983), 'Factor movements and commodity trade as complements', *Journal of International Economics*, **13**, 341–56.

Milner, C.R. and E.J. Pentecost (1993), 'Locational advantage and US foreign direct investment in UK manufacturing', mimeo.

Mundell, R. (1957), 'International trade and factor mobility', *American Economic Review*, **47**, 321–35.

Ray, E.J. (1977), 'Foreign direct investment in manufacturing', *Journal of Political Economy*, **85**, 283–97.

Ray, E.J. (1989), 'The determinants of foreign direct investment in the United States, 1979–1985', in R. Feenstra (ed.), *Trade Policies for International Competitiveness*, Chicago: University of Chicago Press.

Thomsen, S. and P. Nicolaides (1991), *The Evolution of Japanese Direct Investment in Europe*, Hemel Hempstead: Harvester-Wheatsheaf.

Webster, A. (1991), 'Some issues in the measurement of comparative advantage', *Applied Economics*, **23**, 937–48.

7. East Asian foreign direct investment in the EC

V.N. Balasubramanyam and D. Greenaway*

1 EAST ASIAN FDI IN THE EC

East Asian foreign direct investment (FDI), especially Japanese FDI in the EC, is often referred to as a phenomenon, implying that it is an event of significance. It is of significance if for no other reason than that it has grown dramatically since the beginning of the 1980s. Unlike the Americans the Europeans appear to view the surge of FDI from East Asia with equanimity. Indeed, many of the member states of the EC appear to woo such investment with offers of various sorts of incentives. Whether or not such incentives are effective in enticing foreign firms to the EC is a matter of some debate. So, too, are the reasons for the upsurge of East Asian FDI in the EC since the 1980s. Is such FDI a response to 'Fortress Europe'? If so, is it merely a substitute for trade flows? Or is it of the market-seeking variety, lured to the EC with its enlarged market free of barriers to trade? What are the welfare implications of each of these varieties of FDI? What should be the policy framework of the EC towards East Asian FDI? These and other issues constitute the subject matter of this chapter.

The chapter is divided as follows: Section 2 analyses the trends and patterns in FDI in recent years, focusing on East Asian FDI in the EC. The third section reviews the determinants of FDI and the welfare gains from inward FDI. Section 4 is concerned with policy towards investment. From an EC standpoint this involves both internal measures and measures *vis-à-vis* non-EC entities. It also involves both investment incentives and disincentives. In Section 5 we consider how EC 1992 and the completion of the internal market can be expected to affect inward investment, especially from East Asia. This sets the agenda for Section 6, where the focus is on policy coordination in the Community. Finally, Section 7 offers some concluding comments.

* We are grateful to J. Borkakoti for his comments. This chapter draws upon material contained in an earlier paper by the authors on 'Regionalism and Foreign Direct Investment'.

2 TRENDS IN FDI

The total stock of FDI in the world now exceeds $7 trillion. By the end of the 1980s annual outflows of FDI had reached $196 billion. Since 1983 FDI flows have grown at an unprecedented rate of 29 per cent per year, three times faster than the rate of growth of exports and four times that of the growth of world output. Much of this growth in FDI is accounted for by the developed countries, principally the EC, the US and Japan – the so-called triad. The triad accounted for more than four-fifths of the total outward flows and stocks of FDI at the end of 1988. The triad also accounts for more than 65 per cent of inward flows of FDI (Table 7.1). This growth in intratriad FDI in recent years has added a new dimension to the economic links between the triad countries over and above the links created through trade.

Table 7.1 Foreign direct investment and the triad

	Outward FDI		*Inward FDI*	
	Stock (1988) $ billions	*Flows (1985–9)*	*Stock (1988) $ billions*	*Flows (1985–9)*
US	345	18	329	46
EC	332	39	239	19
Japan	111	24	10	
Total triad	788	81	579	65
World	974	105	1 059	65
Triad as % of world	81	77	55	65

Source: UN (1991), *World Investment Report: The Triad in Foreign Direct Investment*.

The most important and dramatic development in the economic relationship between the triad countries is the growth in Japanese FDI. In terms of annual average outflows it increased from $10 billion during the period 1979–81 to $126 billion during 1988–90, a twelvefold increase. Japanese corporations held less than 1 per cent of the total world stock of FDI in 1960, but by 1990 they controlled 15 per cent of that stock. Even more dramatic is the growth of Japan's FDI in the EC and the US. In the case of the US it increased from £4 billion to $65 billion and in the case of the EC it rose from a mere $1 billion to $27 billion (see Table 7.2). Another significant development is the appearance of the newly industrializing East Asian economies on the FDI scene. Taiwan, the Republic of Korea, Singapore and Hong Kong have emerged as significant investors since the early 1980s but until recently much of the FDI was in other developing countries, mostly Asian countries. However, in recent years these East Asian countries have enlarged the orbit of their FDI to include Europe. Taiwan leads the East Asian NICs in terms of outward FDI. The total global stock of Taiwan's FDI stood at $17.6 billion, as opposed to $2.1 billion owned by Korea. Available data show that, over the period 1986–91, total flow of FDI from Taiwan was around $1 billion, of which just under one quarter was in Europe. While Korea and Singapore, too, have begun to invest in Europe, the magnitude of their investment is as yet very low. South Korea's FDI in Europe at the end of 1989 was estimated at $40 million, spread over some 65 projects. South Korean manufacturing presence in Europe is concentrated in consumer electronics, from microwave ovens to colour TV sets. FDI from Hong Kong and Taiwan, mostly concentrated in the UK, is also in electronics and textiles. At the end of 1989, the four newly industrialized countries (NICs) are reported to have invested around $120 million in Britain, providing 3000 jobs.

Table 7.2 Direct investment of the EC (million ecus)

			Inward		
	1984	*1985*	*1986*	*1987*	*1988*
World*	6 177	5 637	6 805	12 578	14 278
US	2 919	1 766	2 484	2 356	606
Japan	390	646	445	1 502	1 461
EFTA	1 661	1 666	3 267	3 543	9 021
Others	1 207	1 559	609	5 177	3 190
			Outward		
	1984	*1985*	*1986*	*1987*	*1988*
World*	17 395	15 349	22 164	30 780	30 711
US	11 650	10 063	17 662	23 901	20 074
Japan	295	36	116	18	187
EFTA	929	760	9	1 826	2 306
Others	4 521	4 490	4 395	5 035	8 144

* Excluding intra-EC investments.
Source: EUROSTAT (1991), *European Community Direct Investment, 1984–88.*

The composition and characteristics of Japanese FDI in Europe has been examined elsewhere by the authors in Balasubramanyam and Greenaway (1992). The key features are that the investment is geographically and sectorally fairly concentrated. About 40 per cent of all investment goes to the UK and around

30 per cent to the Netherlands. This seems to be driven by a number of factors – the long-standing openness of the UK to FDI, relatively low labour costs, the importance of London as a financial centre and the role of the English language. Financial services and commerce account for around 60 per cent of total FDI, the remainder finding its way into manufacturing.

3 THE DETERMINANTS AND BENEFITS OF FDI

There is a copious and controversial literature on both the determinants of FDI and its welfare implications. A number of studies have reviewed this literature in great detail (Agarwal, 1980; Cantwell, 1991; Dunning, 1988). Here we merely note the main elements of this literature which are relevant for an explanation of the current upsurge in East Asian FDI in the EC.

The origins of the various explanations of FDI lie in Hymer's celebrated doctoral thesis on the subject. Hymer's explanation, grounded in industrial organization theory, is that a firm ventures abroad in order to fully exploit the rents inherent in the ownership advantages it possesses. These advantages may range from the possession of superior technology to the ownership of a brand name. Whether the firm would exploit such advantages through licensing or FDI would depend on the nature of the advantages and the degree of imperfections in the market for the advantages it possesses. The higher the imperfections, the greater would be the tendency to undertake FDI and control operations rather than engage in arms'-length transactions. While Hymer was concerned to explain the act of FDI, later theories such as the internalization theory attempt to explain the coming into being of the multinational enterprise whose method of operations is FDI. Well known in this context is the internalization explanation of the multinational enterprise which argues that, faced with imperfections in the markets for intermediary inputs and imperfect information, firms tend to internalize operations. In other words, they internalize operations to minimize costs of transactions and increase productive efficiency. This theory incorporates the idea of market imperfections identified by Hymer and extends it to provide an explanation for the existence of multi-plant firms across national boundaries. Another factor that has figured in explanations of international production is location advantages. Vernon's product life cycle hypothesis, for instance, emphasizes the search for relatively low-cost sources of capital and labour on the part of firms which possess ownership advantages which are transferable across geographical borders. The relative importance of ownership advantages, location factors and the ability of firms to internalize operations and the interrelationships between these factors have all been the subject of considerable debate (see Cantwell, 1991, for a succinct discussion of these issues).

Table 7.3 The OLI paradigm

Ownership advantages

(a) Size
- Obtain inputs more cheaply or exclusive access to inputs
- Better access to product markets
- Product or process diversification
- Economies of scale, both plant-level and firm-level

(b) Intangible assets
- Proprietary knowledge, technology, trademarks, product management, marketing, R&D, bank of human capital

(c) Government
- Policies which favour business in home country

Location advantages

(a) Inputs
- Spatial distribution of inputs and markets
- Input prices, quality and productivity

(b) Economies of scale
- Extent to which plant-level economies of scale make for centralization of production

(c) Government
- Government intervention
- Control of imports (tariffs, etc) tax rates, incentives, investment climate, political stability

(d) Other
- Transport and communications costs
- Infrastructure (commercial, legal, transport)
- Psychic distance (language, culture, business, customs)

Internalization advantages

(a) Market failure in market for final goods
- Reduce costs associated with market transactions
- Compensate for absence of futures markets

(b) Market failure in market for inputs
- Avoid costs of enforcing property rights
- Buyer uncertainty about nature and value of inputs
- Control supplies and conditions of sale inputs

(c) Monopoly power
- Where market does not permit price discrimination
- Control market outlets
- Engage in anti-competitive practices such as cross-subsidization and predatory pricing

(d) Product differentiation
- Need of seller to protect quality of product

(e) Government
- Avoid or exploit government intervention (quotas, tariffs, taxes, price controls)

Source: Adapted from Dunning (1988).

The eclectic paradigm enunciated by Dunning, however, neatly synthesizes the main elements of the various explanations. According to this, the decision to engage in local production and/or intrafirm trade, rather than licence, or engage in arms'-length trade is driven by considerations of ownership, location and internalization. What the 'OLI paradigm' claims is that conditions under all of these headings must be met before FDI can occur.

Take a specific example of a firm which has a valuable proprietary asset – say a strong brand image or a reputation for financial prudence. The positive rate of return which this yields confers an ownership advantage. Now suppose there is a foreign market with no competing brands where this asset can yield a rate of return at least as high as on the home market. Production conditions/transportation costs may lead the firm to decide on a strategy of supplying locally rather than at arm's length. Why should it set up a production plant rather than a licence? One possibility is to ensure that certain quality control conditions are met. Alternatively, the proprietary product may be produced by a proprietary technology of which the firm wishes to retain control. Either way the result is the same: to fully exploit the ownership/locational advantages the firm has to internalize the transaction by setting up a production facility.[1]

Table 7.4 Locational advantages in EC

Advantage	*Applicability to:* EC	Individual member states	*Comments*
a. Inputs: price		√	Especially important in Southern states
quality		√	Especially important in Northern states
b. Economies of scale		√	Given additional importance by 1992 and Single Market
c. Government policy: investment incentives		√	Range of incentives offered, especially in 'regions'. May become more important post-1992
Protected markets		√	May have been a mechanism for side-stepping source-specific restraints
Expectation of Fortress Europe	√		Concern regarding Fortress Europe may have stimulated FDI
d. Infrastructure:			
Political	√		Stability conducive to investment
Transport & communications	√		Good communications and transport systems conducive to investment

Table (7.3) lists possible ownership, location and internalization advantages. Associated with the former there may be advantages attached to size, or intangible assets like reputation or government policy. Where location is concerned, access to particular inputs or economies of scale or government policy or infrastructural factors might be important. Internalization advantages might derive from failures or imperfections in input or output markets. Alternatively, product differentiation or government policy can all play a role. The great advantage of the eclectic paradigm is that it provides a *general* explanation for FDI which encompasses all other model-specific theorems.

In the context of FDI in the EC, there are a number of locational advantages which are or have been influential. Moreover, as we will argue later, these are likely to enhance the firm-specific ownership advantages of Japanese MNEs. These are only provided in Table 7.4 for illustrative purposes at this stage. Later we will investigate EC factors in more detail.

Net Benefits of FDI

Analysis of the welfare impact revolves around, *inter alia*, employment effects, externalities, income redistribution and trade balance effects.

Employment effects

Opponents of FDI argue that it must be employment-reducing, on the grounds that foreign firms replace local firms as suppliers of final goods, and typically the former rely on imported inputs to a greater extent than the latter. Moreover, it is sometimes also argued that those jobs which are created are low value added/low human capital intensity jobs. Evidence from the US does suggest that foreign MNEs in general and Japanese MNEs in particular are more import intensive than indigenous firms (see for instance, Lipsey, 1991; Graham and Krugman, 1991). However, this does not necessarily mean that they will be a source of net employment decline. As Graham and Krugman (1991) point out, aggregate employment has much more to do with supply-side conditions, in particular the occupational and geographical mobility of labour. The 'quality of employment' argument is no more serious. Critics argue that MNEs basically set up 'screwdriver' plants geared towards low value added, low wage functions. Longer-term evidence from US investment in Western Europe, and more recent evidence on Japanese investment in the US and indeed in the UK, suggest that this is not in fact the case.

Externalities

It is possible to argue that FDI has positive spill-over effects through its impact on technology transfer. The contribution of modern endogenous growth theory has been to provide an explicit role for technology in the growth process. FDI is an obvious source of embodied technology – cross-border investment is potentially a major stimulus to growth. Clearly, this is not peculiar to FDI which originates within the Community. There is evidence to suggest that in some sectors – cars in the UK being an excellent example – foreign firms install best practice technology and management techniques and that these 'trickle down' to local producers.

Trade balance effects

Concern here derives from the allegedly high import dependence of foreign firms, combined with the allegedly low value added nature of the operations. This combination has an adverse impact on the trade balance. As noted earlier, there is some evidence from the US (Lipsey, 1991); Graham and Krugman, 1991) to the effect that Japanese firms tend to have a higher import dependence than local firms. Balasubramanyam (1989) among others has argued that this is in fact just a temporary phenomenon. Once the foreign firm becomes established, it sets up local supply networks for sourcing inputs. Moreover, the initial investment itself often brings in its wake investments from downstream producers. Another response is to point out that the goods which are actually produced may replace imports rather than domestically produced import substitutes. This has probably been the case in consumer electronics and cars. Finally, the key point to note is that, fundamentally, it is macroeconomic factors which are responsible for the trade balance at a particular point in time.

Income redistribution

Typically, because market imperfections preclude a potential supplier from fully appropriating the returns to firm-specific assets, FDI allows certain transactions to be internalized. However, the existence of internal markets creates opportunities for MNEs to engage in transfer pricing. In so far as this results in revenues which would otherwise accrue to the host government leaking overseas, it represents a welfare loss. There is evidence from developing countries which shows that transfer pricing does occur on a non-negligible scale. The same kind of evidence is not available for the EC or North America. The practice is likely to be less important in the EC and North America for three reasons: first, the range of controls and restrictions which stimulate it are nothing like as pervasive as in developing countries; second, double taxation agreements are more common; and third, disclosure rules are tighter. The second of these factors is likely to be especially important in the case of Japanese FDI, since full credit for taxes paid in Europe is provided by the Japanese government.

Thus FDI, like international trade, promotes specialization. As with international trade, one can identify static gains (through resource reallocation) and dynamic gains (through exploitations of scale economies, pro-competetive effects on local markets, and a stimulus to growth) which are a corollary of the process. Clearly, the net employment effects or trade balance effects will vary from one industry to another, depending upon supply conditions, market structure and so on. Overall, however, there is a strong presumption that FDI confers net benefits.

4 POLICY TOWARDS INVESTMENT

Since investment is a key determinant of economic growth, policy makers strive to create an environment conducive to investment formation.[2] The pervasiveness of investment codes in developing countries and the diversity of investment incentives in industrialized countries is testimony to this. Historically, investment measures have been regarded as a non-border issue. When economies were relatively closed this was a reasonable simplification; however, with the remarkable growth of trade over the post-war period and the concomitant globalization of production, the border/non-border distinction has become increasingly meaningless. The fact that trade-related investment measures (TRIMs) are an agenda item in the Uruguay Round is a reflection of this. From an EC standpoint this is a two-track issue involving internal measures which might influence cross-border investment and measures *vis-à-vis* non-EC entities. Both will be examined later in greater detail. For the moment we focus on the range of instruments which can be deployed.

Investment Incentives

Many initiatives to encourage capital investment are economy-wide, regionally based or sectorally based. In addition and/or instead of these it is not unusual to find incentives aimed specifically at MNEs considering FDI. The rationale behind discriminatory arrangements is threefold: first, it presumes that FDI supplements indigenous investment, and no crowding out takes place: second, it presumes that there are net benefits to the host economy arising from FDI; third, it presumes that the supply of FDI is responsive to incentives. Table 7.5 lists a range of instruments of investment policy, classified according to whether their initial impact is aimed at the input or output side, and their intended effects. Table 7.6 summarizes empirical evidence on the incidence of investment incentives. As can be seen, they tend to be more prevalent in developing, than in industrialized countries; tend to be geared towards input rather than output support; tend to be aimed at encouraging investment in the export sectors in developing countries and in high-tech sectors in industrialized countries; and are frequently used as an instrument of regional or social policy. There is no evidence at present which links the prevalence, or absence, of these measures to regional trading agreements (RTAs). As we will argue later, however, the trend towards regionalism could mean that they become more widely deployed.

Table 7.5 An inventory of investment incentives

Input incentives	
Instrument	*Intended effect*
Duty drawback	Subsidy on import inputs
Tax exemptions on equipment	Input subsidy
Accelerated depreciation	Subsidy to capital equipment
Investment allowances	Subsidy to capital equipment
Training credits	Subsidy to human capital formation
R&D support	Encourage high technology
Output incentives	
Instrument	*Intended effect*
Export subsidy	Specify that exported output gain bounty
Tax holiday	Exempt profits from taxation for specified period
Market reserve commitments	Local market monopoly conferred on investor
Export retention schemes	Allow MNE to retain foreign exchange earnings

Table 7.6 Incidence of investment incentives

Investment incentives are often used in a non-discriminatory fashion as instruments of regional or social policy
Input incentives are more prevalent than output incentives
Incentive programmes are often enshrined in investment codes in developing countries
Reliance on discretionary incentives is more prevalent in developing countries than industrialized countries
Developing countries make widespread use of incentives to attract MNEs into export sectors
Industrialized countries commonly provide support to encourage investment in R&D intensive sectors

Trade-related Investment Measures

The declaration which initiated the Uruguay Round drew specific attention to the need to examine the applicability of GATT articles to 'the trade restricting and distorting effects of investment measures'. Table 7.7 provides details of TRIMs classified on an input–output basis. They are intended to accomplish three things: first, to influence the location and pattern of economic activity;

second, to ensure that the likelihood of benefits which the host government wishes to secure is greater than it otherwise would be; and third, to redistribute part of the surpluses generated by FDI away from the MNE and towards residents of the host country. These are discussed by Greenaway (1990) under the headings of the *resource allocation, insurance and rent shifting targets*, respectively. The latter is especially important and explains the conjunction of investment incentives and/or protection and TRIMs. In general, TRIMs are second-best instruments and can be 'beggar thy neighbour' policies. The most common TRIMs have trade-distorting effects. Table 7.8 summarizes the evidence on their incidence. As with investment incentives, there is no evidence to link their usage to RTAs. Again, however, as we will argue later, with the proliferation of regional trading blocks they could become more widely used.

Table 7.7 An inventory of TRIMs

Instrument	*Intended effect*
	Input TRIMs
Local content requirements	Specify that some proportion of value added or intermediate inputs be locally sourced
Trade balancing requirements	Link imports of one product to export performance of some other
Laws of similars	Require MNEs to use local substitutes for imported inputs if a 'similar' component is locally manufactured
Limitations on imports	Self-explanatory
Foreign exchange restrictions	Constrain investor in terms of amount of intermediate inputs which can be imported
Local equity participation	Specify that some proportion of equity must be shed locally
Local hiring targets Expatriate quotas National participation in management	Ensure specified employment targets are hit
R&D requirements	Commit MNE to investment in R&D
Technology transfer	Commit MNE to local use of specified technology
	Output TRIMs
Instrument	*Intended effect*
Minimum export requirement	Specify a certain proportion of output to be exported
Trade balancing requirements	As above
Export controls	Specify that certain products may not be exported
Market reserve policy	Specify that local market is reserved for local producers
Product mandating requirements	Oblige the investor to export the mandated product from host country only
Licensing requirements	Oblige investor to license production of output in host country
Technology transfer	Commit MNE to specified embodied technology

Table 7.8 Incidence of TRIMs

The principal TRIMs are local content requirements and minimum export requirements
About one-sixth of (US) affiliates are subject to TRIMs
The incidence of TRIMs in developing countries is four times that in developed market economies (DMEs)
TRIMs are more heavily concentrated in mining and manufactures than in services
The main sectors in manufactures are motor cars, high-tech and petrochemicals
The principal developing countries in terms of incidence are Brazil, Mexico, India and Nigeria
The principal DMEs in terms of incidence are Canada, Australia and Spain
There is a tendency towards rule-based regimes in some developing countries
There is a high correlation between positive investment incentives and TRIMs
There is a high correlation between import protection and TRIMs

5 EC 1992 AND JAPANESE INWARD INVESTMENT

A number of studies have pointed to a connection between economic integration and FDI (UN, 1989; Greenaway, 1987; Shepley, 1992; Yannopolous, 1990; Balasubramanyam and Greenaway, 1992). In each case the data support a positive association, particularly in the case of the EC. This association is tied up with the opportunities which integration offers to exploit firm-specific ownership advantages. The data also show, as we saw earlier, that the EC 1992 programme has been associated with a growth in inward FDI.

There are a number of explanations for the growth of East Asian FDI, particularly that from Japan, since the early 1980s. These can be broadly classified into three groups: finance and cost of capital-oriented explanations, trade policy-oriented explanations and those which emphasize a broad set of factors including globalization strategies of Japanese firms, ownership advantages enjoyed by Japanese firms and the response of Japanese firms to growth in regionalism in the EC and the US.

Finance and Cost of Capital

Finance-oriented explanations attribute the growth of Japanese FDI to the sustained current account surpluses enjoyed by Japan and the appreciation of the Yen. In theory, a current account surplus translates into a capital outflow to preserve balance of payments equilibrium. Also the appreciation of the yen lowers the cost of acquisition of assets valued in dollars and other foreign currencies. There is, however, no suggestion in this theoretical construct that the outflow of capital would necessarily take the form of FDI. These financial factors do pave the way for portfolio capital movements out of Japan, but FDI requires more than mere access to finance. In the absence of some form of ownership advantages related to technology or management, an FDI operation owned and managed by the capital-exporting country cannot be mounted. It is not inconceivable for FDI to occur without a major outflow of capital from the investing country, provided the investing firms possess ownership advantages which are not enjoyed by firms in the host countries. Access to relatively inexpensive sources of finance is neither necessary nor sufficient for FDI to occur. Having said that, however, macroeconomic factors are clearly relevant to explaining why much Japanese FDI is financed from Japan rather than in the host country. Moreover, as we have noted, a large proportion of total Japanese FDI is in financial services, a part of which may simply be the recycling of current account surpluses.

Import Restrictions and FDI

The second set of explanations centres on the impact of import restrictions on inward FDI. Simply put, the argument is that, faced with restriction, exporting firms choose to penetrate foreign markets through FDI. This proposition can be traced back to Mundell's demonstration that trade in goods and international movement of factors are substitutes (Mundell, 1957). This is a much-discussed phenomenon in the context of FDI in developing countries. Several countries, such as India and Indonesia, which have pursued an import substitution strategy have attracted foreign firms into their protected industries. But, as Bhagwati (1978) has argued, protection is one amongst many factors which influence the magnitude of FDI in a country and, with due adjustments for political stability and economic size, it is countries with relatively free foreign trade regimes that attract a relatively high volume of FDI. There is some empirical evidence in support of the opposition. Developing countries pursuing an export promotion strategy of development or a strategy which is neutral appear to harbour a relatively larger volume of FDI per head than countries pursuing an import substitution strategy (see Balasubramanyam and Salisu, 1991).

Evidence from studies on US investment in the EC during the 1960s also suggests that the prospects of growth and an enlarged market rather than restrictions on imports from non-member countries played a major role in the decision of US firms to invest in the EC. Even so, it can be argued that Japanese FDI is on a different footing from FDI in developing countries and American investment in the Community during the 1960s and 1970s. Both the nature and extent of restrictions on Japanese exports differ from those faced by American firms now or in the past. Japanese exports are subject to a number of source-specific restrictions, including anti-dumping actions and voluntary export restraints (VERs), especially so in the case of electronic goods and transport equipment. Most VERs are negotiated by member states and these restrictions have induced Japanese firms to invest in the EC. Such FDI enables them to circumvent VERs; they can also export to markets which are not subject to VERs from their production facilities elsewhere in the EC. By contrast, in developing countries, import restrictions may have failed to induce substantial amounts of FDI because of the absence of a healthy investment climate and a wider regional market.

The logical conclusion of this line of reasoning is that Japanese FDI in the EC is of the tariff-jumping variety. This carries with it the implication that the natural method of foreign market penetration preferred by Japanese and other East Asian firms is exporting as opposed to FDI. It is only when they are deterred from exporting that they resort to FDI. If this were so, FDI tariff- jumping would be inferior to that which takes place spontaneously, for such FDI would not be a result of ownership advantages.

Although one can link some investments to the presence of particular restraints (as in the motor industry sector) it is unlikely that Japanese FDI is undertaken by firms which possess little by way of ownership advantages, in view of the dramatic increase in FDI from Japan and other parts of East Asia since the early 1980s. Tariff-jumping FDI should occur in one or two bursts immediately following the imposition of import restrictions (as may be occurring in some Eastern European countries) rather than expanding steadily over the years. Moreover, evidence shows that managerial practices, if not their technological superiority, are the main ownership advantage most Japanese firms possess and they have transferred such advantages to the host EC countries. Indeed, such managerial know-how appears to be one of the acknowledged benefits to host countries from Japanese FDI. Admittedly, in the initial years a number of Japanese investments were no more than assembly operations, or so-called 'screw-driver' operations. However, over the years these have given way to integrated manufacturing entities. The presumption is that Japanese FDI is motivated by much more than tariff jumping. Evidence based on surveys of Japanese firms in Europe conducted by JETRO suggest that most of the firms surveyed assigned a relatively low rank to import restrictions as a reason for their decision to invest. The group which cited this most frequently was the manufacturers of components for the transport equipment industry. While most other groups cited import restrictions as a factor, they assigned it much less weight compared with other factors such as globalization of Japanese business, catering to the needs of European consumers and the need to supply components to other Japanese manufacturers in Europe.

Bhagwati (1985, 1987) has proposed another novel trade-oriented explanation for FDI from Japan grounded in the political economy of protection. FDI, according to this explanation, takes place not to circumvent tariffs but to defuse the threat of protection. This is quite distinct from the tariff jumping explanation. In the case of the latter, FDI occurs *after* the imposition of protection; in the former it occurs *in anticipation of* its imposition. In this case FDI which transfers technology and promotes employment is in the nature of a bribe paid to the host country in return for allowing free access to the investor country's exports. This exchange is what Bhagwati refers to as *quid pro quo* FDI. The investment undertaken in the first period in anticipation of the threat of tariffs in the second period may not be profitable but, to the extent that it paves the way for exports in the second period, it is in the interest of the investor country. The lobbyists for the exporting countries can cite the benefits from FDI to soften protectionist demands from labour unions and other protectionist lobbies in the host countries. Bhagwati cites several examples of such *quid pro quo* FDI from Japan in the US, including joint ventures between Japanese and US firms.

Quid pro quo FDI obviously serves to preserve liberalized trade regimes and could be a major force in damping the enthusiasm for protection on the part of labour unions and powerful industry-supported lobbies. While there is some evidence in support of *quid pro quo* FDI in the context of Japanese FDI in the US, its incidence in the EC cannot be established with certainty. The bargaining process in the EC is more complicated since an investor may be seeking to appease both member state lobbies and EC lobbies, which may be in different sets. The enthusiasm with which relatively depressed regions in the EC are embracing Japanese FDI may be one sign of the growth of the *quid pro quo* variety of FDI. Part of the FDI in Wales in transport equipment and electronics may have come in response to potential VERs. The fact that it is located in a region which has relatively high unemployment also suggests that warding off demands for protection may be influential.

There is widespread belief that one of the principal factors in the surge of East Asian FDI in the EC in recent years is the concern that the Single Market would be heavily protected and result in a self-sufficient and self-centred Europe. The existing structure of protection with national quotas would give way to Community-wide quotas and a tighter trade regime. Most surveys and interviews with Japanese businessmen indicate that fears of 'Fortress Europe' is one factor in their decision to invest. Is it likely that FDI undertaken in response to perceived threats of protection will succeed in warding off protection, or is it merely a case of getting inside the fortress before the drawbridge is removed? Japan inside the Community may have a better chance of limiting, if not eliminating, protection than a Japan outside. For one thing, increased production by Japanese firms inside the Community would reduce the need to impose tariffs and quotas to the extent that such FDI displaces imports. For another, the visible contribution of Japanese firms to employment and investment in the Community would dilute the case of the lobbies for protection and create counter-forces – the role of the UK government in attempting to resist tight European VERs on Japanese cars is a good example. Moreover, the Community, along with Japanese firms resident in it, would be a strong contender for export markets elsewhere in the world, including Japan. Also protection of the Community's domestic market is hardly likely to open export markets to the European and Japanese firms in the Community. For these reasons a substantial proportion of Japanese FDI in the Community could qualify as *quid pro quo* FDI.

Market Growth and FDI

As well as the threat of protection, growth of regionalism in the EC in the form of the Single Market also has its attractions for foreign investors. The prospects of a vast unified market with 330 million people (360 million with EFTA included) is a major attraction. Although opinion is divided on the issue, the formation of the Single Market is expected to add 5 per cent to the growth rate of the GDP of the Community over the next five years, create two million jobs, provide economies of scale and scope and cut manufacturing costs substantially. Available evidence suggests that these benefits of integration are a major factor in the decision of Japanese firms to invest in the EC. Most Japanese firms in the EC surveyed by JETRO identify the objective of serving consumers in the Community as a major factor in their decision to invest in the EC.

Dynamic effects of integration as opposed to the static trade creation and trade diversion effects have been widely noted in the literature on integration. While increased FDI in response to existing levels of protection or perceived threats of protection would be in the nature of investment diversion, FDI which takes place in response to potential dynamic benefits of integration could be regarded as investment creation. Protection or even threats of protection which induce investment in the EC would displace imports financed by domestic investment. Whether or not it results in domestic production within the Community comparable in price and quality with that of the imports it displaces is arguable. If such domestic production is expensive relative to imports, import-displacing FDI could be regarded as investment diversion analogous to trade diversion.

Investment-creating FDI would create trade and be complementary to it rather than a substitute for it. *Quid pro quo* FDI which does not displace trade would also belong to this category. A characteristic of such FDI would be the exploitation of ownership advantages and the transfer of skills and know-how to which it gives rise. This would promote intra-industry trade within the Community building upon the opportunities for scale and scope economies which integration affords. Recent trends in FDI and trade in the Asian region show that both intra-Asian trade and intra-Asian FDI have increased substantially with FDI. This is also likely to be the case in the Single Market, with both East Asian and American FDI promoting intra-European trade. Moreover, integration in itself is likely to promote ownership advantages for firms resident in the Community.

We have reviewed three sets of explanations for the recent growth in East Asian FDI in the EC. We have argued that, although tariff jumping may be a factor in particular cases, the threat of 'Fortress Europe' is probably a more general factor. FDI induced by the perceived threat of protection could conceivably be of the *quid pro quo* variety; such FDI would not replace trade, but would complement it. In addition, dynamic benefits of integration appear to have been a major factor. A fully fledged econometric test of these propositions is desirable but its execution is hampered by the absence of detailed published data, difficulties of obtaining appropriate proxies, and problems of discriminating between hypotheses. Nonetheless, an attempt is made here to test these propositions.

Econometric Analysis

We first test the proposition that integration-induced benefits such as market size, incomes and infrastructure facilities, rather than trade restrictions have been the main inducements for Japanese FDI in the EC. The estimated regression equation is of the following form:

$$JFD = a + b\, GDP/P + cGDPr + d\, JEX/IECX + U_j \qquad (1)$$

where

JFD refers to annual flows of Japanese FDI into the EC for the years 1980–90;
GDP/P is per capita income for the EC as a whole for the years 1980–90;
$GDPr$ measures the annual average growth rate of GDP in the EC as a whole for the years 1980–90; and
$JEX/IECX$ measures the ratio of Japanese exports to intra-EC exports for the years 1980–90.

The two income variables capture the influence of size of the market and growth of incomes in the Community on inflows of Japanese FDI. The export ratio variable is designed to capture the effect of import restrictions on Japanese FDI in the EC. Ideally, this should be quantified by estimating average tariff rates on Japanese imports which take into account not only the common external tariff but also estimates of tariff equivalent quotas and VERs. However, the data required are not readily available. Moreover, such an estimate of import restriction would not capture the extent of trade diversion arising from these restrictions. The proxy variable for import restrictions included in the equation captures both the import restrictions effect and the trade diversion effect. A negative sign on the coefficient in the estimated equation would suggest that, as the ratio of Japanese imports into the EC to total intra-EC trade declines, FDI from Japan will increase.

Table 7.9 Japanese FDI in the EC: regression analysis

1. $\log(\text{JFDI}) = -5.16 + 0.76\log(GDP/P) + 4.09\log(JEX/ECX) + 0.34\log(GDPr)$
   (1.91) (2.72) (12.03) (4.82)
   Adjusted $R^2 = 0.89$
2. $\text{JFDI} = -2933.40 + 1.18GDP/P + 3608.50JEX/ECX + 785.10GDPr$
   (5.96) (2.94) (6.09) (1.32)
   Adjusted $R^2 = 0.82$
3. $\log(\text{JFDI}) = -16.36 + 1.08\log(GDP/P) + 0.36\log(GDPr)$
   (1.25) (1.25) (0.94)
   $+ 6.41\log(JEX.ECX) + 0.64\log(EC/World)$
   (3.60) (0.15)
   Adjusted $R^2 = 0.8$
4. $\text{JFDI} = -2.972 + 1.18GDP/P + 736GDPr + 3562JEX/ECX + 15.25EC/World$
   (3.06) (2.72) (0.61) (3.05) (0.05)
   Adjusted $R^2 = 0.79$

Table 7.10 Factors rated as important by Japanese companies when considering manufacturing sites in Europe

Factor	*Percentage of firms rating each factor as important*
Reliability/quality of suppliers	74.8
Availability of skilled labour	71.0
Good labour relations	67.3
Communications with other countries	42.1
Accessibility to markets	36.4
Low tax burden	29.0
Response of host government	26.2
Availability of financial assistance	25.2
Low labour costs	23.4
Cost of property	23.4
Presence of Japanese schools	13.1
Presence of Japanese community	8.4

Note: The 107 companies in the sample were asked to identify up to five factors which they regarded as important when considering a site in Europe.
Source: 'Japanese Direct Investment in the United Kingdom, 1986–87', The *Economic Development Briefing*, X. no. 1, 1986, p. 4. See Munday (1990).

We estimated equation (1) in both levels and first differences. None of the estimated equations lends support to the hypothesis that the growth of Japanese FDI in the EC is a response to import restrictions. The coefficient of the trade variable not only bears the wrong sign but it is also statistically significant. These results mirror those reported by Scaperlanda and Mauer (1969) in the context of US investment in the EC during the period 1952–66, with one significant difference. In the equations we have estimated, the coefficient of the trade variable is positive and statistically significant, while in the case of the equations reported by Scaperlanda and Mauer, though positive, it was statistically insignificant. Our findings suggest that Japanese FDI in the EC and Japan's exports to the Community complement one another. Such complementarity may arise because of the observed heavy incidence of intrafirm trade between subsidiaries of Japanese firms in the EC and their parent firms. It is a well-known fact that in the initial years of their operations Japanese FDI in the EC as well as in the US was relatively import-intensive. It is also possible that the positive association between trade and FDI reflects the *quid pro quo* nature of Japanese FDI in the EC. Member countries of the EC which harbour relatively large amounts of FDI may have softened their protectionist stance towards Japan during the 1980s. The UK is a case in point.[3]

These results also suggest that growth in incomes and market size, along with other dynamic effects of integration, exert a stronger influence on Japanese FDI in the EC than trade restrictions. The coefficients of the income variables are positive and statistically significant. We also attempted to assess the impact of growth of intra-EC trade on Japanese FDI. The argument here is that such growth signifies the impact of market size of Japanese FDI. We introduced an additional independent variable in the form of the ratio of intra-EC trade to total EC trade (equations (3) and (4) in Table 7.9) This captures both market size and the trade diversion effect of integration on inflows of FDI into the EC. The coefficient is positive and significant. However, because of multicolinearity between the trade and income variables, the coefficient of the GDP growth rate variable turns out to be statistically insignificant and the coefficient of the per capita income variable is statistically significant only at the 10 per cent level of significance. In sum, these results lend some support to the hypothesis that Japanese FDI in the EC responds to market size, growth in incomes and other integration-induced dynamic benefits.

6 POLICY COORDINATION WITHIN REGIONS

The European Community has a common commercial policy *vis-à-vis* third countries – the common external tariff. Moreover, variations in the level of the tariff, and exceptions to it, are negotiated at the Community level. In recent years, however, this common policy has been eroded by national measures – most notably source-specific restraints such as VERs, and state aid. This seems to be part of a wider process often referred to as 'instrument substitution'. Together with a wide range of other non-tariff measures, these have served to fragment the European market in some sectors (for example, cars, textiles and clothing). The 1992 programme aims to sweep these away. Harmonization of a range of policies, together with the abolition of Article 115 provisions will result in a truly common commercial policy. This reduces the scope for independent action on the part of individual member states.

In the past measures such as VERs have proved attractive as a palliative to adjustment problems. Once that degree of freedom is foreclosed, there is a possibility that, in the same way that VERs substituted for tariffs, investment policy could be substituted for VERs. The extent to which this occurs will be fashioned by adjustment pressures, on the one hand, and the degree to which state aid and regional support policies are harmonized, on the other. The Cecchini Report and other analyses have forecast adjustment pressures in the form of transitional unemployment. From an economic standpoint, this is neither a surprise nor necessarily a problem. After all, adjustment is the price we pay for change. However, from a political economy standpoint, adjustment pressures can be troublesome, particularly when they are non-randomly distributed. It is not easy to forecast exactly which sectors/regions will be most affected. Two points can be made however. First, some recent research suggests that the marked increase in intra-industry specialization may have tailed off recently, and possibly even reversed (Greenaway and Hine, 1991). The importance of this is that both *a priori* theorizing and some empirical evidence suggest that adjustment to trade expansion may be smoother in a setting of intra- as opposed to inter-industry expansion. The second point is that the Community already has a 'regional problem' in that a number of areas, largely on the periphery, are relatively underdeveloped, have relatively low incomes per head and relatively high unemployment. These sectors could be more exposed in the adjustment to market completion.

For these reasons governments *could* come under pressure to provide adjustment assistance of some form. As already noted, source-specific restraints have proved popular in the past; some alternative, such as state aid, could prove popular in the future. A recent Commission study has drawn attention to the level and distribution of state aid in the Community. Between 1986 and 1988, an average of 2.2 per cent of GDP (or 4.5 per cent of total government expenditure) was disbursed as state aid by member states. This amounts to more than twice the Community budget. Moreover, there is a large variance around this figure, from 1.0 per cent of GDP in Denmark to 4.1 per cent in Luxembourg. Already, therefore, there exists quite a wide disparity in the practices of member states. In adjusting to the completed market, and beyond that in preparation for the single currency, there will be obvious pressures on providing state aid to encourage investment. Our statistical analysis suggests that the willingness to provide state aid by member states may have influenced the locational choices of East Asian MNEs. From the Community's standpoint there are dangers associated with uncoordinated action. First, some of the benefits of a common commercial policy could be eroded if member states make greater independent use of regional investment incentives to attract FDI. Second, conflicts over investment policy could spill over to other issues, thereby threatening consensus. Third, from the standpoint of the Community as a whole, competition between member states to attract inward investment redistributes some of the potential gains from FDI away from the host country and towards the investing corporation.

The discussion in the previous section implied that alternative policies can substitute for each other. The basic theory of trade policies confirms that this is so. Recent research has revealed important interconnections between trade policy, investment policy, competition policy and regulation in the services sector. Therefore, in addition to harmonization of investment measures, there is also an issue of the compatibility of investment, and other measures. The problem of policy compatibility arises for three reasons. First, as we have already stressed, increasing openness of economies means that investment policy can no longer be thought of simply as a non-border measure. Many instruments of investment policy have trade effects. Second, and related to the foregoing, different instruments of policy can have equivalent effects. Third, investment policy might have multiple objectives – both macroeconomic and microeconomic. This potentially gives rise to two problems – feedback between policy instruments and porosity across instruments.

Feedback can be positive or negative, reinforcing or counteracting the effects of other policies. An example of positive feedback is seen where tax allowances encourage investment in a particular region where other government policies such as location of central services are in place. An example of negative feedback would be where state aid to encourage investment in a particular sector runs counter to the objectives of competition policy. Clearly, in the latter case policy conflict arises. Not only can this lead to conflict between agencies but it can also stimulate further feedback effects. This is related to the problem of porosity. Because different policy instruments can have equivalent effects, regulation in one area can lead to increased use of unregulated instruments. If, for example, investment grants are tightly regulated, more flexible arrangements on reporting, or intellectual property protection, could be offered to attract a MNE. This is important both from a regional and a multilateral standpoint. If there are perceived to be net benefits from FDI, and if governments compete to secure such investment, the by-product distortions of intervention are minimized with compatible policies. With further integration, this becomes increasingly important. There is also a global dimension to this. One of the major priorities for the Uruguay Round negotiations is to ensure that agreements on TRIMs, subsidies, services and intellectual property rights (IPRs) are compatible. Beyond Uruguay, a key issue for any multilateral trade organization is the compatibility of regulation in these areas with competition policy. These are issues to which we now turn.

From the data provided in Section 2, and subsequent discussion, two points stand out. First, MNEs are key actors, and increasingly so, in the process of international specialization and exchange, a process which is shaped by regionalism. Second, a wide range of policy instruments is available to influence the locational decisions of MNEs. By definition, MNEs are internationally mobile. Their ability to arbitrage between regulatory regimes or support measures can be a source of both policy competition and policy conflict. The growing influence of MNEs has resulted in a great deal of international negotiation and cooperation to set standards regarding the treatment which they face in host countries and, to a lesser extent, to regulate their behaviour.

As noted in Section 3, investment policy has historically been regarded by host governments as a non-border instrument. This being so, it is hardly surprising that bilateral treaties should have proliferated, with close to 300 in existence. Their function is largely as a signalling mechanism – host governments commit themselves to certain standards of treatment relating to nationalization, compensation, most-favoured-nation treatment, dispute settlement and so on. As such, they can offer insurance of sorts to inward investors. As with bilateral trading arrangements, however, the resulting patchwork is a less efficient, less transparent solution than a multilateral regime.

There have been a large number of regional and multilateral agreements relating to MNEs since the early 1960s, especially regional arrangements. The titles of the various treaties, conventions and codes give an indication of their coverage. Mostly they are directed at setting standards relating to, *inter alia*, treatment of investors, investment climate, entry conditions, ownership, conditions of employment, transfer of technology, consumer protection, jurisdiction and dispute settlement. The most active multilateral forum has been the OECD, followed by the World Bank. However, since GATT is now involved in the issue, it could become the lead institution.

As we saw in the previous section, with the growth of FDI and regionalism, there is scope for growing competition to attract FDI within regions. Clearly this can also extend to competition between regions. In so far as MNEs arbitrage between regulatory regimes, and this can distort investment flows and spill over to trade flows, some kind of multilateral arrangements are clearly in order.

TRIMs were explicitly included as an agenda item in the Uruguay Round. At the time of writing, no draft agreement has proved acceptable to all parties. Developing countries in particular have resisted multilateral disciplines on the grounds that many TRIMs do not have direct trade-distorting effects, and even those that do are investment measures rather than border measures. Most industrialized countries are equally adamant that some TRIMs (most notably local content and minimum export requirements) have trade-distorting effects and that their use needs to be disciplined. The principle of a waiver for the least developed countries has been accepted, albeit on a time-constrained basis. Since local content requirements have been found by a GATT panel to be contrary to Article III in at least one important case (against the Canadian FIRA) it is probable that greater discipline can be brought to bear on TRIMs through existing mechanisms. This, together with the (surprising) degree of consensus on the part of industrialized countries regarding the principle of disciplining trade-distorting TRIMs makes an eventual agreement likely.

As we saw in Section 3, investment incentives are also a fairly heterogeneous mix of instruments. The most commonly used are some form of direct subsidy typically operating through a cash grant, accelerated depreciation or development subvention. Several GATT Articles (VI, XVI and XXIII) pertain to subsidies. The first sanctions recourse to countervailing duties (CVDs) if material injury can be associated with a subsidy. Article XVI places an obligation on contracting parties to notify any trade-relevant subsidies, while XXIII sanctions retaliation if rights under XVI are abrogated. The Code on Subsidies agreed in the Tokyo Round supplements and clarifies these obligations but has not worked well. Thus subsidies, too, are an agenda item in the Uruguay Round. Some convergence has occurred on the part of contracting parties (CPs) around the so-called 'traffic light' approach. The sticking point to an agreement here relates not to the traffic light principle but to the components of the various categories. As with TRIMs, if an agreement is reached, it should bring greater discipline to the use of investment incentives.

The final issue we should address on multilateral issues is the way in which disciplines could evolve under the auspices of GATT. This is not to assert that GATT is the only forum in which agreement could be reached – as we have seen, both the UN and the OECD have been active in this respect. If, however, significant progress is to be made, GATT is the key institution as it is in a position to nest any codes in the wider framework of trade rules. The latter is especially important since investment rules are part of a much bigger picture. As borders shift back with increasing openness, and the role of conventional trade instruments, most notably tariffs, declines, issues that were formerly regarded as non-border measures – investment policies, regulation of services, protection of intellectual property and competition policy – are increasingly becoming the subject of trade friction within and between regions. The inclusion of services, IPRs and TRIMs on the Uruguay Round agenda is an acknowledgement of this. Circumstances in the world economy and world trading system have changed profoundly since GATT's inception and the need for a more rules-based system which can accommodate investment, as well as other issues, is paramount.

This of course begs the question of exactly how investment can be accommodated under GATT disciplines. This is an issue recently addressed by Greenaway and Sapir, (1992) in an assessment of progress on all the new issues. It was argued there that GATT disciplines as they apply to merchandise trade could not be transposed to the new issues – complete harmonization is not necessarily desirable, let alone feasible, because differences in regulatory regimes arise for historical reasons, and it is not always clear that one regulatory regime is necessarily more efficient than another. Efforts at complete harmonization would quickly run up against the buffer of national sovereignty. However, the principles on which GATT disciplines are based can be extended to the new issues in general, and investment in particular. Specifically, national treatment, mutual recognition and most favoured nation are all transferable. In the case of investment the first two are especially important. For the Uruguay Round this means identifying those TRIMs which have significant trade-distorting effects and affirming the applicability of appropriate GATT Articles. As argued above, however, TRIMs are only part of the picture and, in the longer term, a code covering direct investment is required, embracing rights of establishment, home and host country obligations and dispute settlement mechanisms.

7 CONCLUSIONS

This chapter has reviewed East Asian FDI in the EC. Both *a priori* reasoning and empirical evidence suggest that the observed upsurge in such investment in the EC is largely due to the potential market size of the EC, although some of it may have been undertaken to ward of threats of trade restrictions. To the extent that such FDI is of the *quid pro quo* variety, it should result in lower levels of protection and reduce the likelihood of a fortress emerging. Japanese FDI is, in fact, actively sought by many of the member states of the EC with a variety of inducements. Such policies testify to the benefits of inward FDI, including employment creation and technology transfer. Whether or not such policies serve to promote the overall volume of FDI in the EC or merely redistribute a given amount between the member states is unclear. But there is some danger that such policies may spill over into other areas of policy. At present multilateral disciplines on the use of investment incentives and disincentives are relatively weak and need to be strengthened. With the inclusion of TRIMs on the Uruguay Round agenda, investment measures are, for the first time, being explicitly embraced by GATT. A Multilateral Trade organization (MTO) agreement would pave the way for more comprehensive disciplines.

NOTES

1. Shepley (1991) has recently criticized this framework as being too static. For purposes of specifying a model which explains a particular investment, this may be so. However, as a means of commenting upon the range of influences which may be relevant, the framework is still useful. Moreover, it is possible to integrate dynamic considerations – for example, technological competence can be thought of as an ownership advantage.
2. The determinants of growth are reviewed in Shaw (1992), Dowrick (1992) and Scott (1992).
3. These conjectures could be more rigorously evaluated with appropriate data changes in country-specific factors, and with data which disaggregated manufactures and services.

REFERENCES

Agarwal, J.C. (1980), 'Determinants of direct foreign investment: A Survey', *Weltwitschaftches Archiv*, **116**(4), 739–73.

Balasubramanyam, V.N. (1989), 'Incentives and disincentives for foreign direct investment in less developed countries', *Weltwitschaftches Archiv*, **120**, 720–35.

Balasubramanyam, V.N. and D. Greenaway (1992), 'Economic integration and FDI; Japanese investment in the EC', *Journal of Common Market Studies*, **30**, 175–94.

Balasubramanyam, V.N. and M. Salisu (1991), 'EP, IS and direct foreign investment in LDCs', in Ad Koekkock and L.B.M. Mennes (eds), *International Trade and Global Development: Essays in Honour of Jagdish Bhagwati*, London: Routledge.

Bhagwati, J.N. (1978), *Anatomy and Consequences of Exchange Control Regimes*, Vol. 1, Studies in International Economic Relations, no. 10, New York: National Bureau of Economic Research.

Bhagwati, J.N. (1985), 'Investing abroad', Esmee Fairbairn Lecture, delivered at Lancaster University, Lancaster, U.K.

Bhagwati, J.N. (1987), 'VERs, *quid pro quo* FDI and VIEs: politics–economics–theoretic analysis, *International Economic Journal*, **1**, 1–4.

Cantwell, J. (1991), 'A survey of theories of international production' in C.N. Pitelis and R. Sugden (eds), *The Nature of the Transnational Firm*, London: Routledge, 16–63.

Dowrick, S. (1992), 'Technological catch up and diverging incomes: paths of economic growth, 1960–88', *Economic Journal*, **102**.

Dunning, J. (1988), *Explaining International Production*, London: Unwin Hyman.

Eurostat (1991), *European Community Direct Investment, 1984–1988*, Luxembourg: Eurostat.

Graham, E. and P.R. Krugman (1991), *Foreign direct investment in the United States*, Washington, DC: Institute for International Economics.

Greenaway, D. (1987), 'Intra-industry trade, intra-firm trade and European integration', *Journal of Common Market Studies*, **26**, 153–72.

Greenaway, D. (1990), 'Trade related investment measures: political economy aspects and issues for the GATT', *The World Economy*, **13**, 367–86.

Greenaway, D. and R.C. Hine (1991), Intra industrial specialisation, trade expansion and adjustment in the European economic space', *Journal of Common Market Studies*, **25**, 603–22.

Greenaway, D. and A. Sapir (1992), 'New issues in the Uruguay round: services, TRIMs and TRIPs', *European Economic Review*, **36**, 509–18.

Hymer, S. (1976), *The International Operations of National Firms: A Study of Direct Foreign Investment*, Cambridge, MA: MIT Press.

Lipsey, R. (1991), 'Foreign direct investment in the US and US trade', Working Paper No. 3623, Cambridge, MA: National Bureau of Economic Research.

Munday, M. (1990), *Japanese Manufacturing Investment in Wales*, Cardiff: University of Wales Publications.

Mundell, R. (1957), 'International trade and factor mobility', *American Economic Review*, **47**, 321–35.

Scaperlanda, A.E. and L.J. Mauer (1969), 'The determinants of US direct investment in the EEC', *American Economic Review*, **59**, 558–68.

Scott, M. (1992), 'A new view of economic growth', *Economic Journal*, **102**.

Shaw, G.K. (1992), 'Policy implications of endogenous growth theory', *Economic Journal*, **102**.

Shepley, S. (1992), 'FOI in the context of European Economic Integration' (mimeo), Brussels: European Commission.

United Nations (1991), *World Investment Report: The Triad in Foreign Direct Investment*, New York.

Yannapolous, G. (1990), 'Foreign direct investment and European integration: the evidence from the formative years of the European Community', *Journal of Common Market Studies*, **27**.

8. Foreign investment in Eastern Europe's transformation process

J. B. Donges and J. Wieners

1 INTRODUCTION

One key element for the successful economic (and political) transformation of the formerly socialist countries is their integration into the world economy. This implies opening up the domestic economy both to foreign trade and to foreign private investment. Massive capital investment over many years to come is essential for generating a positive growth and employment perspective in Eastern Europe. In the short run, new investment is required in existing firms to secure their survival under competitive conditions. In the medium run, it is necessary to rebuild the largely obsolescent capital stock in the enterprise sector, to construct an adequate infrastructure, and to restore the devastated environment. Investment needs might amount to several billion dollars per year in each country, depending on the assumed incremental capital–output ratio and the desired rate of economic growth. Much of the financing for the investments should come from domestic savings, private and public; but, given declining real incomes of private households and severe financial constraints in the public budget, funds from this source cannot be large. The scope for retained earnings in the business sector is still small. Some funds may come from increased foreign borrowing, provided Western countries are prepared to lend more in spite of the existing debt overhang in the region. International agencies, in particular the newly-created European Bank for Reconstruction and Development (EBRD), may also give financial assistance. Expatriates may be willing to make own savings available to their country of origin out of solidarity with the change of the system. Another potentially important source could be foreign direct investment (FDI), as distinct from private portfolio investment which will be of little importance for Eastern Europe as long as there are no functioning stock markets in these countries.

Foreign capital penetration has become a hotly debated issue in Eastern European countries' domestic policy. The main opposition stems from those who still think in terms of Marxist theories of imperialism; apart from their antipathetic attitude towards the whole transformation process and the road towards capitalism, they regard FDI as a threat to the political sovereignty of their country. The main support for FDI comes from those who believe that, on balance, there is much to be gained in economic terms from capital inflows; they want to share the favourable experience of a great number of industrial and developing countries with inward FDI. Furthermore, the debate is provoked by vested interests of particular domestic business and labour groups. While some fear the increased competition from more resourceful and efficient foreign investors and eventual displacement effects associated with it, others welcome foreign investors because they see them as new buyers of local goods and services and as new employers for all categories of personnel (from managers to blue-collar workers), paying salaries above those paid by domestic enterprises. In a sense, foreign investment is a hotly debated issue almost everywhere in the world. At the same time, however, competition among countries for private foreign capital has grown steadily. Policy makers in Eastern Europe will therefore have to decide whether, to what extent and under which conditions they want their countries to share in international investment flows, and they will have to define policies accordingly. They should not take it for granted that potential foreign investors necessarily rank Eastern Europe high in terms of attractiveness.

This chapter is about the role of FDI in the transition of the countries of Eastern Europe from centrally planned economies to market-based economies. It first briefly reviews the historical evolution of investments. Consideration is then given to their prospective role in the privatization programmes of these countries. The questions of why Western firms should invest in Eastern Europe and why Eastern European countries should be interested in attracting them are discussed next. We shall then devote some attention to the policies towards FDI that the host and home countries should or should not pursue.

2 PRINCIPAL TRENDS IN FOREIGN INVESTMENT

Private foreign investment in Eastern Europe has a short history indeed. Under the old socialist regimes it was initially completely forbidden and only gradually and partially permitted from the late 1960s onwards.[1] FDI could be carried out only in the form of joint ventures between domestic and foreign firms. The domestic partner provided the personnel and infrastructure and organized the contacts with local suppliers of inputs, banks and public administration, whereas the foreign partner had to provide know-how and hard currency, but could not claim equity holdings, let alone complete or majority foreign ownership of an enterprise. Not surprisingly, the size of foreign investment was minimal. Until 1987, only 170 joint ventures had been established in the whole of Eastern Europe, with Western capital commitment amounting to just $120 million.[2] It was not until 1989–90, when the intention of Eastern European governments to have their economies changed to a market system finally materialized and new, more liberal laws governing FDI came into force, that joint ventures began to appear in more substantial numbers (Table 8.1).[3] Hungary seems to be the most attractive country, not only measured by the number of joint ventures but also in terms of capital inflows: In 1990–91, those flows amounted to more than $1.6 billion, equivalent to about 40 per cent of total FDI in Eastern Europe as a whole at that time; by the end of 1991, the stock of foreign capital allocated there accounted for more than 50 per cent of the total for this area (Table 8.2).

Table 8.1 Joint ventures in Eastern Europe (at year-end)

	1987	*1988*	*1989*	*1990*	*1991*
Bulgaria	15	25	50	65[a]	800
CSFR	7	16	50	1 600	4 000
Hungary	130	270	980	5 693	10 550
Poland[b]	13	53	867	2 600	4 902[c]
Romania	5	16	40	1 500	10 100
USSR	5[d]	200	1 006	3 000	3 700[e]
Total[f]	175	580	2 993	14 458	34 052

Notes
a September 1990.
b 'Polonia' firms not included (see text).
c October 1991.
d End of 1986.
e July 1991.
f Refers to data shown.

Sources: Own estimates, based on information provided by national and international institutions and on press reports.

Table 8.2 Stock of foreign capital in Eastern Europe (millions of US dollars)

	1987	*1988*	*1989*	*1990*	*1991*
Bulgaria	n.a.	n.a.	4	56	100
CSFR	n.a.	n.a.	50	180	770
Hungary	80	250	850	1 600	2 500[a]
Poland	200[b]	n.a.	200	443[c]	690
Romania	n.a.	n.a.	n.a.	112	343
USSR	50	480	2 300	3 000	3 200[d]
Total[e]	330	730	3 404	5 391	7 603

Notes
a October 1991.
b 1986.
c September 1990.
d July 1991.
e Refers to data shown.

Sources: As Table 8.1.

One striking feature of recent FDI in Eastern European countries is that the foreign capital share is small and has declined. In Poland, for instance, the increase in the absolute number of joint ventures during 1990–91 was accompanied by a decreasing average investment (Jermakowicz and Bochniarz, 1991); by mid-1991, only 37 permits were issued referring to investment projects with a foreign capital share exceeding $2 million (Sadowska-Csieslak and Olszewski, 1991). In Hungary, the average foreign capital commitment fell from 48.2 million forint in 1990 to 23 million forint in the first half of 1991 (Wass von Czege, 1992).[4] Most registered joint ventures (84 per cent) in the former Czech and Slovak Federal Republic (CSFR) have a capital of less than $30 000 (OECD, 1991). In Romania, the situation is similar: more than 90 per cent of joint-venture companies have a foreign capital participation of less than $50 000.[5]

Most of the present stock of foreign capital located in Eastern Europe is of (West) German and Austrian origin. Links of geography and culture, combined with the desire to gain a foothold in untapped markets of countries which happened to be traditional trading partners in the pre-socialist area and could become so again as the reform process makes headway, are a major explanation of this engagement (which, incidentally, is now giving rise to fears about 'German domination' in the host countries, particularly in the former CSFR). Non-European countries, in particular Japan, a leading investing country elsewhere in the world economy, have been reluctant to enter these newly developing markets.

As to sector distribution, FDI has been concentrated thus far in commerce and services. Only recently has a rising trend towards investment in the production sectors (including agriculture) begun to show itself, especially in Hungary (Marrese, 1992). Recently, the biggest foreign investment was undertaken by the German car manufacturer Volkswagen in the former CSFR (about $350 million). In view of cost advantages derived from relatively cheap labour and abundant raw materials, at least in some of the Eastern European countries, one would have expected FDI to occur in manufacturing on a larger scale, but the framework for FDI in the formerly centrally planned economies was not appropriate and the liberalization of FDI regulations in the course of the on-going transformation process could not yet materialize in increasing investment flows because of the still uncertain economic, institutional and political environment in these countries.[6] In particular, the slow pace of privatization may have deterred potential foreign investors.

3 FOREIGN INVESTMENT AND PRIVATIZATION

It is widely agreed that economy-wide privatization is at the core of the transformation process. Without converting a substantial part of productive assets owned by the state into private ownership, a market economy cannot emerge. Nor will the attractiveness of the country for foreign investors improve. When the old centralized systems collapsed and privatization programmes were placed high on the priority list of reform measures, many Western enterprises expected a more or less rapid reduction in the size of the state sector and, correspondingly, ample opportunities for entering hitherto sheltered sectors of the economy. This expectation has proved to be ill-founded.

When a potential foreign investor formed his expectations about a rapid pace of privatization he may have been too optimistic for at least three reasons.

1. The governments of the reforming countries had no blueprint for the privatization (its speed, its sequencing, its scope, its methods). Western experience with privatization of state-owned companies, contrary to initial widespread beliefs, could not serve as a guide, because those privatizations affected only a small number of enterprises and were undertaken in the context of a functioning market economy with a competitive framework in place. In Eastern Europe, any serious privatization policy had to deal with almost the entire economy and competitive environments were still to be created. Moreover, governments were challenged by another distinctive complication: the contention about the restitution principle; that is, whether firms and other assets, which were expropriated under the socialist regimes, should be restored to their former private owners, rather than financial indemnification being provided. Given these very difficult problems, privatization could not be set in motion and proceed as rapidly as expected (and desired).
2. Moreover, there was the problem of valuation of the firms to be privatized. When emerging from a centrally planned economy, there is considerable uncertainty as to what would be the correct price for selling public assets. It is almost impossible to determine the net present value of an asset when the long-term rate of interest required for discounting is unknown. In the face of liberalized product prices and trade reforms, past performance of an enterprise offers no information as to its future performance. The enterprises' balance sheets were in no case informative. The financial infrastructure, such as banks and stock exchanges which are important for the 'technical aspects' of the privatization process, was in a very rudimentary stage of development. There is, then, the fear of selling off too much of the state's assets at too low prices. For all these reasons, even well-meant privatization plans need time before they can be effected.
3. Last, but not least, privatization was from the very beginning of the transformation process also a sensitive political issue. Broad support by the population was needed, but tensions soon emerged. On the one hand, socialist hardliners in the bureaucracy and the army, and conservative state industry managers as well, were interested in keeping control over the

> economy as long as possible, so that rather than providing administrative help in the shaping and execution of privatization programmes, they thwarted them, simultaneously generating confusion and domestic unrest. On the other hand, public opinion became quickly worried about the fact that privatization would lead not only to complete shut-down of firms (because no buyer could be found and public subsidies to preserve them could not be expected) but also to a reduction of jobs in viable enterprises (in order to remove hidden unemployment). Even newly established private firms often wanted state-owned enterprises to stay in the market on the grounds that they could easily exploit them as suppliers or buyers and need not fear them as serious competitors. 'Unholy' alliances between the various special interest groups became strong enough to urge reformist-minded policy makers to go about privatization cautiously, and this the more so as a large part of the population feared that privatization would lead to excessive foreign penetration of their country.

In Hungary and Poland, where privatization began early, the transfer of state enterprises to private hands went along the lines of the British model (Begg, 1991). Enterprises were evaluated *ex ante* by Western consulting and investment firms, and subsequently sold off in public offerings. It soon turned out that this method was unsuitable under the circumstances of an economy in transition because it was too slow and too complicated. In Poland only 30 enterprises were privatized through this method up to March 1992 (Szomburg, 1992). A unique feature in privatizing Eastern European economies was the proposal to distribute shares in public enterprises free of charge to all domestic citizens. Many advantages have been associated with the give-away method: the time-consuming and complicated *ex ante* evaluation of the sale method is circumvented (Lipton and Sachs, 1990; Borensztein and Kumar, 1991); instead, the evaluation of individual enterprises results *ex post* from secondary market trading; privatization is speeded up dramatically (Winięcki, 1990); furthermore, the scope for badly needed new investment is widened as scarce savings need not be used for buying the state assets (Bös, 1991); finally, there is some merit in the argument that state enterprises already belong to the people, because they were financed through forced savings in the past (Hinds, 1990).

Evidently, the give-away method also has its disadvantages. Giving each adult citizen one share in each privatized company effectively means creating thousands of public corporations with highly dispersed ownership. This will result in complicated principal–agent relationships between stockholders and corporate management. A small stockholder will not be in a position to judge whether the management has taken the right decisions. As a consequence, managers can divert company resources for their own personal use. What is probably even more important is the fact that managers favour investments which increase total company turnover rather than company profits because, as has frequently been shown, this raises their salaries and prestige.[7] 'Free' cash flow, that is cash flow in excess of the cash flow needed to fund all investments with a positive net present value, is not disbursed via dividends to stockholders.[8]

Principal–agent problems between stockholders and managers are limited by competition on several markets.[9] In particular, the market for corporate control has received a lot of attention. However, the literature is far from unanimous as regards its efficiency.[10] In the specific Eastern European context there are two additional reasons why hostile takeovers as the main device of the market for corporate control may not work, at least in the immediate future:[11]

1. Takeovers in the Western countries in the 1980s were highly leveraged; corporate raiders financed their transactions largely through loans ('leveraged buyout'). But it is precisely the lack of internal savings in the Eastern European countries which gave rise to give-away schemes. It is thus unclear from which sources the capital to finance takeovers should come (at least as long as foreign borrowing is limited).[12]
2. The financial infrastructure, such as banks and stock exchanges, is still very rudimentary. Highly specialized financial experts are still rare.

Principal–agent problems in enterprises which have been privatized via give-aways will thus be so substantial that the process of restructuring inefficient industries may become almost unworkable (Kirchner, 1992). Shareholders would have insufficient monitoring power in their hands. Furthermore, agency problems might even be aggravated in the transformation period, since old control structures have disappeared, without new ones having yet been established.[13] To cope with principal–agent problems without sacrificing the alleged advantages of give-aways, a multi-step procedure is to be recommended. There are numerous variants, but they all have one common feature: a layer of intermediaries, for example investment funds, is established between the citizens as the ultimate owners and the enterprises.[14] At first, state enterprises are allocated to the intermediaries and subsequently shares in the intermediaries are issued free of charge or only for a nominal fee to the public. Citizens now hold portfolios instead of shares in individual enterprises. The intermediaries will have substantial stakes in the equity capital of their enterprises. Their task is to enforce efficient restructuring in their enterprises, which includes closing down deficit units or dismissing inefficient or uncooperative management. The former CSFR has already established a mass privatization programme which contains elements of this multi-step procedure.[15] There is also a detailed proposal for Poland.[16] In other countries (Russia, Romania) it is being actively considered.

However, there is one aspect which has to be considered when implementing these multi-step privatization schemes. Who controls the intermediaries?

Or to put it differently: the principal–agent problems do not simply disappear; they are shifted to another level, that between the 'funds' and their shareholders. How to establish the appropriate 'mix' of incentives and controls of fund managers still remains unsolved. This leads to the question of whether and to what extent foreign investment should be combined with privatization. Major reasons for doing so are (a) that foreign investors, with their experience in private business, could assume real ownership functions, thereby mitigating principal–agent problems;[17] and (b) that foreign investors, who may be better prepared than potential domestic buyers in assessing future economic opportunities of the firm being privatized, and in absorbing risks as well, would design an entrepreneurial concept that fits best in competition with others. This would enhance the profitability prospects, which in turn would lead to rising prices for the assets in the bidding process and thus alleviate the valuation problem.

These advantages notwithstanding, participation of foreign investment in privatization has been met with scepticism, if not open resistance. The objections[18] are (a) that foreign investors would exploit the lack of experience of national authorities in assessing the value of the firm to be privatized and feign a low market value in order to get the assets at a low price, which would lead to so-called 'squandering of national wealth' to foreigners; and (b) that foreign investors would not reveal their true objectives as to the future activity of the firm, but rather carry out so-called 'asset-stripping' which would mean all employees being dismissed and the acquired real assets being allocated to quite different uses. The last point is not at all convincing. Transformation of the economy also implies restructuring of production and thus a reallocation of resources to (it is hoped) their most efficient uses. If 'asset-stripping' is part of the process, it should not be hampered; domestic investors buying state property would certainly do the same if they expected that they could earn a higher rate of return by embarking upon new business ventures than by staying in the old one.

As to the 'squandering' issue, it is exaggerated. On the one hand, it is far from clear that real asset prices would fall dramatically in bidding (or auctioning) as a result of manipulations and tactics of foreign investors; the opposite seems more plausible. Actual selling prices may be lower than expected by the government, the population, or both; but this may just reflect an underestimation of the degree of obsolescence of the real assets, which is now revealed by market forces. On the other hand, true squandering may occur if the Eastern European governments, in an attempt to attract FDI, start to compete with each other in the field of special incentive policies, in particular tax concessions and subsidies. The more generous those incentives become, the greater the adverse effects on the domestic economy, as such incentives tend to be redundant (other factors are more important in determining the investment decision of a foreign company). The advice therefore is that reforming countries should not engage in special incentive competition. This being said, it should be recalled that capital inflows lead to an increased potential output of the domestic economy and thus to greater employment opportunities within the host country; most of the added income remains as wage income for the local labour force in this country too (even if the foreign investor continuously repatriates all profits from his activity, which seems unlikely to happen). This is a considerable benefit for a reforming country which suffers from an acute short supply of entrepreneurial skills, productive jobs, technology and savings; this benefit has to be set against any claim of squandering.[19] But whatever one's standpoint on this issue, there is nothing in the unfolding scenario to suggest that countries across Eastern Europe are going to be invaded by Western firms keen to snap up state properties at (artificially) depressed prices. The reforming countries face quite another problem: how to overcome the still widespread reluctance of foreign firms to enter their economies. Under such circumstances, these countries cannot afford to involve foreign investors in the privatization process only in a later phase, as has been suggested.[20] The economic costs of putting off FDI would greatly exceed (potential) revenue losses due to low sale prices.

4 INVESTORS' MOTIVES AND HOST COUNTRIES' INTERESTS

Shortly after the breakdown of the socialist regimes all over Eastern Europe, euphoria among Western investors ran high. Two-thirds of multinational corporations had plans to invest directly in Eastern Europe, according to business surveys (Debs, Shapiro and Taylor, 1990; Froot, 1992). As is well known, theories of international investment have put forward many explanations as to why a firm may decide to invest and produce abroad rather than supplying foreign markets through exports. The focus ranges from a great variety of corporate objectives to locational specific advantages. Empirical research has provided supporting and significant evidence for some of the determinants that have been emphasized in the theories. Of various determinants, the following seem to be especially relevant for FDI in Eastern Europe: lower labour costs, abundance of natural resources, and the size and growth potential of the local market. On the investors' side numerous motives exist:

1. Western investors may draw on a pool of cheap labour with which Eastern European countries are abundantly endowed. Wages in this region are among the lowest in Europe. In Poland, for example, average monthly wages in industry amounted to about $200 early in 1992 (World Economy Research Institute, 1992). In Russia, average monthly wages are a mere, $10 calculated at the prevailing enterprise exchange rate of 100 rubles per US

dollar (J. Williamson, 1992). Thus, Eastern Europe appears to be ideally suited for setting up the production of labour-intensive goods which is no longer profitable in the Western high-wage countries. Textiles and other consumer goods are cases in point. By exploiting the comparative advantage of low labour costs, FDI production would be export-oriented in the first place and aim primarily at supplying Western markets. However, the profitability of export-oriented FDI in labour-intensive industries must not be taken for granted, even in the short run. On the one hand, there is already fierce competition in markets for labour-intensive products, induced by dynamic exports from developing countries. On the other hand, market entry is restricted by non-tariff barriers (multi-fibre agreements and the like) almost everywhere in the OECD area. Export-oriented FDI in Eastern Europe will therefore have to concentrate on 'niches', where the input of cheap, but skilled, labour is required. Examples are components and standardized investment goods. In this respect Russia and a few other former Soviet republics are potentially interesting locations, because there are many qualified engineers and mechanical workers who served in the former Soviet military–industrial complex and are now being laid off to a large extent.

2. Eastern European countries, and especially Russia, have abundant natural resources (such as oil, gas, coal, iron ore and non-ferrous metals). It is well known that current exploitation is highly inefficient and that, in particular, the regional distribution of energy supplies within the country is not functioning. Foreign investors could find it attractive to invest in that sector, either to export raw materials elsewhere or to alleviate shortage problems in local production and consumption.
3. Western investors want to have an early stake in the potentially growing domestic markets. Various considerations are involved. One is related to the fact that local consumers have revealed a high preference for Western goods, even if domestic products are of comparable quality and only lack 'Western' design. Foreign investment would bring the desired brand image closer to consumers. It would be possible, of course, to continue supplying these consumers via exports, but setting up production facilities has the advantage that, apart from reducing sellers' and buyers' transaction costs, the foreign firm will be on the spot when, some time in the future, local demand patterns become normalized; that is, more oriented towards domestically produced goods (irrespective of ownership). Moreover, should host country governments maintain or introduce trade barriers in order to promote import-substituting industrialization, 'tariff-jumping FDI' is a way of getting into the protected market. Another consideration is related to government procurement. It is easier for foreign companies to be considered by the national authorities as suppliers when they have local production sites. There is ample experience from all sides that governmental agencies tend to buy from

residential producers. And public demand will be strong, as most of the infrastructure (railways, roads, telecommunications and public utilities) has to be modernized. Furthermore, there is the desire on the part of service firms also to locate activities in Eastern European countries near to their corporate clients in the home countries which have invested there. Commercial banks and insurance companies are obvious examples. Another service sector with market potential is tourism.

4. Finally, FDI is the only way to have a stake in Eastern Europe's potential growth, because opportunities for portfolio investment hardly exist.

Obviously, potential direct investment interests of Western companies can only be realized if government policy in Eastern European countries continues the process of liberalization concerning private foreign capital which was initiated under the old regime. This condition seems to hold. Official attitudes are favourable to FDI almost everywhere in Eastern Europe. Politicians on tour in the West stress the promising investment opportunities in their countries. Legislation has been geared towards encouragement of capital inflows (see next section). From the countries' point of view, FDI could serve numerous purposes:[21]

1. As lending capacities for Eastern European countries seem to be constrained on the international capital market, FDI may be a convenient substitute, to a certain degree. Even without such a constraint, foreign investment is perceived as less risky in macroeconomic surroundings which are highly volatile; dividend payments abroad are due only when profits accrue, whereas foreign loans bear a fixed contractual obligation of interest payments and repayment of principal.
2. Western investment provides badly needed know-how in the marketing and organizational spheres, in addition to modern technology for production. Thus it is expected that both labour productivity and product quality will improve. By creating alternative sources of employment, FDI would help to relieve hardship that results from the inevitable transformation of hidden unemployment into open unemployment. Moreover, bringing foreign capital to domestic workers would be the favoured alternative to emigration to the West, as this could mean an important loss of labour skills and the weakening of the reform process.
3. Foreign investment partners are needed for those domestic enterprises which are probably facing the most formidable adjustment task: the defence-related enterprises, which have to be converted to civilian production, and the nuclear power stations (of the Chernobyl type), which have to be brought up to internationally agreed minimum safety standards. This particularly affects Russia and several of the other former Soviet republics. Moreover, Western engineering and construction industries could be seen everywhere in the East

as very helpful for meeting the extensive infrastructure requirements, including housing.

4. The industry structure in Eastern Europe is highly concentrated, so that domestic local monopolies and near monopolies, especially in the non-tradables sector, which have been freed from pricing regulations wield enormous market power. Experience elsewhere has shown that it is always easier to introduce new competition than to split up an existing monopoly in several competing units. The establishment of foreign companies could play an important role in this regard. Moreover, they could become a yardstick for evaluating the performance of domestic enterprises which are still under state ownership. There is some evidence to show that companies in Eastern Europe with foreign capital participation are on average more profitable than domestic firms (Sadowska-Csieslak, 1991). Hence authorities that may otherwise not be able to get adequate information on the performance record of the enterprises will now obtain it and so be in a better position to exert pressure on unwilling management or replace obviously incompetent management.
5. Foreign investment in banking would help to introduce another medium of corporate control.[22] Foreign private banks with sound balance sheets and highly specific know-how are in a position to harden prevailing soft budget constraints in many domestic firms sooner than the state banks would or could do (Brainard, 1991; Tirole, 1991).[23]
6. Foreign investment may support the host countries' trade policy: export-oriented FDI supports export promotion because the access to foreign hard currency markets is facilitated. If the government follows an import-substituting strategy instead, inward-oriented FDI helps to save scarce foreign currency. The additional supply of goods and services helps to overcome domestic bottlenecks.
7. Foreign investment is a device for reducing an eventual foreign currency debt overhang (for instance in Poland, Hungary and Russia) via debt-for-equity swaps. However, precautions must be taken against increasing the money supply and thereby fuelling inflation. Additionally, the host government should seek to capture most of the market discount from the book value of the loans to avoid inappropriate subsidization of foreign firms.

Whatever the dominant motives for attracting foreign private capital, it should not be expected that inflows would be of such magnitude that all the economic problems of the transition would be solved. Historical experience of, for instance, Hungary and the CSFR shows that, even in the inter-war period, when both countries were highly integrated into the world economy, the share of foreign capital in the total domestic stock of real capital did not much exceed 27 per cent (Csáki, 1992; Begg, 1991). As at that time, FDI may also nowadays be important for economic growth and employment, but the driving forces will have to be mobilized at home.

5 POLICIES TOWARDS FOREIGN INVESTMENT

At the beginning of the 1990s global competition for risk capital has intensified.[24] This raises important policy issues for the Eastern European countries: should host governments offer special incentives for foreign investors and, if so, in which forms should they provide them? Or should governments concentrate on general economic policies and, if so, what does this mean during the process of transformation? We shall advocate that reforming countries should give primacy to devising a favourable general economic framework and that special incentive measures should be considered with great caution.

Scepticism about special incentives rests on the common experience in many other countries (in particular the developing countries) and which tells us that such incentive measures are usually both quite ineffective in attracting private capital inflows from abroad and inefficient from an allocation point of view.[25] This is particularly true of those instances where foreign enterprises received tax concessions, public subsidies and trade protection, when the kind and the extent of incentives varied among foreign firms and between foreign and domestic private investors, and when host governments competed with each other in the provision of special incentives. The impact of the incentive on a foreign firm's investment decision seems to be small. While it is most unlikely that a much greater amount of private capital could be attracted from abroad than would have been possible under alternative and broader policy arrangements which had from the outset emphasized a sound general investment environment, special incentive measures simply raise rents for the foreign firms which would have made the investment anyway. There is the very real danger that all this could happen again in the Eastern European countries. And yet most governments have decided to grant special incentives to foreign investors, mainly tax incentives of various kinds. Whether they are overdoing it in terms of social cost–benefit considerations is still too early to judge; but the possibility cannot be ruled out.

If there is a rationale for special incentive measures during the process of transformation, it must be argued as a case of necessity: the lack of adequate infrastructure and competent administration may be a critical constraint on foreign investment, so that special incentives may be required to offset such impediments. However, it is very difficult, if not impossible, to draw a clear line between incentive measures that are reasonable on these grounds and those which are excessive. Strict criteria are therefore needed, in particular

1. that special incentives are provided on a temporary basis only and that they are reduced over time (in order to avoid moral hazard problems);
2. that a ceiling on the overall financial commitment is placed and announced in advance (in order to avoid delays in the indispensable budget consolidation); and
3. that trade policy concessions in the form of tariffs or quotas against competing imports are not considered at all (in order to avoid a restructuring of the economy in isolation from the principle of comparative advantage).

This having been said, the general rule for the host government should be to create an appropriate investment climate in the first place. The former CSFR, Hungary and Poland have already made progress in implementing the necessary policies; the other countries are following them or are expected to do so shortly. One common feature of the actions which the countries have taken to build a good image and create confidence is the promulgation of new, rather liberal foreign investment codes almost everywhere.[26] But there are noteworthy differences among the countries:

1. While some of them (in particular Hungary and Poland) guarantee the protection of foreign property and prompt and full compensation at a realistic market value in the event of expropriation, other countries have not yet elaborated specific provisions on this key issue.
2. While profit remittances abroad (in hard currency) are now generally allowed, rules on the repatriation of capital are much less straightforward, especially in Bulgaria, Romania and some former Soviet republics.
3. While complete foreign ownership is permitted almost without sectoral or other restrictions in some countries, this is not the case in others, or there is a requirement for prior approval by the national authorities.
4. While dispute settlement procedures have been determined everywhere, questions about the impartiality of arbitration are raised in various countries because it is the national court, not an international institution, which has the decisive vote.

Apart from enhancing the attractiveness of Eastern European countries to foreign investors through the implementation of a liberal legal framework for international capital flows, there is much more to be done in order to strengthen the credibility of the continuation of the transformation process. The 'point of no return' has not been reached in all countries – especially in Russia and the other republics of the former USSR.

Western firms may find it best to wait, rather than to invest in the East, as long as the needed economic reforms are not making sufficient progress. Among the deterring factors that are being mentioned, for instance by German firms at present, are the deep macroeconomic imbalances (revealed by runaway budget deficits, hyperinflationary pressures and a considerable volatility in the real exchange rate), the prevalence of large state monopolies, the persistence of distorting regulations and interventionist policies in product and labour markets, the arbitrariness reigning at different levels of bureaucracies, the lack of reasonable legal reform and the delays in the privatization process. The political instability and (possible) armed conflicts are further overriding factors which make potential Western investors hesitant; property rights cannot be guaranteed effectively in such unstable environments. It seems that for foreign investors the 'option value of waiting' (Blanchard *et al.*, 1991) is still high.

In a sense, Eastern European governments face a dilemma: they need and want private foreign capital, but they have great difficulties in pursuing economic reforms in a way that dispells foreign investors' doubts about the successful transition of these countries to market economies. Time has become a very critical factor. To be sure, there is no ready recipe for resolving this dilemma, given the fact that even well-conceived reform measures often come to a standstill at a quite early stage, and have to be withdrawn, because they are fiercely opposed by powerful special-interest groups, or the population as a whole, who are unwilling to make adjustment-related sacrifices. Under such circumstances, it may be of some help at least to embark on controlled experiments carrying reasonable chances of rapid success. One example is the development of so-called 'free economic zones', as has been suggested especially for Russia (Busch, 1992). It should be recalled that a number of developing countries have been using this instrument as part of their industrialization strategy (with mixed results in terms of social welfare). The idea is to allow economic activities to be set up in clearly delineated areas of the country (such as St Petersburg), these areas being equipped with the necessary infrastructure facilities, being freed from the many market regulations otherwise hampering the economy and being efficiently integrated into the international division of labour through free trade and payments provisions. In principle, such selective 'islands of stability and freedom' could attract private foreign capital quickly, in particular export-oriented investment and, by providing positive impulses for the economic development of the host country through linkages of various kinds between the free zone and the rest of the domestic economy, they could increase public support for the transformation process so that the attractiveness of the whole country for FDI would improve in the medium run. But two caveats are necessary: on the one hand, host governments may be tempted to use the free economic zones as a substitute for completing the whole reform programme; if this happens, the potential net benefits of experimenting with free economic zones will be marginal at best when compared with the overall social cost of not progressing towards the market economy. On the other hand, even if the host government is reform-minded, foreign investors could misinterpret the decision of developing free economic zones as a lack of reformist determination and discount this particular country as a location for investment.

There is also an active role for Western governments and international institutions in paving the way for more steady and significant private capital flows to Eastern European countries. This role should focus on imponderable risks concerning the general economic framework in the countries in transition, risks which are rooted either in the lack of political stability or in the eventuality of confiscatory tax policies or price controls by host governments. Such general country risks cannot be quantified and therefore privately insured against; nor can they be adequately covered through bilateral investment guarantee treaties (which already exist between many Western and Eastern European countries). There are a number of ways in which the West could help to reduce the general country risks. For example, Western governments could take an equity stake in a joint venture (Schulmann, 1992). Another possibility, based on the Auerbach–Jorgenson method of the first-year capital recovery system, consists in allowing a firm that invests in Eastern Europe to deduct from its tax liabilities the present value of future depreciation in the same year the investment is made; should the general country risk arise in subsequent years and generate a negative cash flow, the foreign firm would automatically be exempted from its tax liability (Donges *et al.,* 1992). It is by no means clear, however, whether such measures would provide a significant stimulus to FDI in economically, socially and politically unstable countries.

6 CONCLUDING REMARKS

In this chapter we have focused on the private capital needs of Eastern European countries in transition towards market-based economies and the policy conditions for substantial direct investment flows from the West. The picture is admittedly somewhat impressionistic, as detailed and reliable information on all relevant aspects is not yet available and empirical research on foreign investment in the reforming countries is still quite rudimentary.

Three fundamental points should be recognized at this stage of the analysis. Firstly, foreign investment is not a panacea for resolving the many problems that inevitably arise during the process of transformation. These problems have to be tackled by the national governments through appropriate macro and micro policies, including an adequate institutional set-up. Secondly, the reforming countries have to generate the bulk of their massive capital needs out of their domestic savings. FDI is to be seen as a complementary source of finance, apart from its great value for delivering technological know-how, managerial skills and marketing expertise. And thirdly, foreign investors will not move in great numbers to Eastern Europe in view of the many uncertainties surrounding the process of transformation; they have plenty of promising choices in the OECD area and in many developing countries as well. Hence xenophobic attitudes, should they arise, are the last thing that reform-minded countries in the region could afford.

NOTES

1. The first country to change legislation and allow the entry of foreign private capital was (former) Yugoslavia (in 1968). In the 1970s, a group of three countries took similar steps (Romania in 1971, Hungary in 1972, Poland in 1976). Another group of three countries followed in the 1980s (Bulgaria in 1980, Czechoslovakia in 1986 and the former USSR in 1987). The former GDR did not pass legislation on capital imports until early 1990, after the Berlin Wall had tumbled and the possibility of unification with the FRG had begun to show on the political horizon. Before that, the GDR was only prepared to consent to licensing agreements for Western technology.
2. Source: UNECE (1989) and Institut der deutschen Wirtschaft (1990). It should be mentioned, however, that in 1976 Poland allowed Polish expatriates to set up fully foreign-owned enterprises. Until 1989 some 700 of these so-called 'Polonia' firms were established. However, their economic impact was minimal. See Breitkopf, Górski and Jaszczynski (1991) and Sadowska-Csieslak (1991) for details.
3. The figures refer to joint ventures which were registered with the national authority. It is unknown how many registered joint ventures became operational and in which year. Data on foreign investment in Eastern Europe are incomplete, ambiguous and sometimes contrived, and should be used with great caution.
4. However, in real terms the foreign capital share decreased even more substantially, since the Hungarian currency lost considerable purchasing power.
5. Source: Bundesstelle für Aussenhandelsinformationen (1992).
6. An exception is East Germany, where West German laws and regulations were adopted immediately after the reunification. Capital inflows are increasing rapidly. However, most 'foreign' investment comes from West Germany. For details, see the regular publications by Treuhandanstalt.
7. For a classical exposition of this argument, see Baumol (1959).
8. See Jensen (1986, 1988).
9. The disciplining effect of competition on the market for managerial talent is discussed by Alchian (1977) and Fama (1980). For competition on product markets as a control device, see de Alessi (1973).
10. Grossmann and Hart (1980) highlight free-riding among shareholders as a reason why takeovers as the main device of the market for corporate control might fail. Scherer (1988), Shleifer and Vishny (1988) and Stein (1988) argue that the market for corporate control may be socially harmful if the incumbent management behaves myopically as a result of constant takeover threats. Easterbrook and Fischel (1981) and Gilson (1981/2) analyse anti-takeover measures used by the incumbent management.
11. The two following arguments are considerably qualified as soon as foreign investors are also taken into consideration, as will be shown in detail below.
12. This argument has to be qualified to a certain degree: when borrowing facilities are limited, the real interest rate presumably will be high. However, it is an empirical fact that prices of real assets tend to be low when real interest rates are high, because investors substitute stocks for bonds. So the notion may be submitted that only a very small amount of capital is required for takeovers in Eastern Europe, which may well come from domestic sources of savings.
13. See Moore (1981) for agency problems in centrally planned economies.
14. See, for example, the proposals by Blanchard and Layard (1990), Lipton and Sachs (1990) and Dornbusch (1991).

15. See OECD (1991).
16. See Ministry of Privatization (1992).
17. For a detailed discussion, see Bofinger (1991).
18. See Jonscher (1991); O.E. Williamson (1992).
19. In any case, remaining squandering concerns may be dissipated if the revenues from the sale of state property to foreigners are distributed to domestic citizens on a regular basis. For details, see Schmieding and Koop (1991) and Bofinger (1991).
20. Begg (1991) argues for a later participation of foreigners in privatization on the grounds that future political uncertainty will have diminished and so will risk discounts which have to be granted to foreign investors. Froot (1992) has stated that a sequence in which foreign participation in privatization only becomes acceptable after state assets have been distributed to domestic citizens will give them a larger bargaining power.
21. See Sadowska-Csieslak (1991); Winiecki (1991).
22. See Stiglitz (1985) for the general argument on banks as institutions of corporate control.
23. Schmieding and Buch (1992) present an interesting proposal on how to create better banks in Eastern Europe.
24. In particular, the developing countries have gained ground. See Agarwal *et al.* (1991) for details.
25. See, for instance, World Bank (1985); International Monetary Fund (1985).
26. It is hardly possible to keep track of the newest developments as the legislation is subject to frequent amendment. The full version of the paper presented at the conference includes detailed information on foreign investment legislation as of year-end 1992. It is available from the authors upon request.

REFERENCES

Agarwal, J.P. *et al.* (1991), *The International Competitiveness of Developing Countries for Risk Capital,* Kieler Studien Nr.242, Tübingen: J.C.B. Mohr (Paul Siebeck).

Alchian, A. (1977), 'Corporate management and property rights', in A. Alchian (ed.), *Economic Forces at Work,* Indianapolis: Liberty Press, 227–57.

Baumol, W. (1959), *Business Behaviour, Value and Growth,* New York: Macmillan.

Begg, D. (1991) 'Economic reform in Czechoslovakia: should we believe in Santa Klaus', *Economic Policy*, **13**, October, 244–86.

Blanchard, O. *et al.* (1991), *Reform in Eastern Europe,* Cambridge, MA: MIT Press.

Bofinger, P. (1991), 'Privatisierung in Osteuropa aus Sicht der Principal-Agent-Theorie', mimeo.

Borensztein, E. and M.S. Kumar (1991), 'Proposals for privatization in Eastern Europe', *IMF Staff Papers,* **38**, June, 300–26.

Bös, D. (1991), 'Privatization in East Germany: a survey of current issues', *IMF Working Paper*, November.

Brainard, L. (1991), 'Strategies for economic transformation in Central and Eastern Europe: role of financial market reform', in H. Blommestein and M. Marrese (eds), *Transformation of Planned Economies: Property Rights and Macroeconomic Stability,* Paris: OECD, 95–109.

Breitkopf, M., M. Górski and D. Jaszczynski (1991), 'Privatisation in Poland', *Economic and Social Policy Series No. 6* , Warsaw: Friedrich-Ebert-Foundation Poland, March.

Bundesstelle für Aussenhandelsinformationen (1992), 'Rumänien hofft auf mehr Auslandsinvestitionen', *Nachrichten für Aussenhandel,* 19 March, 3.

Busch, B. (1992), 'Sonderwirtschaftszonen als Instrument der Systemtransformation', Beiträge zur Wirtschafts- und Sozialpolitik Nr. 198, Cologne: Institut der deutschen Wirtschaft, April.

Csáki, G. (1992), 'East–West corporate joint ventures; promises and disappointments', Working Paper No. 3, Budapest: Institute for World Economics of the Hungarian Academy of Sciences, January.

De Alessi, L. (1973), 'Private property and dispersion of ownership in large corporations', *Journal of Finance,* **28** (September), 839–51.

Debs, R.A., H. Shapiro and Ch. Taylor (1990), *Financing Eastern Europe – A Study Group Report,* Washington, DC: Group of Thirty.

Donges, J.B. *et al.* (1992), *Zur Wirtschaftsreform in Osteuropa,* Frankfurter Institut für wirtschaftspolitische Forschung, January.

Dornbusch, R. (1991), 'Priorities of economic reform in Eastern Europe and the Soviet Union', Occasional Paper No. 5, London: Centre for Economic Policy Research, January.

Easterbrook, F.H. and D.D. Fischel (1981), 'The proper role of a targets management in responding to a tender offer', *Harvard Law Review,* **94**, April, 1161–2003.

Fama, E. (1980), 'Agency problems and the theory of the firm', *Journal of Political Economy,* **88**, 288–307.

Froot, K.A. (1992), 'Foreign direct investment in Eastern Europe: some economic considerations', paper presented at the Conference on 'Transition in Eastern Europe' in Cambridge, MA, 26–9 February.

Gilson, R.J. (1981/2), 'The case against shark repellents: structural limitations on the enabling concept', *Stanford Law Review,* **34**, 775–836.

Grossman S. and O.D. Hart (1980), 'Takeover bids, the free-rider problem and the theory of the corporation', *Bell Journal of Economics,* **11**, 42–64.

Hinds, M. (1990), 'Issues in the introduction of market forces in Eastern European socialist economies', World Bank Internal Discussion Paper, April.

Institut der deutschen Wirtschaft (1990), 'Mehr Spielraum', *iwd*, 23 August, 6–7.

International Monetary Fund (1985), 'Foreign private investment in developing countries', Occasional Paper No. 33, Washington, DC, January.

Jensen, M. (1986), 'Agency costs and free cash flow, corporate finance and takeovers', *American Economic Review,* **76**, May, 232–329.

Jensen, M. (1988), 'Takeovers: their causes and consequences', *Journal of Economic Perspectives*, **2**, Winter, 21–48.

Jermakowicz, W.W. and Z. Bochniarz (1991), 'Direct foreign investment in Poland, 1986–1990', in H. Bak, P. Pysz and R. Scharff (eds), *Das Balcerowicz-Programm,* Erlangen: Deutsche Gesellschaft fur zeitgeschichtliche Fragen e.V., 259–303.

Jonscher, Ch. (1991), 'The role of foreign investment in Poland's privatization program', in the Meeting Report of the Workshop on 'The Social and Political Consequences of Decentralization and Privatization', Gdansk, 10–12, April.

Kirchner, Chr. (1992), 'Privatization plans of Central and Eastern European States', *Journal of Institutional and Theoretical Economics,* **148**, 4–19.

Lipton, D. and J. Sachs (1990), 'Privatization in Eastern Europe: the case of Poland', *Brookings Papers on Economic Activity*, **2**, 293–341.

Marrese, M. (1992), 'Hungary emphasizes foreign partners', *RFE/RL Research Report,* **17**, 24 April, 25–32.

Ministry of Privatization (1992), 'Mass privatization – proposed program', Warsaw.

Moore, J.H. (1981), 'Agency costs, technological change, and Soviet central planning', *Journal of Law and Economics,* **24**, 189–214.

OECD (1991), *Economic Survey: Czech and Slowak Federal Republic,* Paris.

Sadowska-Csieslak, E. (1991), 'Summary and conclusions', in *Foreign Investments in Poland – Regulations, Experience and Prospects*, Warsaw: Foreign Trade Research Institute, 80–84.

Sadowska-Csieslak, E. and J. Olszewski (1991), 'Analysis of permits granted by the foreign investment agency', in *Foreign Investments in Poland – Regulations, Experience and Prospects*, Warsaw: Foreign Trade Research Institute, 40–56.

Scherer, F.M. (1988), 'Corporate takeovers: the efficiency arguments', *Journal of Economic Perspectives,* **2**, Winter, 69–82.

Schmieding, H. and C. Buch (1992), 'Better banks for Eastern Europe', Kieler Diskussionsbeiträge Nr.197, Kiel: Institut für Weltwirtschaft, December.

Schmieding, H. and Michael Koop (1991), 'Privatisierung in Mittel- und Osteuropa: Konzepte für den Hindernislauf zur Marktwirtschaft', Kieler Diskussionsbeiträge Nr.165, Kiel: Institut für Weltwirtschaft, February.

Schulmann, H. (1992), 'Economic reform in the former Soviet Union? What is needed and how the west can help', speech delivered at the International Economics Workshop, Harvard University, 4 March.

Shleifer, R. and R.W. Vishny (1988), 'Value maximization and the acquisition process', *Journal of Economic Perspectives,* **2**, Winter, 7–20.

Stein, J.C. (1988), 'Takeover threats and managerial myopia', *Journal of Political Economy*, **96**, 61–80.

Stiglitz, J.E. (1985), 'Credit markets and the control of capital', *Journal of Money, Credit, and Banking,* **18**, February, 133–52.

Szomburg, J. (1992), 'Privatisierung von Staatsbetrieben in Polen', mimeo.

Tirole, J. (1991), 'Privatization in Eastern Europe: incentives and the economics of transition', paper presented at NBER Macroeconomic Meeting, 8–9 March.

Treuhandanstalt, *Monatsinformationen der THA,* various issues.

United Nations Economic Commission for Europe (1989), *New Joint Ventures and Foreign Investment Regulations, and Listing of Joint Ventures Domiciled in the European CMEA Member Countries at the Beginning of 1989,* February.

Wass von Czege, A. (1992), *Ordnungspolitische Standortbedingungen für Direktinvestitionen in Mittel- und Osteuropa: Ungarn,* Hamburg: Verlag Weltarchiv.

Williamson, J. (1992), *The Economic Opening of Eastern Europe,* Washington, DC: Institute for International Economics.

Williamson, O.E. (1992), 'Private ownership and the capital market', in H. Siebert (ed.), *Privatization – Symposium in Honor of Herbert Giersch,* Tübingen: J.C.B. Mohr (Paul Siebeck), 27–54.

Winiecki, J. (1990), 'Privatization in communist economies: crucial differences and problems', *Economic Affairs*, April/May, 36–43.

Winiecki, J. (1991), 'Competitive prospects in Eastern Europe – a parting of ways', *Intereconomics*, July/August, 187–91.

World Bank (1985), *World Development Report*, New York: Oxford University Press.

World Economy Research Institute (1992), *Poland International Economic Report 1991/92,* Warsaw: Warsaw School of Economics.

9. Capital flows and the excess burden of the exchange rate regime

T.C. Mills and G.E. Wood*

1 INTRODUCTION

When floating exchange rates were adopted in the 1970s there was relief, almost pleasure, among economists, for an artificial, arbitrarily imposed restriction on national economies and economic policy making had been removed. But views have changed. There is now a widespread, although of course not universal, belief that fixed exchange rates and ultimately a single currency within Europe are desirable; and exchange rate stability is once again taken seriously as an object of policy in countries outside the EC. In the European case, the argument has two quite separate strands. One is that only by fixing exchange rates to an anchor currency – the DM – can price stability be achieved: national monetary authorities, other than that of Germany, are not trusted. The other is that fixed exchange rates (and then a single currency) are *important* to the 'Single Market Program': only with such an exchange rate regime will the full benefits which could accrue from the free intra-European movement of goods, labour and capital be realized.[1]

The argument for this latter position is based both on transactions costs and on uncertainty. Moving to a single currency could reduce the costs of transacting within Europe by eliminating the costs of changing from one currency to another. Whether it does so depends, of course, on how the costs of money transmission (essentially explicit bank charges plus interest lost to both buyer and seller while payment is in transit) change; but in any event, although the prospective saving here could be large for the tourist, it is not substantial for firms (Chown and Wood, 1991).[2] The other, more important, argument is that removing the possibility of exchange rate change will do away with a significant 'non-tariff barrier', for the possibility of exchange rate changes will deter some traders and investors altogether, while others will have to pay a substantial cost to fix the domestic value of their foreign currency receipts. Floating exchange rates, in other words, are said to impose additional volatility, and hence costs, on international markets. If this is correct, there is a case for pegged exchange rates,

* We are indebted to Kevin White for research assistance and to Cletus Coughlin, Mervyn King and Paul Mizon for their very helpful comments. We are, of course, responsible for any remaining errors.

and a particularly strong one for any group of countries which is keen to encourage mutual international trade and investment. On the other hand, if they do not impose such costs, then the reasoning in favour of pegged rates based on advantages to trade from lower volatility is overcome. It is this argument that the present chapter addresses.

The chapter is in four main sections. First, we briefly describe the doubts we have about the above belief, and set out how we propose to test whether our doubts are well founded. We then describe the data set on which our tests are carried out and present the tests and their results. This section is followed in turn by a discussion of the results and of some qualifications to them. The chapter concludes with an overview of the approach and of the main conclusions.

2 TRADE, CAPITAL AND THE EXCHANGE RATE REGIME

There was undoubtedly once a consensus that exchange rate flexibility was harmful to trade flows. The argument was straightforward: exchange rate risk is an implicit cost, and this cost in any given transaction is proportional to the prospective variability of the bilateral exchange rate applicable to the transaction concerned. That was generally as far as a statement of the relevant theory went, and that seemed far enough, as for a number of years studies supported the proposition; see, for example, Cushman (1983) or DeGrauwe and deBellefroid (1987). But as time passed an increasing number of studies have contradicted these findings.

Examples of these are Gotur (1985); the IMF's (1984) extension of Cushman's (1983) paper so as to cover the exports of the seven largest industrial countries – Canada, France, Germany, Italy, Japan, the UK and the US – to each of the other six; Bryant (1985), Bailey, Tavlas and Ulan (1986, 1987), Bailey and Tavlas (1988) and Ascheim, Bailey and Tavlas (1987). Of these studies (and others not listed), Bailey and his co-authors appear to be unique in paying serious attention to the underlying theory. When this is done, the theory looks rather less plausible. Essentially three distinct (and non-competing) criticisms were advanced by Bailey *et al.* First, they set out a simple two-country example. They assumed (perversely, in view of the results of the trade financing literature, summarized below) that both countries invoice exports in the importers' currency. In this case the cost to one country may indeed be the forward discount; but as *both* currencies cannot be at a discount to each other, the other country's exports will be encouraged by a forward premium. More generally (and conforming better with the data), they remark that traders have all sorts of ways of protecting themselves against risk. These may enable them to learn about the foreign exchange markets and to speculate in them; traders and speculators need not be distinct groups and, by acquiring information, traders may take their place among the intramarginal speculators. And finally, we should also consider the consequences for trade of what would have happened had the exchange rate not been allowed to change.

All in all, the weight of evidence has shifted. Martin Feldstein (1992) has summarized the prevailing consensus as being that floating rates do *not* impede trade. Indeed, he went so far as to suggest that floating rates are *more* favourable to trade than are fixed rates (as did Gottfried Haberler in 1986). Even a glance at international trade relative to national income shows no manifest effect of the shift from pegged to floating exchange rates (see Table 9.1). It is perhaps slightly surprising in view of such data that the idea that flexible exchange rates impede trade for a time gained such ready acceptance. One might, of course, argue that trade would have been even greater with pegged rates; but the stability or, in some cases the steady growth, of these series would not make that easy.

Table 9.1 Trade in country's own currency as a percentage of nominal GDP

	Canada	*France*	*Germany*	*Italy*	*Japan*	*UK*	*US*
1970	36.42	26.06	34.78	26.22	18.75	33.30	8.42
1971	36.16	26.40	34.16	26.39	18.96	32.49	8.38
1972	37.54	27.29	33.74	27.71	17.36	32.13	8.96
1973	40.16	29.18	35.30	30.18	18.16	37.40	10.68
1974	44.20	36.55	41.70	38.09	25.54	46.58	14.43
1975	41.62	31.23	39.54	34.67	22.75	40.80	13.55
1976	40.26	34.19	42.73	38.83	23.51	44.11	14.11
1977	41.81	34.71	42.57	38.43	21.97	46.36	14.37
1978	44.77	33.27	41.18	37.62	18.23	44.17	14.87
1979	48.75	35.57	43.68	40.19	21.11	44.12	16.42
1980	49.17	37.76	49.82	39.49	25.56	41.77	17.82
1981	48.06	38.91	49.91	41.87	25.17	39.85	16.90
1982	42.63	38.52	50.64	39.88	24.79	40.25	14.96
1983	43.00	38.18	49.29	36.57	23.04	41.51	13.97
1984	48.95	40.36	52.69	38.62	24.17	46.04	15.10
1985	49.03	39.89	54.94	38.61	22.79	45.91	14.15
1986	48.31	34.71	48.83	32.58	16.99	41.54	14.28
1987	45.83	34.46	47.07	31.79	15.80	41.31	14.95
1988	46.74	36.01	48.06	31.73	15.60	40.29	15.96
1989	44.08	38.67	51.67	33.75	16.86	42.13	16.34
1990	43.59	37.79	50.63	32.12	17.69	41.82	16.51
1991	42.49	—	50.46	30.51	16.39	38.88	16.41

Note: 'Trade = exports + imports, both with the same sign.

Source: *International Financial Statistics*.

All this applies to trade in goods and services, but what about capital flows? Except in the case where trade grew without growth in trade imbalances (which does not appear to be the case in the OECD area: see Table 9.2), international movements of capital must also have been larger. The view suggested by Table 9.2 is supported by Cushman's (1985) study of the effect of exchange rate volatility on direct investment. Exchange volatility, Cushman notes, might reduce overseas investment; or it might increase it, or diversify it across more countries as a means of reducing risk through portfolio diversification. The conclusion of his empirical work was that exchange rate volatility had no significant effect on international direct investment. And very recently, Rutter (1991), whose data period ended in 1989, found that international direct investment had grown *more* rapidly than trade flows.[3]

Table 9.2 Trade imbalances in country's own currency as a percentage of nominal GNP

	Canada	*France*	*Germany*	*Italy*	*Japan*	*UK*	*US*
1970	2.92	0.72	2.32	1.65	0.21	1.97	0.03
1971	1.97	0.33	2.12	0.74	1.84	1.26	0.44
1972	1.04	0.28	2.46	0.52	1.71	2.29	0.80
1973	1.35	0.42	3.60	3.36	0.33	4.89	0.18
1974	0.17	2.47	5.17	5.64	1.38	8.07	0.78
1975	1.20	0.27	3.63	1.68	0.41	4.15	0.19
1976	0.18	2.05	3.08	3.18	0.42	4.54	0.89
1977	0.72	4.71	3.22	1.15	1.36	2.87	1.89
1978	1.02	0.50	3.21	0.14	1.86	2.45	1.80
1979	0.70	1.08	1.62	1.51	0.77	3.17	1.44
1980	1.95	2.83	0.65	4.99	1.09	1.04	1.16
1981	0.91	2.47	1.81	4.06	0.78	0.07	1.14
1982	4.33	3.60	3.23	3.34	0.66	0.51	1.22
1983	3.63	2.08	2.52	1.65	1.74	1.77	1.89
1984	3.65	1.34	3.08	2.57	2.66	2.61	3.24
1985	2.95	1.30	4.03	2.62	3.40	1.86	3.31
1986	1.33	0.64	5.85	0.35	4.11	3.44	3.63
1987	1.34	1.14	5.91	1.21	3.32	3.37	3.75
1988	0.87	1.24	6.11	1.25	2.67	5.33	2.80
1989	0.37	1.41	6.06	1.43	2.23	5.46	2.46
1990	0.76	1.49	4.35	1.08	1.79	4.08	2.24
1991	0.40	—	0.80	1.12	2.31	2.44	1.53

Source: *International Financial Statistics*.

How can this apparent invulnerability to the exchange rate regime be explained? The literature on foreign trade financing, pioneered by Sven Grassman in 1973 and developed by several authors subsequently, may provide an explanation so far as trade in goods goes. That literature showed that traders used a very wide range of devices to protect their home currency receipts from exchange rate fluctuations; it was unusual to resort to forward or futures markets in currency for such protection. Accordingly, costs of such protection were seldom explicit. That, of course, need not mean the costs were invariably small. Unfortunately, none of the studies of trade financing tried to cost the techniques they discovered, but as the weight of evidence suggests that exchange rate floating does not affect trade, this may suggest that these costs were small.

That argument cannot, however, be extended to capital flows. They, too, appear to have been unaffected by the exchange rate regime, while many of the techniques used to protect trade flows – holding imported inventory equal in value to foreign currency indebtedness, for example – are not applicable to international trade in capital. Why then is it not the case that capital flows are not affected by the exchange rate regime, and that restricted capital flows restrict, if not trade, certainly trade imbalances? Our answer to this question, the answer which is the focus of our empirical work, is that floating exchange rates impose no additional volatility on international markets. There is, therefore, no reason to expect them to inhibit flows of goods, services or capital. The argument behind this is as follows.

Like any other market, the foreign exchange market is subject to shocks. There can be shocks which impinge directly elsewhere, but have repercussions on the foreign exchange market (a bad harvest, for example); or the shocks can affect initially the foreign exchange market and then spread through the economy from there. Examples would be a sudden monetary expansion, or even a long-lasting change of sentiment about the currency. *The fact that the exchange rate is pegged does not make the shocks disappear.* They simply impinge elsewhere, leading, of course, *inter alia*, to the well-known 'policies to defend the exchange rate'.[4] How do we test this?

The exchange rate regime can affect the economy in two ways. If there is a pegged exchange rate, it is unlikely to stay pegged without policy actions. These can take several forms. Most common are foreign exchange intervention and manipulation of short-term interest rates. Accurate figures on official intervention or the stock of foreign exchange reserves are not always available. But interest rates are, and several authors (Batchelor and Wood, 1982; Wood, 1983; Belongia, 1988) have found, the last two in the context of the exchange rate mechanism (ERM), that unpredictable interest rate variability increased after exchange rates were pegged.[5] There is also, of course, the possibility that choice of exchange rate regime can affect the longer-run behaviour of the economy, influencing trends and cycles in important macroeconomic variables.

If it does not, then all that the choice of exchange rate regime does is shift the distribution of short-run fluctuations from one market to another and it then becomes quite unsurprising that trade and capital flows are unaffected by that particular policy choice.

To discover whether this is true we examine the behaviour over trends and cycles of various key macroeconomic variables and assess whether this behaviour changed with the exchange rate regime. If, as we hypothesize, it did not, then floating exchange rates do not create an 'excess burden'. In contrast, if there is some change, such as an increase in the variability of these variables when floating exchange rates are adopted, then they do create such a burden, and there is a *prima facie* case for fixed rates. (The case is no more than that; for it might be cheaper to bear a greater burden in the exchange market than a lesser burden elsewhere.)[6]

It is now appropriate to set out our data and examine their properties in relation to the proceeding discussion.

3 THE STOCHASTIC PROPERTIES OF UK MACROECONOMIC SERIES

In this section we consider the stochastic properties of five major UK macroeconomic time-series since the mid-nineteenth century, these being output, prices, money and short and long interest rates: Table 9.3 provides the definitions and sources of the data. Given the discussion of Section 2, particular attention is paid to whether the stochastic properties of the different series altered across regimes.

Table 9.3 Data definitions and sources

Series	*Definition*	*Source*
Output	GDP at factor cost	Mills (1991, 1992)
Price	Retail price index	Capie and Webber (1985)
Money	M3	Capie and Webber (1985)
Short interest rate	3-month prime bank bill rate	Capie and Webber (1985)
Long interest rate	Consolidated yield	Capie and Webber (1985)

Output

Annual UK output (measured in logarithms) over the period 1855 to 1990 is shown in Figure 9.1, while Table 9.4 reports augmented Dickey–Fuller (1979)

(*ADF*) statistics, calculated over various sample periods, for testing whether the series contains a unit root. Also reported are the estimates of the largest autoregressive root, $\hat{\rho}$, and accompanying 95 per cent confidence intervals constructed using Table A.1 of Stock (1991).

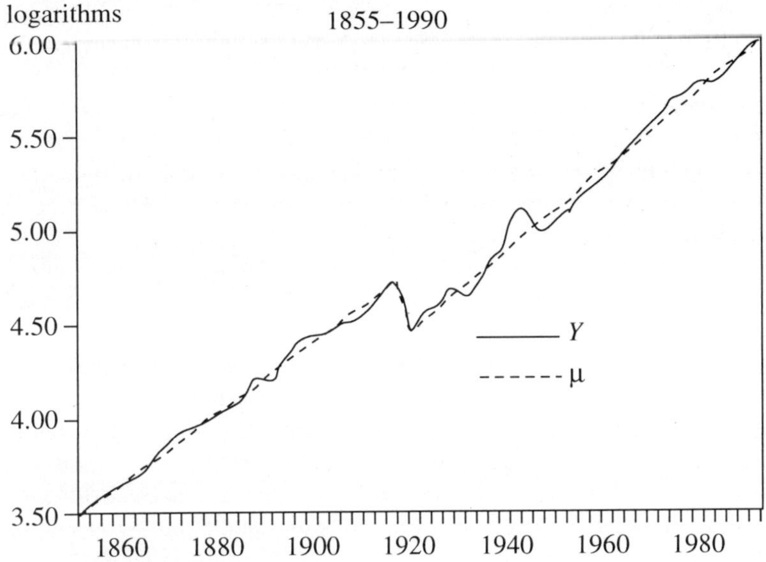

Figure 9.1 Annual UK output

Table 9.4 Unit root tests for annual UK output

			95% confidence interval	
	ADF	$\hat{\rho}$	ρ_L	ρ_U
1855–1990	–2.54	0.93	0.86	1.03
1855–1918	–4.29**	0.57	<0	0.81
1922–1990	–3.47*	0.78	0.50	1.03
1922–1939	–2.05	0.60	0.27	1.25
1946–1972	–5.22**	0.51	<0	n.a.
1973–1990	–1.84	0.65	0.40	1.26

Note: *ADF* is the *t*-ratio on $\hat{\rho}$–1 from the regression $Y_t = \alpha + \beta t + \rho Y_{t-1} + \theta \nabla Y_{t-1} + a_t$, where Y_t is the logarithm of output; ** and * denote significance at 1 per cent and 5 per cent levels using the critical values given by MacKinnon (1990).

While the unit root (that is, difference stationary) hypothesis cannot be rejected for the complete sample of data or for the inter-war and post-1972 sub-periods, it can be rejected at the 1 per cent level for both the pre-1919 data and the 1946–72 'Bretton Woods' period and at the 5 per cent level for the post-1921 data. Perhaps more informative are the accompanying confidence intervals. Using the complete data set, the interval for ρ is reasonably tight, whereas for the sub-samples, many of which have only a small number of observations, the intervals are considerably wider. Nevertheless, that for the pre-1919 data confirms the much reported trend stationary behaviour of output in that period (Mills, 1991; Capie and Mills, 1991; Crafts and Mills, 1992) while the others suggest that trend stationarity can by no means be ruled out: this is particularly so in the light of the well-known power problems associated with such tests (see DeJong *et al.*, 1992a, 1992b).

The source of the anomaly is readily apparent from Figure 9.1: there is a break in the trend function in 1919 that is not instantaneous but lasts for two years, being completed by 1921, whereupon the series continues on a new trend path. As, for example, Perron (1989) shows, unit root tests are not consistent against trend stationary alternatives when such trend functions contain shifts in slope: in these circumstances $\hat{\rho}$ converges asymptotically to unity under the alternative. The question now is whether these two trend functions are stochastic or deterministic: if the former then output remains a difference stationary process.

The approach taken by Perron (1989) is to suppose that output reacts to a shock to the trend function in the same way as it reacts to any other shock. This leads to the following estimating equation:

$$Y_t = \alpha + \beta t + \gamma DU_t + \delta DT_t + \psi D(TB)_t + \rho Y_{t-1} + \theta \nabla Y_{t-1} + a_t \qquad (9.1)$$

where $DU_t = 1$ and $DT_t = t$ if $t > T_B$, and 0 otherwise, while $D(TB)_t = 1$ if $t = T_B + 1$ and 0 otherwise. T_B is the time of the break in trend, here assumed to be 1918 $(T_B = 64)$.

Under the difference stationary null, $\rho=1$, $\beta=\delta=0$ and, in general, $\alpha\neq0$ and $\psi\neq0$. Under the trend stationary alternative, $\rho<1$, $\psi=0$ and, in general, $\alpha\neq0$, $\beta\neq0$ and $\delta\neq0$: γ can be non-zero under both hypotheses.

Estimation of equation (9.1) obtained the following parameter estimates, with (absolute) *t*-ratios shown in parentheses (for $\hat{\rho}$, for obvious reasons, we provide the *t*-ratio for $\hat{\rho}-1$):

$$\underset{(6.05)}{\hat{\alpha} = 0.992} \;;\quad \underset{(5.89)}{\hat{\beta} = 0.0055} \;;\quad \underset{(5.16)}{\hat{\gamma} = -0.141} \;;\quad \underset{(1.26)}{\hat{\psi} = -0.037} \;;$$

$$\underset{(3.07)}{\hat{\delta} = 0.00078} \;;\quad \underset{(5.98)}{\hat{\rho} = 0.717} \;;\quad \underset{(4.77)}{\hat{\theta} = 0.334}$$

Given that the break point, 1918, is roughly half-way into the sample, the 1 per cent point of the asymptotic distribution of the *t*-ratio for $\hat{\rho} - 1$ is, from Perron (1989, Table VI.B), –4.90: our value of –5.98 represents a clear rejection of the null of $\rho = 1$. Furthermore, α, β and δ are clearly significantly, while ψ is insignificantly, different from zero, all in accord with the alternative of a trend stationary model.

Given this clear result in favour of the trend stationary hypothesis, it is instructive to follow a related approach to modelling the series. A plausible trend function is a segmented trend, having breaks at 1918 and 1921; that is, if output can be decomposed as $Y_t = \mu_t + n_t$, the trend function μ_t is

$$\mu_t = \alpha + \beta t + \lambda_1 D_{1t} + \lambda_2 D_{2t}$$

where $D_{it} = (t - T_i)$ if $t > T_i$ and 0 otherwise; $T_1 = 64$ and $T_2 = 67$ being the break points 1918 and 1921. Campbell and Perron (1991) suggest detrending Y_t by μ_t and then performing an *ADF* test on the residuals, that is, $\hat{n}_t = Y_t - \hat{\mu}_t$. Doing this yields a test statistic of –5.24. Although the distribution of this statistic depends on the number of deterministic regressors contained in the trend function μ_t, with the (absolute) critical values increasing as more regressors are included, such a value would seem to be sufficiently large to warrant rejection of the difference stationary null: for example, it well exceeds the 1 per cent critical value of this statistic obtained from Monte Carlo simulation by Balke and Fomby (1991) using similar models estimated over a similar time period.

We may also model the segmented trend μ_t and the 'cyclical' component n_t jointly: this latter component is found to be adequately modelled as an AR(2) process, leading to the fitted model (standard errors shown in parentheses)

$$\begin{aligned} Y_t &= \underset{(0.025)}{3.474} + \underset{(0.0006)}{0.0196t} - \underset{(0.0098)}{0.1109D_{1t}} + \underset{(0.0097)}{0.1136D_{2t}} + n_t \\ n_t &= \underset{(0.083)}{1.092n_{t-1}} - \underset{(0.083)}{0.347n_{t-2}} + a_t \end{aligned} \tag{9.2}$$

This model has some simple and pleasing properties. Trend growth is 1.96 per cent per annum up to 1919 and 2.23 per cent from 1922, the level of trend output falling 27.4 per cent in the intervening three years. The component n_t implies that output exhibits stationary cyclical fluctuations around the trend growth path, the cycles having an average period of 8.1 years. The residual standard error is 2.33 per cent, which compares favourably with 2.47 per cent from the regression of equation (9.1).

We thus conclude that, apart from the three years immediately after the First World War, during which period the series fell dramatically, the stochastic process generating output has remained remarkably stable: output is a trend stationary process, irrespective of, for example, the exchange rate regime in force.

Prices

Figures 9.2 and 9.3 present plots of the (logarithmic) UK price level annually from 1870 to 1990 and monthly from January 1922 to May 1992, respectively, excluding the war years 1940 to 1945, while Table 9.5 presents *ADF* and accompanying statistics for the two data series. On the face of it, these tests provide little or no evidence against the hypothesis that prices are difference stationary ($I(1)$). However, two aspects of these results are worth further investigation.

The first is the behaviour of the price level before the abandonment of the gold standard in 1931. Mills (1990) analyses the 'long' gold standard period from 1729 to 1931 and obtains an estimate of ρ of 0.93, identical to that obtained for the shorter sample here, beginning in 1870. The corresponding *ADF* test, though, is able to reject the unit root null at the 5 per cent significance level and the process found to generate the price level (an autoregression of order two) yields cycles having periods of around 50 years, close to the 'long swings' thought to have characterized prices during this period: see Cagan (1984) for an extended discussion of this view.

Table 9.5 Unit root tests for UK prices

			95% confidence interval	
	ADF	$\hat{\rho}$	ρ_L	ρ_U
1870–1913	-1.77^a	0.93	0.77	1.11
1870–1931	-1.56^a	0.96	0.85	1.09
1870–1939	-1.40^a	0.97	0.91	1.07
1922–1939	-2.75^a	0.77	<0	1.21
1946–1990	-1.56^b	0.97	0.82	1.11
1946–1972	-2.14^b	0.79	0.47	1.16
1973–1990	-2.03^b	0.87	0.28	1.25
1922.01–1939.12	-2.26^a	0.98	0.93	1.02
1946.01–1992.05	-1.76^b	1.00	0.98	1.01
1946.01–1972.12	-1.67^b	0.98	0.97	1.01
1973.01–1992.12	-2.64^b	0.99	0.91	1.02

Note: *a* denotes the *t*-ratio on $\hat{\rho}-1$ from the regression $Y_t = \alpha+\rho Y_{t-1}+\Sigma_i\theta_i\nabla Y_{t-i}+a_t$, where Y_t is the logarithm of the price level; *b* denotes the *t*-ratio on $\hat{\rho}-1$ from the regression $Y_t=\alpha+\beta t+\rho Y_{t-1}+\Sigma_i\theta_i\nabla Y_{t-1}+a_t$, and where the lag length is set at one for annual data and twelve for monthly data.

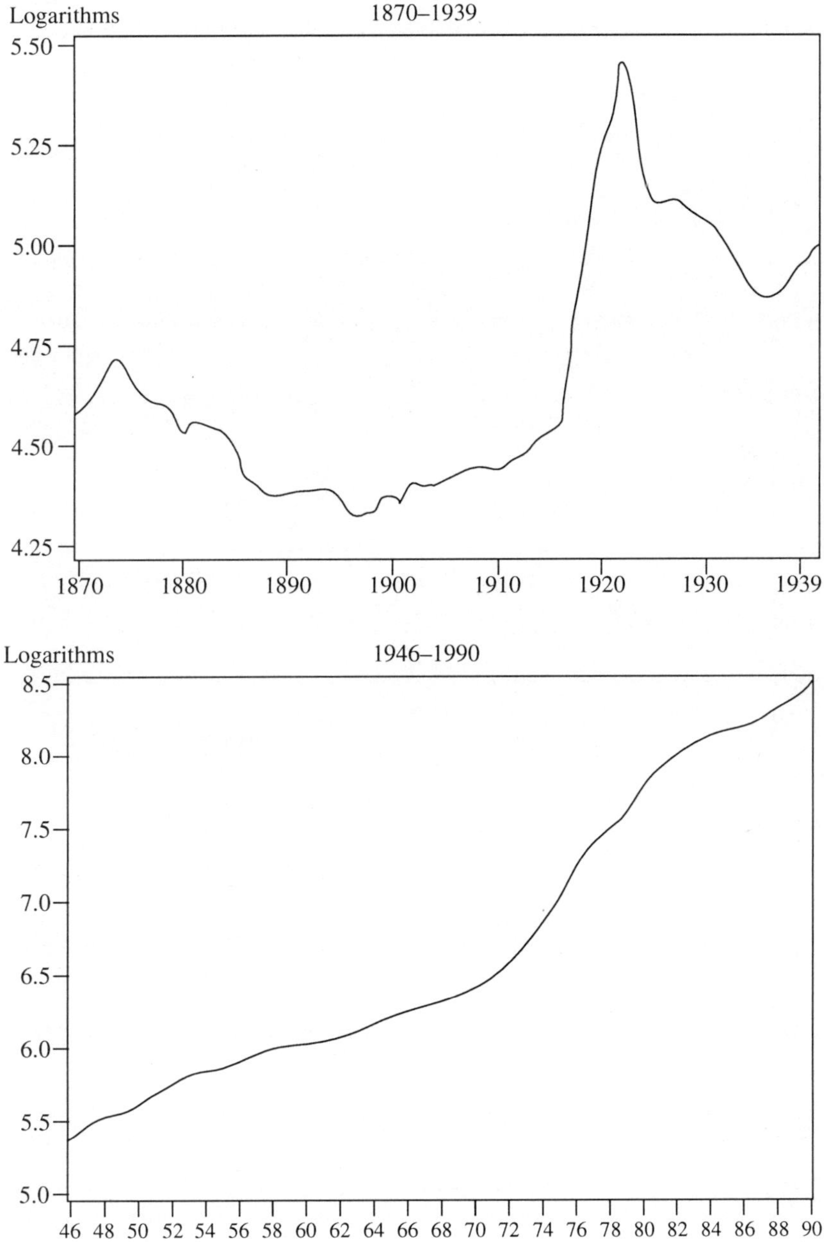

Figure 9.2 UK price level (annually)

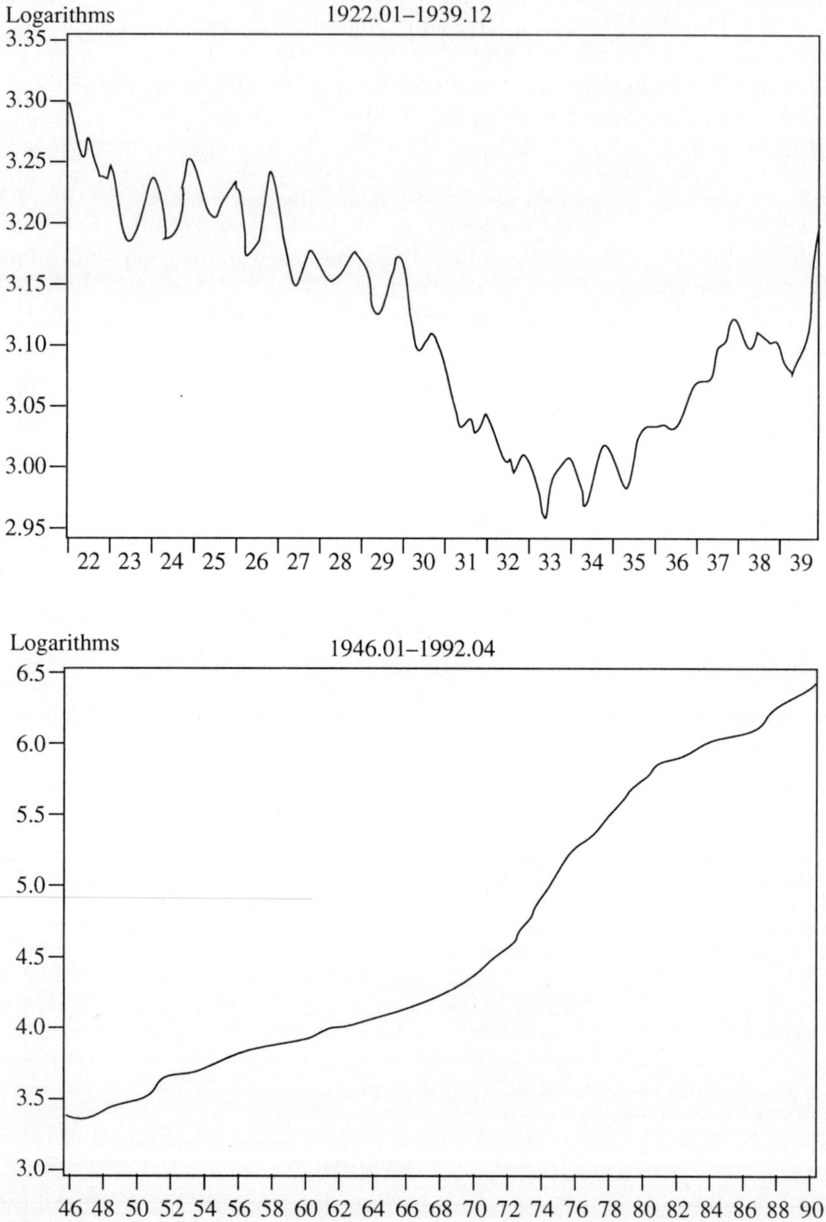

Figure 9.3 UK price level (monthly)

The second aspect concerns the post-1946 behaviour of prices. From Figures 9.2 and 9.3 the series is seen to have undergone slope changes around 1973 and 1983, the reasons for these being well known. Statistically, this is behaviour typical of an $I(2)$ process and Table 9.6 thus reports *ADF* statistics for the (logarithmic) price changes. From these results there is some evidence that post-war prices are an $I(2)$ process, particularly for the post-Bretton Woods era beginning in 1973.

The results are therefore suggestive of UK prices undergoing two shifts in its generating process. The first might be associated with the abandonment of the gold standard, shifting the series from an $I(0)$ to an $I(1)$ process, although from Figure 9.3 it is clear that prices did not start a secular increase until mid-1933, some two years after the move off the gold standard: see the discussion in Capie, Mills and Wood (1986a). The second shift is around 1973, and could be associated with both the move to floating exchange rates and the first oil price shock.

Table 9.6 Unit root tests for UK price changes

	ADF	$\hat{\rho}$
1933–1990	–3.21*	0.71
1933–1972	–3.95**	0.46
1946–1990	–2.64	0.72
1946–1972	–4.01**	0.15
1973–1990	–1.91	0.63
1933.01–1992.05	–3.42*	0.77
1933.01–1972.12	–3.95**	0.54
1946.01–1992.05	–2.92*	0.81
1946.01–1972.12	–3.37*	0.47
1973.01–1992.12	–1.95	0.83

Note: *ADF* denotes the t-ratio on $\hat{\rho}-1$ from the regression $\nabla^2 Y_t = \alpha + \rho\nabla Y_{t-1} + \Sigma_i\theta_i\nabla^2 Y_{t-i} + a_t$, where Y_t is the logarithm of the price level, and where the lag length is set at one for annual data and twelve for monthly data; ** and * denote significance at the 1 per cent and 5 per cent levels using the critical values given by MacKinnon (1990).

Money

Figure 9.4 plots annual observations on the logarithms of M3 from 1871 to 1912, while Figure 9.5 plots monthly observations from 1922 to 1989, excluding the war years. Unit root test results are presented in Table 9.7. For all sample periods, the null hypothesis of a unit root cannot be rejected. Moreover, the series is indeed $I(1)$, for we could not establish that further differencing was required for stationarity.

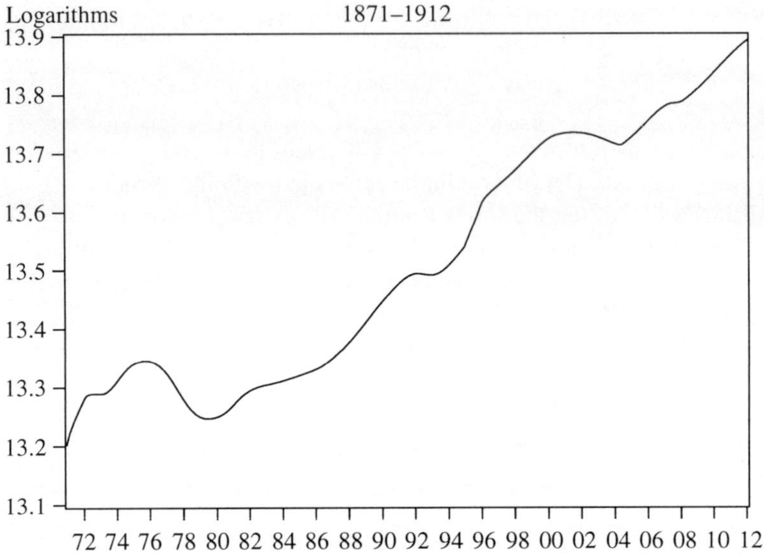

Figure 9.4 Money supply: M3 (annual)

Table 9.7 Unit root tests for UK money

			95% confidence interval	
	ADF	$\hat{\rho}$	ρ_L	ρ_U
1870.01–1913.12	–1.77	0.93	0.77	1.11
1923.01–1939.12	–2.43	0.96	0.93	1.02
1946.01–1989.06	0.19	1.00	0.98	1.01
1946.01–1972.12	–0.55	0.98	0.97	1.01
1973.01–1989.06	–1.02	0.99	0.91	1.02

Note: *ADF* denotes the *t*-ratio on $\hat{\rho}-1$ from the regression $Y_t = \alpha+\beta t+\rho Y_{t-1}+\Sigma_i\theta_i\nabla Y_{t-i}+a_t$, where Y_t is the logarithm of M3, and where the lag length is set at one for annual data and twelve for monthly data.

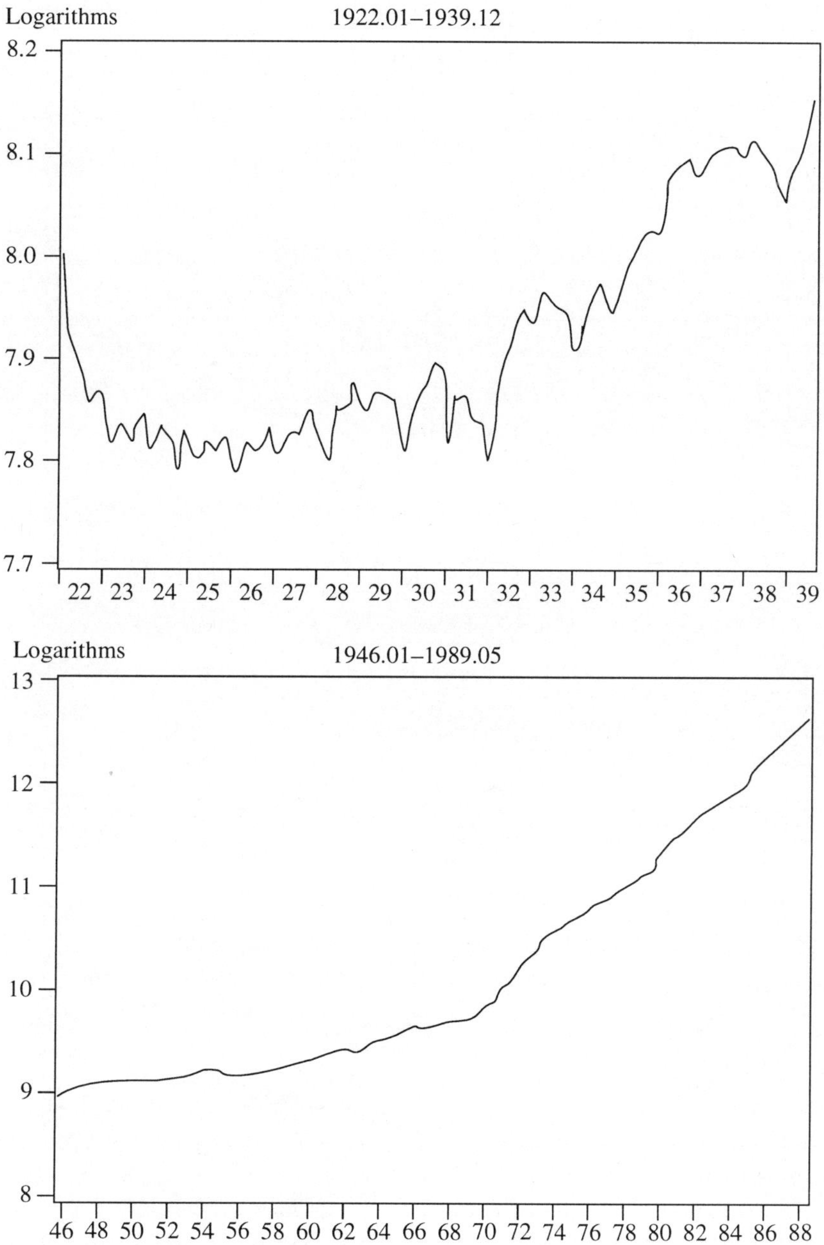

Figure 9.5 Money supply: M3 (monthly)

Interest Rates

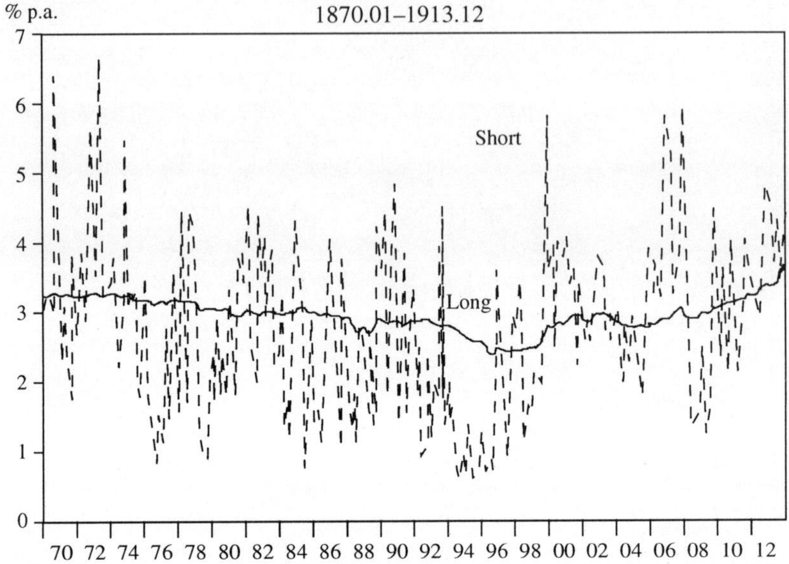

Figure 9.6 UK interest rates (1870–1913)

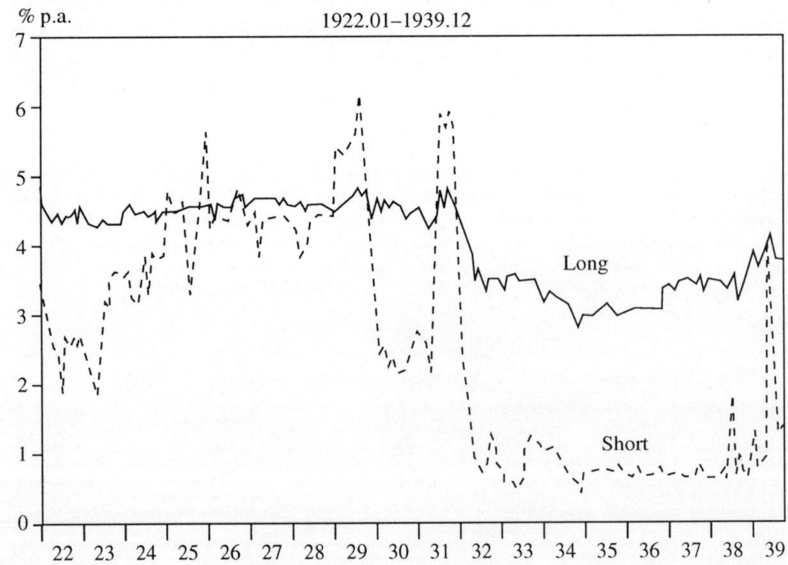

Figure 9.7 UK interest rates (1922–1939)

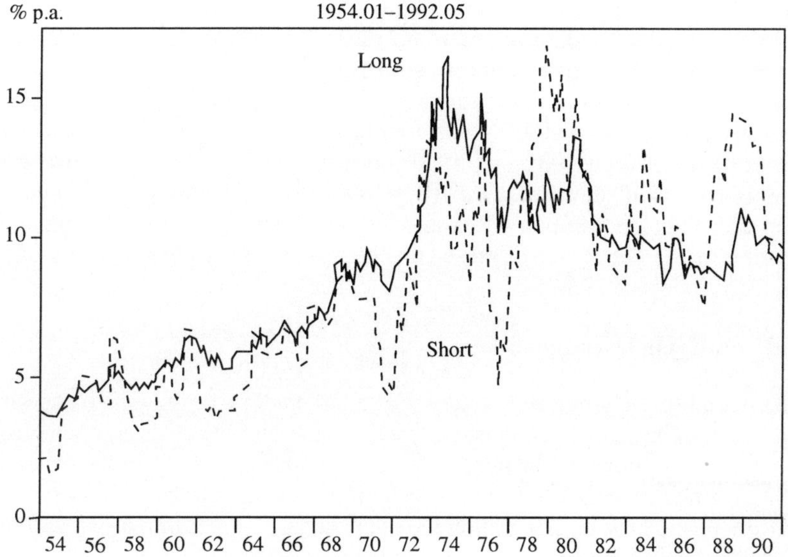

Figure 9.8 UK interest rates (1954–1992)

Table 9.8 Unit root tests for UK interest rates

			95% confidence interval	
Short rate	*ADF*	$\hat{\rho}$	ρ_L	ρ_U
1870.01–1913.12	–7.70**	0.80	n.a.	n.a.
1922.01–1931.12	–2.04	0.92	0.89	1.04
1932.01–1939.12	–6.60**	0.68	n.a.	n.a.
1954.01–1972.12	–1.90	0.97	0.95	1.02
1973.01–1992.04	–2.47	0.98	0.92	1.02
			95% confidence interval	
Long rate	*ADF*	$\hat{\rho}$	ρ_L	ρ_U
1870.01–1913.12	–0.34	1.00	0.99	1.01
1922.01–1931.12	–5.11**	0.68	n.a.	n.a.
1932.01–1939.12	–3.44*	0.90	0.66	1.02
1954.01–1972.12	–0.30	1.00	0.99	1.02
1973.01–1992.04	–1.94	0.97	0.95	1.02

Note: *ADF* denotes the *t*-ratio on $\hat{\rho}-1$ from the regression $Y_t = \alpha+\rho Y_{t-1}+\Sigma_i\theta_i\nabla Y_{t-i}+a_t$, where Y_t is the interest rate and where the lag length is set at zero for the short rate and two for the long rate; ** and * denote significance at the 1 per cent and 5 per cent levels using the critical values given by MacKinnon (1990).

Figures 9.6 to 9.8 plot monthly observations on short and long interest rates from 1870 to 1992, excluding war years and related periods of interest rate restriction, while Table 9.8 reports unit root test results.

Since the lifting of restrictions after the Second World War, both interest rates have been $I(1)$ processes, but their behaviour before 1939 is rather different. Both are stationary between 1932 and 1939, but during the 1920s long rates are stationary ($I(0)$) and short rates are $I(1)$, while before 1914 the orders of integration are reversed. (Capie, Mills and Wood, 1986b, provide an extended discussion of the behaviour of these two interest rate series in relation to the Stock Conversion of 1932.)

Trend and Cycle Decompositions

Has the variability about trend of the series altered across regimes? To answer this question we need to decompose each series into trend and cycle components. There are many ways to do this, ranging from the use of a predetermined moving average to calculate trend to designing a signal extraction filter based on the stochastic process generating the data and a set of assumptions relating to the behaviour of the unobserved components.

For output, equation (9.2) provides the appropriate decomposition. Table 9.9 thus reports the standard deviations of the cyclical component n_t for a variety of sample periods. From these statistics one gets the impression that variability about trend has increased during the twentieth century: in particular, the abandonment of the gold standard in 1931 seems to have been accompanied by an increased variability of output about trend, even after the war years are excluded.

Table 9.9 Variability of the cyclical component of output (per cent)

1855–1913	2.69
1855–1931	2.82
1855–1913, 1922–1931	2.89
1922–1931	3.40
1922–1939	3.84
1932–1939	3.70
1932–1990	5.43
1932–1939, 1946–1990	4.13
1946–1990	4.24
1946–1972	4.37
1973–1990	3.68

For the other series, we have presented evidence of shifts in the stochastic processes generating them, so that signal extraction techniques would be rather difficult to apply. We have chosen, therefore, to use a technique that has proved popular in recent years for examining the 'stylized facts' of macroeconomic time-series, the detrending filter originally proposed by Hodrick and Prescott (1980) and used in, for example, Kydland and Prescott (1990). Although there can be serious drawbacks with using this filter (see King and Rebelo, 1989; Harvey and Jaeger, 1991), for our exploratory purposes it provides a simple and computationally convenient method of detrending.

Tables 9.10 to 9.13 report statistics assessing the variability of the trend and cycle components of the price level, money supply and short and long interest rates, while Figures 9.9 to 9.12 present graphs of these components.

Table 9.10 Component variability of prices

	$\bar{x}$	s_x	s_T	s_C
1922.01–1939.12	3.12	0.85	0.87	0.20
1946.01–1992.05	4.60	0.94	0.94	0.01
1946.01–1972.12	3.88	0.30	0.30	0.01
1973.01–1992.05	5.61	0.51	0.51	0.01

Notes
$\bar{x}$: sample mean.
s_x: sample standard deviation.
s_T: sample standard deviation of trend component.
s_C: sample standard deviation of cycle component.

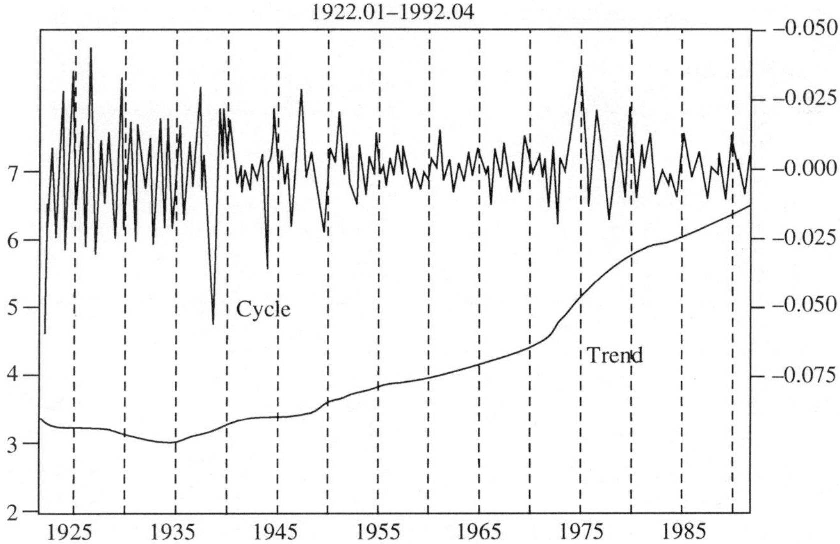

Figure 9.9 Price level: trend and cycle

Table 9.11 Component variability of money

	$\bar{x}$	s_x	s_T	s_C
1922.01–1939.12	7.90	0.10	0.10	0.02
1946.01–1992.05	10.03	1.08	1.08	0.02
1946.01–1972.12	9.27	0.27	0.27	0.02
1973.01–1992.05	11.28	0.66	0.66	0.02

Notes
$\bar{x}$: sample mean.
s_x: sample standard deviation.
s_T: sample standard deviation of trend component.
s_C: sample standard deviation of cycle component.

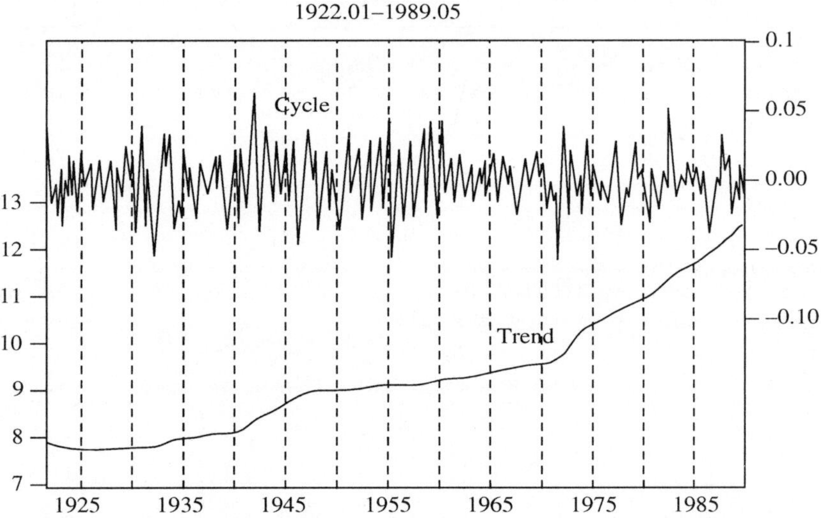

Figure 9.10 Money supply: M3 trend and cycle

Table 9.12 Component variability of short interest rates

	$\bar{x}$	s_x	s_T	s_C
1870.01–1913.12	2.73	1.18	0.76	0.81
1922.01–1931.12	3.74	1.08	0.68	0.77
1932.01–1939.12	0.86	0.71	0.51	0.53
1954.01–1972.12	5.42	1.76	1.54	0.67
1973.01–1992.04	11.43	2.44	1.84	1.22

Notes
$\bar{x}$: sample mean.
s_x: sample standard deviation.
s_T: sample standard deviation of trend component.
s_C: sample standard deviation of cycle component.

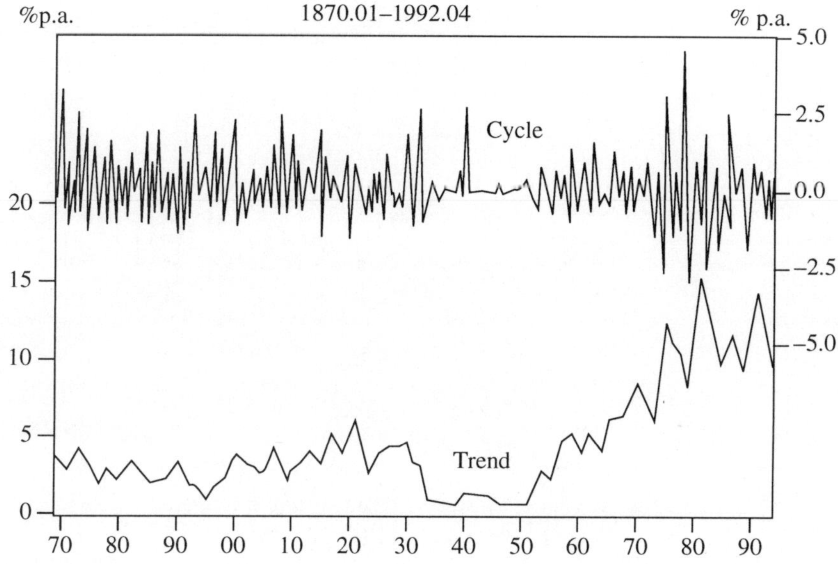

Figure 9.11 Short interest rate: trend and cycle

Table 9.13 Component variability of long interest rates

	$\bar{x}$	s_x	s_T	s_C
1870.01–1913.12	2.94	0.23	0.22	0.06
1922.01–1931.12	4.44	0.14	0.11	0.13
1932.01–1939.12	3.29	0.35	0.30	0.15
1954.01–1972.12	6.35	1.71	1.67	0.24
1973.01–1992.04	11.32	1.91	1.74	0.61

Notes
$\bar{x}$: sample mean.
s_x: sample standard deviation.
s_T: sample standard deviation of trend component.
s_C: sample standard deviation of cycle component.

For the inter-war years, the trend of the price level was relatively flat, with a slow decline until 1933 and an upward drift thereafter. The cyclical component, in contrast, is relatively volatile. After 1946, however, the trend is smooth and monotonic, while the cyclical component is less volatile than before. Trend money is rather similar to trend prices, but cyclical variability is stable throughout the sample period.

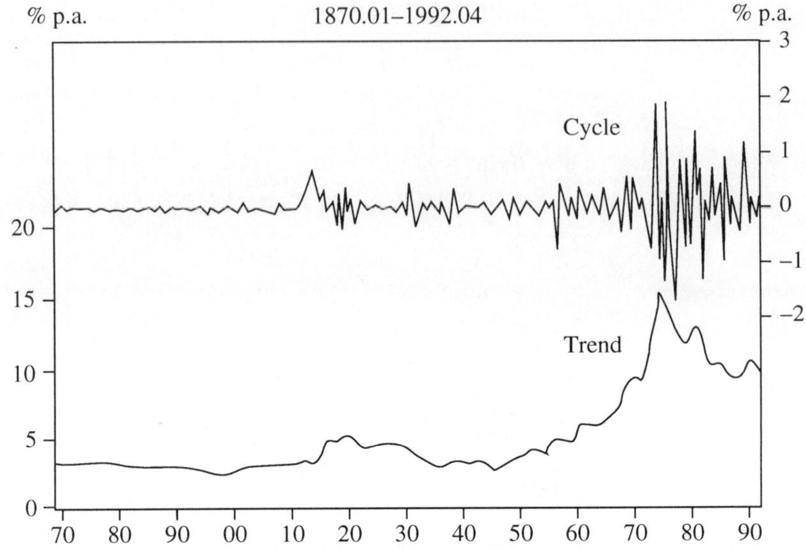

Figure 9.12 Long interest rate: trend and cycle

Pre-1914 trend interest rates fluctuate around 3 per cent, although the far greater stability of long rates is reflected in the almost constant components of this series relative to short rates. Volatility is, indeed, fairly stable until 1972, after which both trend and cycle components become considerably more variable.

4 INTERPRETATION AND CONCLUSIONS

When discussing the above findings, it is convenient to consider together the trend and cyclical behaviour of each series. We start with output: as was noted above, the trend growth of output changed, from 1.96 per cent per annum to 2.23 per cent per annum, between 1919 and 1922. Speculating on what produced that welcome change is outside the scope of this chapter. What we would note is the stability of the post-1922 trend in the face of a wide variety of monetary experiences and exchange rate regimes: a clear demonstration of the long-run neutrality of money. In contrast to that long-run neutrality, the cyclical behaviour *was* affected. The variability of output rose substantially with the abandonment of the gold standard; the significance of this is discussed below.

Turning now to prices, what do we find? The first notable feature is the essentially flat trend, with long swings around it, under the gold standard – again a result to be expected from the nature of the system and consistent with the behaviour of interest rates described below. Rather more dramatic – and equally revealing about the nature of the monetary regime – is the post-1946 period. The trend of prices was positive after 1946, accelerated sharply around 1973, and slowed around 1983. Britain went to a floating exchange rate in 1972, but there was also the first oil price shock and the Heath–Barber monetary expansion. That the acceleration of prices was the result of these factors rather than of the new exchange rate system is suggested by the slowing of prices around 1983, still under a floating rate regime. (The role of the exchange rate regime in the 1973 episode is also discussed in Williamson and Wood, 1976. The conclusion that the exchange rate regime was not at fault was also, by different means, argued there.) The cyclical component of prices became much smoother and was unaffected by the exchange rate regime; its variability was unchanged from 1946 to 1992 and identical over sub-periods and the period as a whole.

Money's trend was unexciting, the series being difference stationary throughout. The trend of money conforms to that of prices, but the cyclical component's variability does not change.

Finally, we come to interest rates. The striking contrast is in the situation before the First World War, when long rates were stable and short rates volatile, an observation usually interpreted as reflecting expectations of long-run price level stability (see Mills and Wood, 1982; Fisher, 1930; Friedman and Schwartz, 1982; Mills and Wood, 1992, all of whose explanations of the Gibson Paradox depended on stable price expectations), and post-1972 behaviour, when inflation first accelerated and then slowed, and both interest rate series displayed markedly increased variability.

How do these findings as a whole bear on the hypothesis that the exchange rate regime is not a source of volatility? They provide support. Of the variety of exchange rate regimes after 1913 (we turn to the gold standard in a moment), none seemed to increase the volatility of any series examined to any significant extent. The policy changes necessary to hold rates pegged may have appeared in a series that, in the absence of reliable data, we did not examine, foreign exchange reserves, and *did* appear in higher frequency movements than the trends and cycles we isolate (Batchelor and Wood, 1982; Wood, 1983; Belongia, 1988). Interest rate cyclical variability did increase with the movement to floating exchange rates in 1972; but there are numerous other factors to explain this. Shocks to the price of oil disturbed financial markets very substantially in this period. On these shocks were also superimposed two others: there was a commitment to reduce inflation – what this meant in terms of the operation of monetary policy was unknown, so the commitment increased uncertainty for a time; and, further, monetary targets were adopted. These affected the way in which the authorities used short-term interest rates; and, as a commitment to monetary targets became increasingly credible, the relationship between movements in short and long rates changed.[7]

It cannot but be observed that there was greater stability – of output, interest rates and prices – under the gold standard than under any subsequent exchange rate regime. But, of course, the gold standard was more than an exchange rate regime. It was a system, a set of rules, for the conduct of *monetary policy*; and there is abundant evidence that variable or unpredictable monetary policy can disturb key macroeconomic series.

All in all, then, it appears clear that the exchange rate regime is not a source of volatility for the main macroeconomic variables.[8] In view of that, it is not surprising that neither international trade nor international capital movements are affected by the exchange rate regime in place. It also, therefore, follows that arguments for fixed exchange rates in Europe and exchange rate pegging elsewhere cannot gain support from claims that floating rates are harmful to the international economy. Arguments for fixed rates must depend only on their traditional supports – the desire to import price level performance and the optimum currency area discussions.

NOTES

1. This argument usually takes as axiomatic that trade creation will outweigh trade diversion. Whether it will is important, but completely outside the scope of this chapter.
2. Firms sufficiently large to maintain their own treasury operations would in most cases still require these organizations, as such firms will be trading outside the EC as well as inside it.
3. This may, of course, reflect a burden imposed by floating exchange rates. Firms may build plants abroad as a way of protecting themselves from exchange rate fluctuations. We turn again to this below.
4. It is the effect on trade of these policies that Martin Feldstein (1992) had in mind when he suggested that pegged exchange rates might inhibit trade.
5. In Wood (1983) there was an exception to this: the Republic of Ireland after it joined the ERM. Unpredictable interest rate variability fell in that country, but increased in every other ERM member.
6. It must, of course, be recollected that the exchange rate regime is not exogenous to the shocks which have affected the economy (except perhaps in the case of the ERM, and that case is arguable). We turn to this issue once our results have been presented.
7. Initially, rises in short rates produced rises in long rates, but, as markets became convinced that the authorities were serious, short and long rates started to move much more independently of each other.
8. This suggests that the increasing international diversification of investment does not result from a desire to avoid foreign exchange risk. An alternative explanation is that it reduces the risk of suddenly facing tariff barriers; this would certainly be consistent with Japanese interest in the US and in the UK (the latter, of course, being in the EC).

REFERENCES

Ascheim, J., M.J. Bailey and G.S. Tavlas (1987), 'Dollar variability, the new protectionism, trade and financial performance', in D. Salvatore (ed.), *The New Protectionist Threat to World Welfare*, Amsterdam: North-Holland.

Bailey, M.J. and G.S. Tavlas (1988), 'Trade and investment under floating exchange rates: the U.S. experience', *Cato Journal*, Fall, 421–42.

Bailey, M.J., G.S. Tavlas and M. Ulan (1986), 'Exchange rate variability and trade performance: evidence for the big seven industrial countries', *Weltwirtschaftlichen Archiv*, **122**, 466–77.

Bailey, M.J., G.S. Tavlas and M. Ulan (1987), 'The impact of exchange rate volatility on export growth: some theoretical considerations and empirical results', *Journal of Policy Modelling*, Spring, 225–43.

Balke, N.S. and T.B. Fomby (1991), 'Shifting trends, segmented trends, and infrequent permanent shocks', *Journal of Monetary Economics*, **28**, 61–85.

Batchelor, R.A. and G.E. Wood (1982), 'Floating exchange rates: the lessons of experience', in R.A. Batchelor and G.E. Wood (eds), *Exchange Rate Policy*, London: Macmillan, 12–34.

Belongia, M.T. (1988), 'Prospects for international policy coordination: some lessons for the EMS', *Federal Reserve Bank of St. Louis Review*, July/August, 19–27.

Bryant, R.C. (1985), 'International financial intermediation: underlying trends and implications for government policies', Washington, DC: The Brookings Institute.

Cagan, P. (1984), 'Mr. Gibson's paradox – was it there?', in M.D. Bordo and A.J. Schwartz (eds), *A Retrospective on the Classical Gold Standard 1821–1931*, Chicago: University of Chicago Press, 587–604.

Campbell, J.Y and P. Perron (1991), 'Pitfalls and opportunities: what macroeconomists should know about unit roots', Princeton University, Economic Research Program Research Memorandum No. 360.

Capie, F.H. and T.C. Mills (1991), 'Money and business cycles in the U.S. and U.K., 1870 to 1914', *Manchester School*, **59**, (Supplement), 38–56.

Capie, F.H. and A.J. Webber (1985), *A Monetary History of the United Kingdom*, London: Allen & Unwin.

Capie, F.H., T.C. Mills and G.E. Wood (1986a), 'What happened in 1931?', in F.H. Capie and G.E. Wood (eds), *Financial Crises and the World Banking System*, London: Macmillan, 120–48.

Capie, F.H., T.C. Mills and G.E. Wood (1986b), 'Debt management and interest rates: the British stock conversion of 1932', *Applied Economics*, **18**, 1111–26.

Chown, J. and G.E. Wood (1991), 'The road to monetary union', London: Institute of Directors.

Crafts, N.F.R. and T.C. Mills (1992), 'British economic fluctuations 1851–1913: a perspective based on growth theory', in N.F.R. Crafts and S.N. Broadberry (eds), *Britain in the International Economy 1870–1939*, Cambridge: Cambridge University Press.

Cushman, D.V. (1983), 'The effects of real exchange rate risk on international trade', *Journal of International Economics*, **15**, 45–63.

Cushman, D.V. (1985), 'Real exchange rate risk, expectations, and the level of direct investment', *Review of Economics and Statistics*, **67**, 297–308.

DeGrauwe, P. and B. deBellefroid (1987), 'Long-run exchange rate variability and international trade', in S. Arndt and J.D. Richardson (eds), *Real Financial Linkages Among Open Economies*, Cambridge, MA: MIT Press.

DeJong, D.N., J.C. Nankervis, N.E. Savin and C.H. Whiteman (1992a), 'The power problems of unit root tests in time series with autoregressive errors', *Journal of Econometrics*, **53**, 323–43.

DeJong, D.N., J.C. Nankervis, N.E. Savin and C.H. Whiteman (1992b), 'Integration versus trend stationarity in time series', *Econometrica*, **60**, 423–33.

Dickey, D.A. and W.A. Fuller (1979), 'Distribution of the estimators for autoregressive time series with a unit root', *Journal of the American Statistical Association*, **74**, 427–31.

Feldstein, M. (1992), 'The case against EMU', *The Economist*, 13 June, 19–22.

Fisher, I. (1930), *The Theory of Interest*, New York: Macmillan.

Friedman, M. and A.J. Schwartz (1982), *Monetary Trends in the United States and the United Kingdom*, Chicago: University of Chicago Press.

Gotur, P. (1985), 'Effects of exchange rate volatility on trade: some further evidence', *IMF Staff Papers*, **32**, 475–512.

Grassman, S. (1973), *Exchange Reserves and the Financial Structure of Foreign Trade*, Farnborough: Saxon House.

Haberler, G. (1986), 'The international monetary system and prospects for international coordination', Washington, DC: American Enterprise Institute.

Harvey, A.C. and A. Jaeger (1991), 'Detrending, stylized facts and the business cycle', London School of Economics Discussion Paper No. EM/91/230.

Hodrick, R.J. and E.C. Prescott (1980), 'Postwar U.S. business cycles: an empirical investigation', Carnegie-Mellon University Discussion Paper No. 451.

International Monetary Fund (1984), 'Exchange rate volatility and World trade', Occasional Paper No. 28.

King, R.G. and S.T. Rebelo (1989), 'Low frequency filtering and real business cycles', University of Rochester Working Paper No. 205.

Kydland, F.E. and E.C. Prescott (1990), 'Business cycles: real facts and a monetary myth', *Federal Reserve Bank of Minneapolis Quarterly Review*, **14**, 3–18,

MacKinnon, J. (1990), 'Critical values for cointegration tests', UC San Diego Discussion Paper 90–4.

Mills, T.C. (1990), 'A note on the Gibson paradox during the gold standard', *Explorations in Economic History*, **27**, 277–86.

Mills, T.C. (1991), 'Are fluctuations in U.K. output transitory or permanent?', *Manchester School*, **59**, 1–11.

Mills, T.C. (1992), 'How robust is the finding that innovations to U.K. output are persistent?', *Scottish Journal of Political Economy*, **39**, 242–55.

Mills, T.C. and G.E. Wood (1982), 'Econometric evaluation of alternative money stock series, 1880–1913', *Journal of Money, Credit and Banking*, **14**, 265–77.

Mills, T.C. and G.E. Wood (1992), 'Money and interest rates in Britain from 1870–1913', in N.F.R. Crafts and S.N. Broadberry (eds), *Britain in the International Economy 1870–1939*, Cambridge: Cambridge University Press.

Perron, P. (1989), 'The great crash, the oil shock, and the unit root hypothesis', *Econometrica*, **57**, 1361–1401.

Rutter, J. (1991), 'Trends in international direct investment', US Department of Commerce, Office of Trade and Investment Analysis, Staff Paper, No. 91–5.

Stock, J.H. (1991), 'Confidence intervals for the largest autoregressive root in U.S. macroeconomic time series', *Journal of Monetary Economics*, **28**, 435–59.

Williamson, J. and G.E. Wood (1976), 'The British inflation, indigenous or imported?', *American Economic Review*, **66**, 520–31.

Wood, G.E. (1983), 'The European monetary system: past developments, future prospects and economic rationale', in R. Jenkins (ed.), *Britain and the EEC*, London: Macmillan.

10. Privatization, debt–equity conversions and capital repatriation

P.N. Snowden

1 INTRODUCTION

Recent debt reduction agreements in Latin America have taken place against the background of domestic economic liberalization in which privatization programmes have played a significant part. The most striking example is provided by Mexico which began a privatization programme in January 1989, the year of her debt reduction agreement. There have followed a series of 200 individual sales which are estimated to have raised a total of $17 billion (or 6.6 per cent of annual GDP). Telmex, the country's telephone monopoly, raised $4 billion and the sale of 12 banks a further $10 billion of this total (Fraser, 1992). The Venezuelan government, which negotiated a debt reduction agreement in March 1990, began to sell state-owned assets later in the year. Revenues during 1991 reached $2.2 billion. Argentina, having concluded an outline debt reduction agreement in June 1992, is hoping to sell nearly all state companies during 1993 for at least $6 billion (ibid.).

While these privatization and debt reduction programmes are components of wider economic liberalization strategies, governments have varied in their willingness to use privatization as a *vehicle* for achieving reductions in outstanding domestic and foreign public debt. Only in the sale of three state-owned steel companies in November 1991 did the Mexican authorities accept payment in the form of debt rather than cash. While Venezuelan privatizations exclude debt–equity swaps, privatization issues have contributed through this mechanism to some of the $12 billion reduction in Argentina's external debt since 1990 (Crawford, 1993). They will make a further contribution in the current agreement mentioned above. The Brazilian government, which is attempting to conclude a debt reduction agreement at the time of writing, has imposed a 25 per cent discount on any debt for privatization equity exchanges. This provision appears to have been prohibitive (Fraser, 1991, 1992).

A further striking feature of the post-debt reduction Latin American reforms has been the beginning of a return of substantial quantities of capital which fled the region prior to, and following, the debt crisis of the early 1980s. One estimate suggests that a net sum of over $10 billion returned to Chile and the four countries mentioned above in the two years 1989 and 1990 (Chartered West LB, 1991).

The purpose of the present chapter is to attempt to assess the relevance of privatization sales both as a means of reducing the external debt 'overhang' (through debt–equity exchanges) and for encouraging capital repatriation. Reflecting the scale of some recent privatization programmes, the chapter will examine these issues using a macroeconomic framework. A subsidiary purpose is to offer thereby a macroeconomic interpretation of arguments found in recent literature on external debt restructuring which has drawn primarily from the theory of finance (for example, Frenkel *et al.*, 1989).

The attraction of privatization programmes as a vehicle for debt–equity exchanges arises from the earlier difficulties of programmes in which foreign creditors received domestic currency (at an effectively preferential exchange rate) in exchange for their debt instruments. This method carried the risk that the use of the money to purchase domestic shares would lead to inflationary pressure. The auction of debt for newly privatized equity claims appears to remove this problem and is increasingly seen as the model for future debt–equity swaps. Nevertheless, the macroeconomic focus of the chapter will emphasize that there is an opportunity cost to these asset exchanges and it is against these that the possible benefits to the country concerned must be judged.

Section 2 below uses a portfolio framework to examine the macroeconomic impact of privatization in the context of a country making net transfers to foreign creditors and whose residents hold a stock of external assets. This analysis will be exclusively of portfolio effects, with the introduction of efficiency gains being delayed until Section 3. While these two sections will help to clarify the mechanics of privatization in the domestic context, Section 4 will introduce the possibility of foreign purchases of some of the equities issued. Both foreign cash purchases and debt–equity swaps will be considered.

2 PRIVATIZATION IN THE CONTEXT OF EXTERNAL PUBLIC DEBT AND PRIVATE CLAIMS

The macroeconomic significance of privatization in economies characterized both by external debt and significant private foreign asset holdings may be clarified by a simple portfolio framework in which domestic wealth holders divide their portfolios between money, equities and foreign bonds. While the latter, representing the outcome of prior capital flight, may be sold, it is assumed that the proceeds would be 'repatriated' through purchase of the other two assets if incentives were to change.

To clarify the overall effects of privatization sales, the analysis proceeds in three stages. The initial assumption, to be relaxed in the following section, is that there are no supply-side efficiency effects of privatization; the assets have positive market value based on the existing profitability of the enterprises under state control. This assumption probably excludes the principal potential gain from privatization, but the nature of these gains is best illustrated by introducing them separately into the portfolio calculation. The final stage of the analysis, in the fourth section, introduces foreign purchases of privatization assets both for cash and in exchange for debt.

Excluding these transactions for the present, privatization issues must be absorbed into domestic portfolios, W, made up as follows:

$$\text{money} = M = mW \tag{10.1}$$
$$\text{equities} = R/r_k = eW \tag{10.2}$$
$$\text{foreign bonds} = C/r_b = bW \tag{10.3}$$
$$m + e + b = 1 \tag{10.4}$$

where equation (10.4) reflects the balance sheet constraint. In equations (10.2) and (10.3), expected annual returns on equities, R, together with the fixed coupon, C, on foreign bonds are discounted at their appropriate rates. Whereas r_k can change in the short run, reflecting changes in share prices, the rate on foreign bonds r_b is assumed to be given. In this case, the portfolio decision is to determine how many bonds to hold (that is, changing the value of C).

In the short run, the money supply is taken as being exogenously determined with the authorities adjusting bank reserves consistent with the maintenance of a trade surplus required to effect payments on foreign public debt. The model is illustrated in Figure 10.1, with formal results presented in Appendix 1.

The suggested link between the return on equities, (r_k) and the rate of investment spending in the right-hand part of the diagram reflects the 'q' theory, where the demand for new capital goods depends on the market valuation of the existing capital stock. The saving schedule $(S_{(p+g)})$ represents (yield-sensitive) private and (given) government saving out of *national* income. As shown in Appendix 2, these flows are in addition to the surpluses from domestic product which are supporting net external debt service payments. Defined in this way, the point at which the saving and investment schedules intersect will involve an external trade surplus equal to the debt service transfers. The accompanying equilibrium structure of rates depicted in the left-hand part of the diagram is therefore consistent with constant money holdings of $0a$ by domestic wealth holders. Given, also, the prevailing return on foreign bond holdings, (r_b), the demand for these rises with falling domestic returns. The fraction of external assets held in the portfolio is therefore given by the distance bW in Figure 10.1.

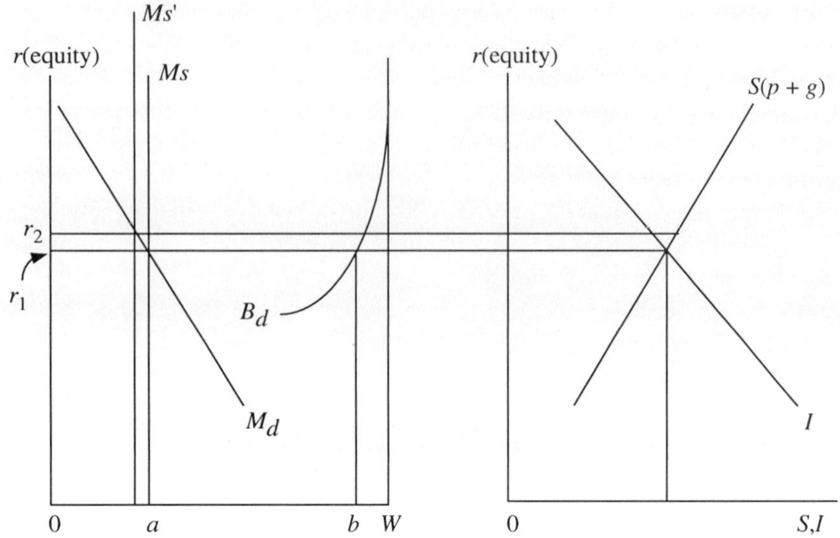

Figure 10.1 Portfolio and macro balance effects of privatization sales

The remainder of the portfolio (*ab* in the diagram) is composed of holdings of domestic equities.

Noting that both of the asset demand schedules shown on the left of Figure 10.1 are drawn for constant rates of return on foreign bonds and money (r_b and r_m), the *immediate* effects of privatization sales are indicated by the leftward shift of the money supply schedule (to M_s') and the implied rise in equity returns to r_2. Thus the privatization sales, which enter the model as a rise in the expected returns on equity instruments (R), are shown in the figure to result in reduced holdings of money and foreign bonds. This repatriation of capital is confirmed in Appendix 1 with the condition that bonds and equities are closer portfolio substitutes than are equities and domestic money balances. Over a period, however, an expanded current account surplus would tend to restore the initial money stock, as implied by the figure. With no further policy actions, the government sector would ultimately have exchanged domestic (equity) for foreign (exchange) assets held at the central bank. The latter would support replenished money holdings in an expanded private sector portfolio.

While this result is analogous to the conventional effects of a domestic bond sale, a realistic assumption in this case is that the government would wish to use the proceeds of the sale, especially in view of the implied decline in future public revenues. If thc authorities were simply to buy a portfolio of shares with the money raised, the portfolio consequences of the privatization would be neutralized. One set of similar assets would have been exchanged by the public for another. An alternative, and perhaps more likely, use of the funds would be to repurchase government debt held by the banking system. The consequence for bank balance sheets of this strategy would be to extinguish loan assets as well as deposits while leaving reserves unchanged. If the banks were to expand their balance sheets once more by buying shares, the final result would again be a neutralization of the privatization sales from the portfolio viewpoint; the system would return to the initial portfolio composition shown in Figure 10.1. For the non-bank private sector, money, bond and equity holdings would be unchanged.

It is clear in practice, however, that one of the difficulties associated with large-scale programmes is in selling the quantities of shares involved without depressing their prices. Mexico's successful programme, for example, has attempted to maximize demand by breaking up large enterprises before flotation and by making a controlling interest easier to acquire for local investors (Fraser, 1990). The tendency for large-scale sales to push prices down could be explained in terms of Figure 10.1 in two ways. Firstly, banks may be reluctant to absorb the new equities as a replacement for the government debt being extinguished. In this event, they may be thought of as choosing to hold a higher reserve ratio, with the result that the money supply would not return immediately to the initial equilibrium. The overall current account surplus implied on the right-hand panel of the diagram by a money supply remaining below $0a$, however, would eventually return portfolios to that position as foreign exchange reserves accumulated.

It may be noted from equations (10.1) to (10.3) above that the flotation-induced increase in R implies, when all rates of return have regained their initial values, that C (foreign bonds at the constant rate r_b) and M must have grown proportionately. The financial wealth of the domestic portfolio holders has increased (as reflected in a foreign exchange-induced expansion of the money supply) to the point that all assets are willingly held at their long-run values. It is worth noting in this simple framework that the privatization alone eventually *increases* rather than reduces the holding of foreign assets. If illegal, these outflows may be thought of as being accomplished simply by over- and under-invoicing of imports and exports, respectively. In Figure 10.1, this practice would result in narrower measured trade surplus and some (policy) induced further raising of rates of return given the surplus required for external debt service.

A second explanation for equity returns to be increased by privatization sales would be the government's simply spending the receipts (thus replenishing the money supply) without extinguishing domestic debt. In this case, the private sector must absorb an enhanced supply of equity instruments at an unchanged level of money supply. Since their financial wealth is initially increased in this case, the demand for money schedule in Figure 10.1 would shift right. While the enhanced wealth would also shift (left) the foreign bond schedule, the net effect would be a rise in the returns on equity made necessary by their excess supply at the initial array of rates of return.

This case emphasizes that the government can only spend the receipts of privatization sales on current output by temporarily 'crowding out' private activity. The private sector is obliged to save for a transitional period, during which its portfolio will be rebalanced with extra money holdings supplied through a net trade surplus (as indicated on the right of Figure 10.1 when equity yields are at r_2). Once more, privatization which does not extinguish equivalent claims against the government must eventually lead to a rise in financial wealth of the private sector sufficient to absorb the new equity at their long-term values. In this case, however, the government's potential fiscal position will have been weakened by the sale of a profitable asset. If wealth holders were to be the population of taxpayers, their 'real' wealth would be unchanged, in contrast to the previous example. They would have achieved a position reminiscent of a 'Ricardian' equilibrium, with the extra financial assets generating the necessary tax payments.

The possibility that governments will face difficulties in making very large privatization sales, given unfavourable portfolio preferences by both banks and public, has important practical implications. An immediate consequence is that lower realized prices for assets sold would imply a smaller benefit for state finances (for example, for the repurchase of debt held by banks) than would be achievable in more favourable conditions. If the authorities were to try to overcome this difficulty by staggering the sales over a long time period, any further benefits of privatization not so far identified would also be delayed in their realization. The introduction of these further benefits is the subject of the following section.

3 EFFICIENCY GAINS FROM PRIVATIZATION: MACROECONOMIC EFFECTS

The key benefit usually associated with privatization in practice is the efficiency improvement which private ownership may confer. The ability of governments to sell previously loss-making enterprises for positive market values (sometimes after initial restructuring) suggests a major potential benefit in terms of the model used above. In selling entities which otherwise would continue to be a net drain on the state budget, two separate implications may be identified. Firstly, the positive price received for a loss-making enterprise can be used to retire existing debt or be placed in new investments. Secondly, the elimination of the enterprise deficits from the future accounts of the public and private sectors produces a further lasting improvement in macroeconomic balances.

When privatization is associated with an improved budgetary position (and perhaps with other policy reforms) an important and potentially beneficial change in the portfolio adjustments discussed earlier becomes possible. The initial discussion suggested that privatization alone had no obvious merits as a means of inducing the return of flight capital on a long-term basis. With unchanged preferences, foreign holdings would be expected to rise. It is the association of privatization with improved fiscal balances and, through these, reduced risks to local currency assets of future devaluation which produces the possibility of a shift in preferences away from foreign bonds towards domestic equities.

The budgetary benefits of privatization appear to be very significant. In the case of Mexico, government subsidies to state-owned companies have been reduced from an estimated 8 per cent of GDP in 1982 to 4 per cent at the end of 1990 (Fraser, 1990). As we saw in the previous section, the return of flight capital in response to improved economic prospects which privatization may help to herald suggests (portfolio) stock adjustment. In addition, however, lasting flow effects need to be considered. These two elements are illustrated in Figure 10.2, which depicts the response to an anticipation that the privatization programme, by helping the government budget, will reduce future inflation and, with it, exchange rate risks. At each rate of return shown, money demand increases and foreign bond demand declines (from Bd to $Bd_{2)}$ to leave a greater fraction of the portfolio devoted to domestic equities. Appendix 3 confirms this movement out of foreign bonds unambiguously, as well as the need for some monetary accommodation if r_k is not to rise. The extent of the accommodation depends on the proportionate increase in outstanding share capital represented by the privatization issues and the impact of the improved outlook on the relative asset demands for money and equities.

With the repatriation implying a foreign exchange inflow, the authorities must choose a domestic money supply which is consistent with their target external surplus. Figure 10.2 illustrates the case where the improved budget position permits greater public or private saving (the shift from $S_{(p+g)}$ to $S_{(p+g)}'$) and, therefore, a reduction in required rates of return.

The suggested improvement in the accounts of the public sector produces a shift in portfolio preferences towards domestic assets which will have implications for the domestic banking system. To the extent that the demand for domestic money balances increases, the proceeds from foreign bond sales will be deposited directly with the banks. Alternatively, if privatization sales are used to repay debt held by domestic banks, foreign exchange holdings will be correspondingly increased in the banking sector. In effect, foreign bonds are exchanged at the national level for foreign exchange held by the banking system and its ability to make foreign currency loans for equipment purchase is thereby increased.

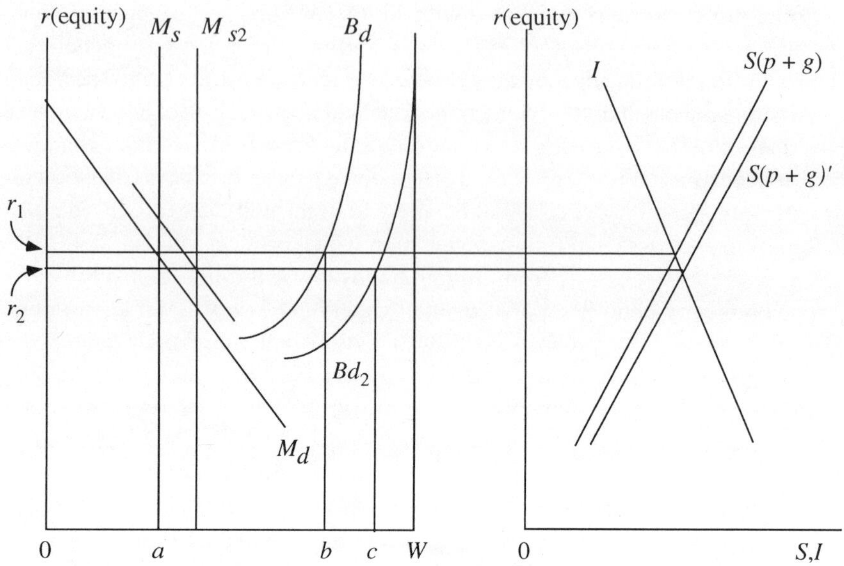

Figure 10.2 Privatization with anticipated efficiency gains

The welfare implications of this switch may be noted before introducing foreign purchases of privatization issues, since they are also relevant in that context. In aggregate terms, the net benefit of the repatriation-induced foreign exchange inflow arises from the difference between the returns to the new domestic investments which it permits and the previous returns on the foreign bonds. That there should be an excess return is a likely outcome of the assumed burden of foreign debt. In view of country risk, interest rates charged on any loans which the country might be able to attract will tend to be higher than world interest rates, suggesting the same for the marginal return to domestic investment (see, for example, Claessens and Diwan, 1989).

In the case of a resident currently holding foreign assets, the superior returns available on domestic investments are needed to compensate for the risks of devoting more of a given portfolio to domestic currency-denominated assets; country risk is as relevant for these as for foreign investors. With this in mind, the following section discusses the role of foreign cash and debt-related purchases of privatization equity.

4 FOREIGN PARTICIPATION IN PRIVATIZATION ISSUES

Foreign cash purchases of newly privatized shares have similar financial implications to those already discussed with respect to the return of domestic flight capital. If the auction is open to foreign cash bids, the only further financial benefit would arise if these investors required a lower anticipated return than domestic residents in considering the repatriation of their funds. Given that the latter will usually have left the country illegally in the first place, there may be further risks for residents in declaring the possession of large quantities of foreign exchange.

If, for reasons of this type, foreign investors are willing to bid a higher price than nationals for the privatization issues, the stock and flow benefits identified above will be enhanced. Realization by the government of higher prices will permit, as previously assumed, a greater volume of domestic government debt to be repurchased from the banking system or to be invested in new infrastructure. This stock reduction in government net indebtedness would, through the reduction in future interest payments, contribute to the flow improvement in the government's accounts which the efficiency effects of the privatization have been assumed to promise. Given the continuing need to make transfers with respect to foreign debt, it is this long-term improvement which will sustain the reduction in the cost of new investment.

In the circumstances described, it makes little difference whether domestic or foreign investors take up the shares offered. Nevertheless, in a number of recent programmes, an attempt has been made to encourage domestic participation in preference to that of foreign nationals. While such discrimination could, of course, be justified on the basis of a preference for domestic over foreign ownership of the economy's capital stock, the present argument suggests an alternative interpretation.

For one reason or another, domestic residents holding foreign assets may be attaching a risk premium to domestic investments which is higher than that applied by foreign participants *and which they will later discover to have been unjustified.* The decision to offer domestic residents specific inducements to buy would then be interpreted as encouraging them to carry out the portfolio shifts they would eventually have wanted to make, thereby raising their, and therefore national, welfare. The cost of the inducement, however, is the lower price for the shares sold to residents and the diminished assistance to the budget in future years.

If the benefits of foreign cash purchases of privatized entities seem to have been clear to governments in recent programmes, the merits of debt–equity conversions in this context have not been so widely perceived. Despite the enthusiasm of foreign banks and their regulators for the conversion of debt into privatization equity, as the provisions of the US Regulation K suggest (McKenzie and Thomas, 1992, p.144), host government restrictions have been common. In the cases of Uruguay and Venezuela, sales are for cash only (*Financial Times*). To what extent can the above analysis be used to assess this suspicion? Despite an early and apparently successful example, provided by Chile after May 1985, subsequent debt–equity swap programmes were subject to a number of criticisms, of which two are especially relevant here. Whereas Chile's programme took place in a general environment of monetary restriction (McKenzie and Thomas, 1992, p.153) other programmes were associated with aggravation of inflationary pressure. As in the Chilean case, the swaps typically involved the central bank exchanging debt purchased at a discount by residents or foreigners for an amount approaching its face value in local currency. When the latter was used to purchase equities, the implication was that the domestic money supply would rise.

In terms of Figures 10.1 and 10.2, it is clear that such a policy, by shifting the money supply schedule to the right, would raise share prices (and lower r_k) with consequences for inflation and/or the external balances. It would amount to an expansionary policy unsupported by foreign exchange inflow, and a number of earlier programmes were abandoned ostensibly on these grounds (see, for example, McKenzie and Thomas, 1992, p.154). If this had been the fundamental objection to debt–equity swaps, however, the new wave of programmes associated with privatization would have been a satisfactory response, since no domestic net money creation is implied.

The second objection concerned the efficacy of swaps in reducing an external debt overhang (Bulow and Rogoff, 1988). In this argument, the external creditor is seen as holding defaulted debt which has a market value equal to the present value of the aggregate payments which it is anticipated that the country will make, divided by the nominal debt outstanding. Thus the price is equal to the *average* value of the debt and a potential participant would want to realize a similar value in acquiring shares in exchange. From the country's viewpoint, however, it has only succeeded in extinguishing a *marginal* amount of its debt which will be much below the average when full repayment is not envisaged. Thus, while Chile was able to swap around 16 per cent of its outstanding debt for equity (McKenzie and Thomas, 1992, p.125), the terms on which this was achieved are open to doubt (Crawford, 1993).

Since the assumed efficiency gains arise from privatization itself, rather than from the identity of the new shareholders, the decision to allow debt–equity swaps can be examined in terms of the initial analysis in which such gains were ignored and the privatized enterprise was assumed to be profitable at the time of sale. In those circumstances, the proceeds of the sale were thought of as being used to repurchase domestic government debt held by the banking system. Against this benchmark, the decision to allow external debt–equity exchanges could only be justified if the future relief to the budget which resulted was at least as great as that arising from the cancellation of domestic claims with the proceeds from a cash sale. This possibility would seem to be ruled out by the assumed partial default on external debt and the average/marginal terms of its cancellation described above.

This reasoning suggests that privatization-based debt–equity swaps would only be beneficial if the country was already anticipating more or less full repayment on its external debt, perhaps as a consequence of the economic reforms on which it was embarked. Since the debt overhang would have been eliminated in these conditions, the risk-sharing benefits of equity participation would come into play as a case for encouraging swaps. The country would be exchanging contractual claims to receive interest for a share in an income stream which would be more closely related to realized returns on the underlying assets (Lessard, 1989). The benefits of debt–equity exchanges, therefore, arise as a *result* of debt reduction; they are not a means of achieving it.

5 CONCLUSIONS

The chapter has examined the relationship between a number of phenomena associated with economic liberalization in debtor countries. The key issues examined have been the relationship between large-scale privatization programmes, debt reduction and the repatriation of flight capital.

Using a portfolio framework, the macroeconomic benefits arising from privatization have been shown to depend on two main factors deriving from potential efficiency improvements. Firstly, the private buyers are offering a price to the government which reflects the potential of the assets to generate profits in the private sector. The revenues generated by this valuation can be used to improve the budgetary position directly, perhaps by the repurchase of existing internal debt. Secondly, and additionally from the viewpoint of the national economy, the elimination of future public sector deficits associated with these loss-making enterprises will permit a higher rate of investment spending for a given fiscal stance.

While these are substantial potential gains, the analysis also suggests that the reluctance of some governments to permit shares in privatized enterprises to be exchanged for outstanding debt may be well founded. While there are advantages to foreign equity rather than debt contracts, these only materialize when the debt in question is being fully serviced, or nearly so. In the conditions of a debt overhang, the debt is already a quasi equity claim with repayments depending on the current economic conditions facing the economy. The implication must be that debt–equity swaps are not directly relevant to dealing with the debt overhang. They are beneficial only when the external debt position has been normalized by a debt reduction agreement with creditors.

Since these agreements typically involve the exchange of senior bonds for old debt, one possibility would be to permit the exchange of the *new* instruments for privatization share issues. In this case the budget saving would be as great as the value of the assets being sold, with the added advantage of a better structure of external claims from the country's viewpoint.

REFERENCES

Bulow, J. and K. Rogoff (1988), 'The buyback boondoggle', *Brookings Papers on Economic Activity*, **2**, 675–98.

Chartered West LB (1991), Reported data in *Latin Finance*, (27), May, 7.

Claessens, S. and I. Diwan (1989), 'Liquidity, debt relief and conditionality', in I. Husain and I. Diwan (eds), *Dealing with the Debt Crisis*, World Bank, 213–25.

Crawford, L. (1993), 'Chile closes book on pioneering debt-swap experiment', *Financial Times*, 19 January.

Financial Times (1992), Latin American Finance Survey, 4, 6 April.

Fraser, D. (1990), 'A record breaking sell-off programme', in *Financial Times*, Mexico supplement, 25 October.

Fraser, D. (1991), 'Mexico prepares for toughest privatisation', *Financial Times*, 6 November.

Fraser, D. (1992), 'Mexico: an envied programme,' in *Financial Times*, Latin American Finance Supplement, 6 April.

Frenkel, J.A., M.P. Dooley and P. Wickham (eds) (1989), *Analytical Issues in Debt,* Washington, DC: IMF.

Lessard, D. (1989), 'Beyond the debt crisis: alternative forms of financing growth', in I. Husain and I. Diwan (eds), *Dealing with the Debt Crisis*, 294–306.

McKenzie, G. and S. Thomas (eds) (1992), *Financial Instability and the International Debt Problem*, London: Macmillan.

APPENDIX 1 PRIVATIZATION WITH UNCHANGED EXPECTATIONS

The portfolio composition equations in the text were as follows:

$$M = mW \qquad (10A.1)$$

$$R/r_k = eW \qquad (10A.2)$$

$$C/r_b = bW \qquad (10A.3)$$

$$m + e + b = 1 \qquad (10A.4)$$

The proportions m, b and e are determined by relative rates of return, as follows:

$$m = m(\overset{+}{r_m}, \overset{-}{r_b}, \overset{-}{r_k}) \qquad (10A.4a)$$

$$b = b(\overset{-}{r_m}, \overset{+}{r_b}, \overset{-}{r_k}) \qquad (10A.4b)$$

$$e = e(\overset{-}{r_m}, \overset{-}{r_b}, \overset{+}{r_k}) \qquad (10A.4c)$$

With money supply assumed exogenous in the short run, and the return on foreign bonds and domestic money remaining constant throughout, this system reduces to two reduced-form equations which determine the return on domestic equities (r_k) and the quantity of foreign bonds held (indicated by C when r_b is given). Using equations (10A.1 and (10A.3)

$$C = r_b bM/m \qquad (10A.5)$$

Equations (10A.1) and (10A.2) give:

$$r_k = mR/eM \qquad (10A.6)$$

Differentiating logarithmically for proportionate changes:

$$\dot{C} = \dot{r}_b + \dot{b} + \dot{M} - \dot{m} \qquad (10A.5')$$

$$\dot{r}_k = \dot{m} + \dot{R} - \dot{e} - \dot{M}, \qquad (10A.6')$$

where dots equal proportionate changes. From the above, and using (10A.4a), (10A.4b) and (10A.4c) with r_b and r_m constant, the following expressions result:

$$\dot{r}_k = \{\dot{R} - \dot{M}\} / z \tag{10A.7}$$

$$\dot{C} = \{x/z\}\dot{R} + \{y/z\}\dot{M} \tag{10A.8}$$

where $x = r_k(\dot{b}_{rk} - \dot{m}_{rk})$, $y = [1 + r_k(\dot{e}_{rk} - \dot{b}_{rk})]$ and $z = [1 + r_k(\dot{e}_{rk} - \dot{m}_{rk})]$.

Expressions (10A.7) and (10A.8) confirm that, when $\dot{R} = \dot{M}$, the return on capital, r_k remains constant and $\dot{C} = \dot{R}$ when $\dot{R} = \dot{M}$.

APPENDIX 2 THE RELATIONSHIP BETWEEN NATIONAL SAVING AND DEBT SERVICE PAYMENTS

When $(X - M)$ is defined as the balance of exports and imports of goods and services, C as private consumption spending, I as private investment and G as government spending on goods and services, the following defines total expenditure on GDP:

$$Y = C + I + G + X - M$$

Subtracting taxes (T) and debt service transfers (Tr) from both sides yields an expression for disposable national income:

$$Y - T - Tr = C + I + (G - T) + (X - M - Tr)$$

Private saving from national income is defined as:

$$S_p = (Y - T - Tr) - C$$

Substitution of this definition into the expression for national disposable income yields the following on rearrangement (where $S_g = T - G$):

$$(X - M - Tr) = (S_p + S_g) - \mathrm{I}$$

This is the relationship depicted on the right-hand side of Figures 10.1 and 10.2. Saving–investment equality as defined implies a trade surplus equal to the debt service transfers.

APPENDIX 3 PRIVATIZATION AND ANTICIPATED POLICY IMPROVEMENTS

When the privatization sales are anticipated to improve the budget and, thereby, to stabilize macroeconomic policy, a shift in favour of domestic assets may be anticipated. This effect may be incorporated by introducing a new influence on the choice of portfolio composition, as follows:

$$m = m(\overset{+}{r_m}, \overset{-}{r_b}, \overset{-}{r_k}, \overset{-}{p^e}) \qquad (10A.4a')$$

$$b = b(\overset{-}{r_m}, \overset{+}{r_b}, \overset{-}{r_k}, \overset{+}{p^e}) \qquad (10A.4b')$$

$$e = e(\overset{-}{r_m}, \overset{-}{r_b}, \overset{+}{r_k}, \overset{-}{p^e}) \qquad (10A.4c')$$

Where p^e is the expected rate of inflation and is used as an index of domestic financial instability. Thus a rise in p^e *encourages* foreign bond holdings at the expense of both domestic money and equities.

The final expressions with the additional expectational effects are as follows:

$$\dot{r}_k = (\dot{R} - \dot{M})/z - \{(\dot{e}_p - \dot{m}_p)/z\}dp^e \qquad (10A.7')$$

$$\dot{C} = \{x/z\}\dot{R} + \{y/z\}\dot{M} + [\dot{b}_p - \dot{m}_p(y/z) - \dot{e}_p(x/z)]dp^e \qquad (10A.8')$$

These expressions confirm that, when the proportionate asset demand changes, for example, $\dot{m}_p$, $\dot{e}_p$ are satisfied fully by a proportionate increase in respective asset supplies ($\dot{M}$, $\dot{R}$) the rate of return on equity (r_k) is unchanged. The shift out of foreign bonds is then exactly $\dot{b}_p.dp^e$. Otherwise, accommodating monetary expansion would be necessary taking into account relative impact on asset demands [($\dot{e}_p$ - $\dot{m}_p$) dp^e].

11. Malaysia's inverse saving–investment correlation: the role of public and foreign direct investment

Maxwell J. Fry*

1 INTRODUCTION

In 1980, Martin Feldstein and Charles Horioka highlighted the strong positive correlation between national saving and investment ratios across countries. Since then, many researchers have corroborated this relationship both across countries and over time (for example, Dooley, Frankel and Mathieson, 1987; Frankel, 1991). The topic has been kept alive not by dispute over the existence, but rather by disagreement over the interpretation, of this relationship (for example, Dornbusch, 1991; Feldstein and Bacchetta, 1991).

In contrast to most other countries, Malaysia's domestic investment ratio *IY* and national saving ratio *SNY* have been negatively correlated over the period 1979–91 (*t* statistics in parentheses):[1]

$$\begin{aligned} IY &= 0.622 \;-\; 1.000SNY. \\ &\quad (5.421)\;(-2.585) \\ &\quad \bar{R}^2 = 0.321 \end{aligned} \tag{11.1}$$

A one percentage point *decrease* in the saving ratio has been associated with a one percentage point *increase* in the domestic investment ratio. Hence a one percentage point decrease in the saving ratio has also been associated with a two percentage point deterioration in the current account. This scissors movement of saving and investment ratios since 1979 is shown in Figure 11.1.

This chapter investigates the causes of this inverse relationship by estimating saving, investment and current account functions for Malaysia over the period 1971–91. The next section presents the saving, investment and current account

* My thanks go to Chan Ali Ha, Latifah Merican Cheong, Jungsoo Lee, Mark Mitchell and David Sapsford. This chapter expands on a report entitled 'Factors Affecting the Saving Ratio in Malaysia' commissioned by the Asian Development Bank. While I wish to acknowledge its financial support, the views expressed in this chapter do not necessarily reflect the views and policies of the Asian Development Bank.

estimates. Section 3 examines the extent to which Malaysia's inverse saving–investment correlation has been caused by public sector and foreign direct investment. Section 4 offers a conclusion.

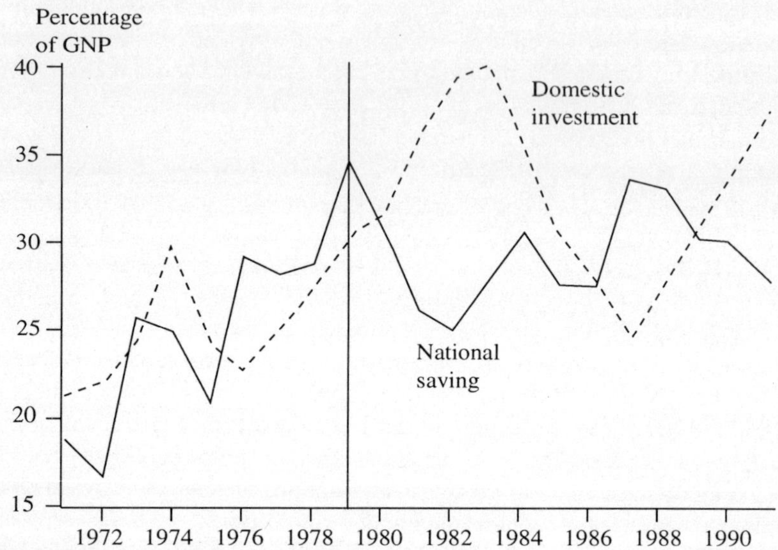

Figure 11.1 Malaysia's national saving and domestic investment ratios

2 MALAYSIA'S CURRENT ACCOUNT BEHAVIOUR

The balance of payments on current account can be defined as

$$CAY \equiv SNY - IY, \tag{11.2}$$

where CAY is the balance of payments on current account divided by GNP, SNY is the national saving ratio and IY is the domestic investment ratio, all expressed in current prices. Following Lloyd Metzler (1968) the behaviour of Malaysia's current account is explained using the same factors that determine the national saving and domestic investment ratios.

Modern saving theories indicate that the rate of growth in aggregate real income is a key determinant of a country's ratio of national saving to GNP SNY. Hence this saving function for Malaysia incorporates the rate of growth in aggregate income as well as the following additional explanatory variables:

$$SNY = a_0 + \overset{+}{a_1}INCG + \overset{-}{a_2}DEPR + \overset{+}{a_3}GINIL + \overset{-}{a_4}IGY + \overset{-}{a_5}FDIY, \qquad (11.3)$$

where *SNY* is gross national saving/GNP (current prices), *INCG* is the rate of growth in gross national income (constant prices), *DEPR* is the population dependency ratio (population under 15 and over 64 divided by the population aged 15 to 64), *GINIL* is the natural logarithm of the Gini concentration ratio for income, *IGY* is gross public sector investment/GNP (current prices) and *FDIY* is foreign direct investment/GNP (current prices).

The rate-of-growth effect in the life-cycle saving model refers to the rate of growth in aggregate real income. Typically, empirical tests use the rate of growth in aggregate real output – real GNP – defined here as *YG*. In an open economy, however, the rate of growth in gross national income *INCG* differs from the rate of growth in gross national product *YG* as the result of terms-of-trade changes. Real gross national income can be defined as $y + x(P_x/P_m - 1)$, where y is real GNP, x is exports measured at constant prices, and P_x/P_m is the price of exports divided by the price of imports or the gross barter terms of trade. Here the rate of change in real income derived from this measure of real gross national income is used.

The population dependency ratio, *DEPR*, can be expected to exert a negative effect on the national saving ratio; a large body of empirical evidence suggests that the presence of more children in a household raises consumption in relation to income (Fry and Mason, 1982). Indeed, one might expect that total consumption over the household's entire lifetime will be higher when it raises more children. In other words, households may not save more when their children have become independent to offset completely the lower saving during the child-rearing period. In the terminology of the life-cycle saving theory, this is known as 'the level effect'. Although a higher population dependency ratio may reduce the level of saving over the household's lifetime, having more children could increase a household's desire to leave a larger bequest, so increasing the level effect. Hence the level effect of household size on saving behaviour is ambiguous in theory. The level effect, which can be influenced by any explanatory variable, incorporates the bequest motive for saving.

A more unequal distribution of income could raise the saving ratio, in which case the coefficient of the natural logarithm of the Gini concentration ratio, *GINIL*, would be positive. As an alternative to *GINIL*, Homi Kharas (1989, pp. 13–14) proposes using the real effective exchange rate expressed in natural logarithms as a proxy.

Until the mid-1970s, the choice between national (including net factor income from abroad) and domestic (excluding net factor income) saving was fairly unimportant, because net factor incomes from abroad tended to be small. With the rapid rise in workers' remittances and foreign debt service (both components of net factor income from abroad) since the mid-1970s, the choice has become non-trivial. In part, national saving is chosen here as the dependent variable in preference to domestic saving because of the high degree of substitutability between domestic saving and workers' remittances. As household heads go abroad, their domestic household income, and hence saving out of such income, plunge. However, remittances sustain living standards of these households and saving out of domestic income plus remittances may actually increase. Hence, while domestic saving falls, national saving need not. One might reasonably anticipate that a drop in workers' remittances resulting from the return of household heads would be largely offset by an increase in domestic saving. In other words, there is likely to be strong substitutability between domestic saving and the workers' remittance component of national saving.

In the second place, interest payments on foreign debt reduce national saving but not domestic saving. It seems irrational to ignore interest payments, while recognizing income from and expenditures on all other current account transactions. Individuals ignore their interest payment obligations at their peril; so do nations. Furthermore, national saving measures the resources available locally to finance domestic investment. While domestic saving may indicate effort, national saving indicates the net result of that effort.

Current price rather than constant price data are used to calculate the national saving ratio for two reasons. First, the primary motive for saving is future consumption. Hence a constant price saving series should use the price of consumption goods as a deflator. In fact, however, constant price saving data for Malaysia are deflated implicitly by the investment price index, since national saving is derived by adding the balance of payments on current account to investment. Second, the balance of payments on current account measured at constant prices can easily produce a positive figure when a deterioration in the terms of trade has actually produced a large current account deficit. In such a case, the positive constant price measure of the current account is misleading and the relevant measure for the purposes of economic analysis is the negative current price measure of the current account deficit.

The investment function, *IKY*, specified here as the ratio of investment to GNP (both in constant prices) is based on the flexible accelerator model. Mario Blejer and Mohsin Khan (1984, pp. 382–3) describe some of the difficulties of estimating neoclassical investment functions for developing countries. Without data on the capital stock and the return to capital, there is little choice in practice but to use some version of the accelerator model.

The speed of adjustment in this flexible accelerator investment function is determined by the natural logarithm of the terms of trade index, *TTL*, the ratio of public sector investment to GNP, *IKGY*, and the ratio of foreign direct investment to GNP, *FDIY*. Torsten Persson and Lars Svensson (1985) show that an improvement in the terms of trade could raise the investment ratio by increasing the return to capital. The coefficient of the public sector investment ratio indicates the extent to which public sector investment crowds out private sector investment; a coefficient of one implies that there is no such crowding out. In recent years, Malaysia's investment ratio has undoubtedly also been influenced by the large inflow of foreign direct investment. Again, the coefficient of the foreign direct investment ratio indicates the extent to which this form of investment crowds out both domestically financed private investment and public sector investment.

The investment function derived in this way is:

$$IKY = b_0 + \overset{+}{b_1}YG + \overset{+}{b_2}TTL + \overset{+}{b_3}IKGY + \overset{+}{b_4}FDIY + \overset{+}{b_5}IKY_{t-1}, \qquad (11.4)$$

where *YG* is the rate of growth in GNP at constant prices.

Combining the determinants of saving and investment, a standard specification search suggests the following selection of explanatory variables for the current account ratio in the case of Malaysia:

$$CAY = c_0 + \overset{+}{c_1}INCG + \overset{-}{c_2}DEPR + \overset{-}{c_3}DDCY + \overset{+}{c_4}GINIL + \overset{-}{c_5}IGY + \overset{-}{c_6}FDIY, \qquad (11.5)$$

where *DDCY* is the change in domestic credit divided by GNP and *IGY* is gross public sector investment/GNP (current prices).

Table 11.1 presents the estimates for Malaysia's national saving, domestic investment and current account ratios over the period 1971–91 using data from government of Malaysia official sources.[2] Because real income and GNP growth could well be endogenous to the saving and investment process, these variables were treated as endogenous in two-stage least-squares estimates. In fact, however, the results of the two-stage least-squares estimates were virtually the same as those of the ordinary least-squares estimates. Jerry Hausman's (1978) test for simultaneous equation bias does not reject exogeneity of these two explanatory variables at the 99 per cent confidence level. As several of the diagnostic tests are inapplicable to two-stage least-squares estimation, only the ordinarily least-squares estimates are reported in Table 11.1. The estimates satisfy standard stability tests as well as all the diagnostic tests for white noise residuals reported in Table 11.1.

Table 11.1 shows that, on the one hand, Malaysia's national saving ratio has been increased significantly by a higher rate of growth in gross national income expressed at constant prices and a higher Gini concentration ratio. On the other hand, it has been decreased significantly by a higher population dependency ratio, a higher ratio of public sector investment to GNP, and a higher ratio of foreign direct investment to GNP. Table 11.1 also shows that domestic investment is increased significantly by higher real GNP growth, improved terms of trade, higher public sector investment and higher foreign direct investment.

Table 11.1 Estimates of Malaysia's national saving, domestic investment and current account ratios, 1971–91

National saving SNY		Domestic investment IKY		Current account CAY	
Variable	*Coefficient*	*Variable*	*Coefficient*	*Variable*	*Coefficient*
Constant	1.646	Constant	–0.457	Constant	1.466
	(8.584)		(–2.018)		(8.068)
INCG	0.288	*YG*	0.373	*INCG*	0.238
	(5.654)		(2.100)		(4.741)
DEPR	–1.176	*TTL*	0.112	*DEPR*	–1.117
	(–8.587)		(2.167)		(–8.708)
GINIL	0.561	*IKGY*	0.511	*DDCY*	–0.300
	(4.994)		(2.204)		(–2.948)
IGY	–0.468	*FDIY*	0.955	*GINIL*	0.535
	(–3.554)		(3.599)		(4.850)
FDIY	–0.617	IKY_{t-1}	0.429	*IGY*	–1.435
	(–3.064)		(2.286)		(–10.868)
				FDIY	–1.455
					(–6.272)
$\bar{R}^2$	0.902	$\bar{R}^2$	0.894	$\bar{R}^2$	0.954
SEE	0.014	SEE	0.017	SEE	0.013
SNY mean	0.275	*IKY* mean	0.300	*CAY* mean	–0.021
DW	2.343			*DW*	1.749
LM(1,14)	1.174	*LM*(1,14)	1.682	*LM*(1,13)	0.048
	(0.297)		(0.216)		(0.831)
B–P Q (1 lag)	1.23	*B–P Q* (1 lag)	1.36	*B–P Q* (1 lag)	0.07
	(0.267)		(0.243)		(0.798)
L–B Q (1 lag)	1.42	*L–B Q* (1 lag)	1.57	*L–B Q* (1 lag)	0.08
	(0.234)		(0.211)		(0.784)
ARCH(1)	0.032	*ARCH*(1)	1.055	*ARCH*(1)	1.712
	(0.860)		(0.318)		(0.207)
ARCH(3)	2.050	*ARCH*(3)	0.434	*ARCH*(3)	1.566
	(0.153)		(0.732)		(0.242)
JB	0.526	*JB*	2.529	*JB*	0.922
	(0.770)		(0.282)		(0.631)

Note: Figures in parentheses are *t* statistics under the coefficients and probabilities under the diagnostic test statistics. *B–P* is Box–Pierce, *L–B* is Ljung–Box, *LM*(ℓ, *T–k–*ℓ) is the Breusch–Godfrey *F* statistic for residual autocorrelation of order ℓ after fitting *k* regressors, *ARCH*(ℓ) is an *F* statistic for Engle's *ARCH* heteroscedasticity test with ℓ lagged squared residuals, and *JB* is the Jarque-Bera statistic which has χ^2 distribution with two degrees of freedom.

Finally, Table 11.1 shows that the current account is improved by higher income growth and a more unequal distribution of income; both these variables raise Malaysia's saving ratio. The current account is worsened by a higher population dependency ratio and faster domestic credit expansion; a higher population dependency ratio reduces Malaysia's saving ratio. Faster domestic credit expansion probably reduces saving and increases investment. While domestic credit expansion is not a significant explanatory variable in either the saving or the investment function, its combined negative effect on saving and positive effect on investment in the current account is significant.

3 EFFECTS OF PUBLIC SECTOR AND FOREIGN DIRECT INVESTMENT ON MALAYSIA'S CURRENT ACCOUNT

Both the direct estimate of the current account and an indirect estimate derived from the estimated saving and investment ratios pinpoint public sector and foreign direct investment as the two main causes of Malaysia's inverse saving–investment correlation. The current account estimate in Table 11.1 shows that a one percentage point increase in the foreign direct investment ratio reduces the current account surplus by 1.5 percentage points, indicating that it reduces national saving by 0.5 of a percentage point. A similar magnified effect on the current account is produced by public sector investment; a one percentage point increase in the public sector investment ratio worsens the current account by 1.4 percentage points. Again, this happens because an increase in public sector investment reduces national saving as well as increasing domestic investment.

The negative effects of public sector and foreign direct investment ratios on the national saving ratio provide the key to an explanation of Malaysia's inverse saving–investment correlation over the period 1979–91. The negative effect of the public sector investment ratio on Malaysia's national saving ratio may spring from the fact that higher public sector investment reduces private sector investment. The coefficient of *IKGY* in the investment function is positive but significantly less than one; the domestic investment estimate in Table 11.1 indicates that, while public sector investment crowds out private sector investment in the short run, foreign direct investment does not. When private sector investment is crowded out, the incentive to save in order to provide an equity component for the financing of such investment is also reduced.

A rather different explanation may hold for a negative impact of the foreign direct investment ratio *FDIY* on the national saving ratio shown in Table 11.1. Since foreign direct investment does not crowd out any other type of investment, its negative influence may be produced as a statistical artifact. If some residents realize that terms and conditions for foreign direct investment are more favourable than they are for locally financed investment, they have an incentive to remove capital from Malaysia and to bring it back again in the form of foreign direct investment. To the extent that these individuals wish to conceal the capital outflow, they will over-invoice imports and under-invoice exports.[3] This method of removing capital from a country reduces measured national saving, even if the true level of saving remains constant, because saving is measured residually as investment plus the current account ($SNY \equiv IY + CAY$). Hence an increase in foreign direct investment would be accompanied by a reduction in recorded national saving.

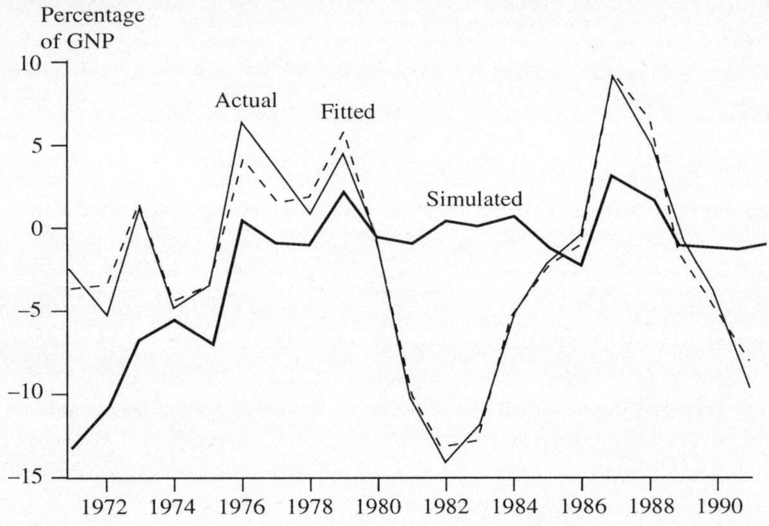

Figure 11.2 Malaysia's actual, fitted and simulated current account ratio

Hal Hill (1990, p. 24) points out that the Malaysian authorities may prefer foreign direct investment to local non-indigenous (non-Bumiputera) investment.[4] Hill (1990, p. 26) concludes: 'In Malaysia, ownership is perhaps a more sensitive issue than in any other East Asian country, but the concern relates as much to *domestic* ownership shares as to foreign penetration.'[5] In general, Malaysian investments require 30 per cent Bumiputera equity participation. However, where a foreign investment is permitted a maximum 70 per cent ownership, the local participation need not include any Bumiputera participation. This concession could therefore permit 100 per cent ownership where the foreign direct investment originates from non-Bumiputera Malaysians for investment in industries where domestically financed investment would require a 30 per cent Bumiputera participation.

This chapter now examines what might have happened to Malaysia's current account had public sector and foreign direct investment ratios remained constant. To do this, the saving, investment and current account ratios are simulated with public sector and foreign direct investment ratios set at their mean values throughout the period 1971–91. Figure 11.2 shows the actual current account ratio, the current account ratio fitted from the current account estimate in Table 11.1 and the simulated current account ratio with both public sector and foreign direct investment ratios set at their mean values throughout the period 1971–91. While the fitted current account ratio tracks the actual current account ratio quite well, the simulated current account ratio exhibits far less volatility, particularly over the period 1979–91. Indeed, there is virtually no correspondence between the simulated and actual current account ratios over this period. This is hardly surprising since the inverse correlation between saving and investment which emerged after 1979 coincided with the upsurge in public sector and direct foreign investment in the early 1980s. Since then, both these forms of investment have been more prominent and more volatile than they were in the 1970s.

The final proof that the inverse saving–investment correlation over the period 1979–91 was caused primarily by fluctuations in public sector and foreign direct investment ratios lies in the regression of a simulated investment ratio, *IYS*, on a simulated saving ratio, *SNYS*, again derived from the estimated equations simulated with both public sector and foreign direct investment ratios set at their mean values throughout the period 1971–91.[6] For the period 1979–91, the relationship between *IYS* and *SNYS* is:

$$\begin{aligned} IYS &= 0.264 + 0.160 SNYS. \\ &\quad (3.829)\ (0.688) \\ &\quad \bar{R}^2 = -0.046 \end{aligned} \tag{11.6}$$

While the simulated saving and investment ratios show no correlation at all, the fitted saving and investment ratios using the actual public sector and foreign direct investment data exhibit virtually the same relationship displayed in equation 11.1: a coefficient for the fitted saving ratio of –0.974 and $\bar{R}^2$ of 0.367 for the period 1979–91. When only the public sector or the foreign direct investment ratio is set at its mean value for the period 1971–91, the negative coefficient of the simulated national saving ratio falls to about –0.5 in the simulated domestic investment estimate for the period 1979–91. Therefore, the two variables are jointly responsible for Malaysia's inverse saving–investment correlation over the period 1979–91.

4 CONCLUSION

Tamim Bayoumi (1990) examines three alternative explanations for the positive saving–investment correlation in the OECD countries – capital immobility, endogenous private sector behaviour and government policy. After finding that private saving–investment correlations are substantially weaker than total saving–investment correlations and that total saving–investment correlations were weak during the gold standard period, Bayoumi (1990, p. 80) concludes that government policy has been the predominant cause of the post-war saving–investment correlations in the OECD countries.

In Malaysia's case, the total saving–investment correlation over the period 1979–91 is significantly negative, while the private saving–investment correlation is non-existent. Hence government policy has caused the inverse relationship between saving and investment in Malaysia. In the early 1980s, an expansionary fiscal policy mainly in the form of increased public sector investment produced double-digit government deficits (Claassen, 1992). The subsequent real appreciation of the exchange rate and dramatic deterioration in Malaysia's terms of trade in 1985 and 1986 caused a recession which pushed the deficit back into double digits in 1986. Only when foreign debt rose to uncomfortable levels in the mid-1980s did the government's attention focus on the balance of payments. Clearly, government budgetary policies could be used to reduce Malaysia's inverse saving–investment relationship.

In addition to the government's own saving and investment behaviour, its encouragement of foreign direct investment has also contributed to Malaysia's inverse saving–investment correlation. The analysis presented above indicates that foreign direct investment exerts a negative effect on the national saving ratio and a positive effect on the domestic investment ratio. The inverse relationship between saving and investment did not exist before the upsurge in foreign direct investment in the early 1980s. Were this upsurge financed in part from concealed capital outflows from Malaysia, this could explain the inverse relationship between investment and measured national saving ratios. In such a case, the inverse correlation could be reduced or eliminated in the future by removing any incentive for round-trip capital flows. Hence another way to reduce this inverse correlation between saving and investment ratios in the future would be to ensure that domestically financed investment was offered exactly the same terms and conditions, particularly with respect to ownership restrictions, that are offered to foreign direct investment.

NOTES

1. For consistency with the definition used by the government of Malaysia, the national saving ratio is defined here as domestic investment plus exports of goods and services plus net factor income from abroad minus imports of goods and services plus net transfers from abroad

divided by GNP. The domestic investment ratio is defined as domestic fixed investment plus the change in stocks divided by GNP.

2. The foreign direct investment data correspond to those reported in *International Financial Statistics*. As shown by Thomas Parry (1988, Table 4.1, p. 96), IMF and OECD sources provide wildly different figures.
3. An exporter submits an invoice for a smaller sum than that actually received for the exports when surrendering foreign exchange to the central bank; the difference can then be deposited in the exporter's bank account abroad. Conversely, an importer submits an invoice for an amount exceeding the true cost of the imports in order to siphon the difference into his foreign bank account.
4. The Malaysians refer to the indigenous or Malay population as the Bumiputera community; the non-indigenous population consists, in the main, of Chinese and Indians.
5. The World Bank (1991, p. 138) also notes that there has been discrimination against minority businesses in Malaysia.
6. The current account imbalance simulated indirectly from these simulated saving and investment functions is very similar to the direct simulation shown in Figure 11.2. The correlation coefficient of a regression of the direct simulation on this indirect simulation for the period 1971–91 is 0.806.

REFERENCES

Bayoumi, Tamim (1990), 'Saving–investment correlations: immobile capital, government policy, or endogenous behavior?', *International Monetary Fund Staff Papers,* **37**, (2), June, 360–87.

Blejer, Mario I. and Mohsin S. Khan (1984), 'Government policy and private investment in developing countries', *International Monetary Fund Staff Papers,* **31**, (2), June, 379–403.

Claassen, Emil-Maria (1992), *Financial Liberalization and Its Impact on Domestic Stabilization Policies: Singapore and Malaysia,* Singapore: Institute of Southeast Asian Studies.

Dooley, Michael P., Jeffrey A. Frankel and Donald J. Mathieson (1987), 'International capital mobility: what do saving–investment correlations tell us?', *International Monetary Fund Staff Papers*, **34**, (3), September, 503–30.

Dornbusch, Rudiger (1991), 'National saving and international investment: comment', in B. Douglas Bernheim and John B. Shoven (eds), *National Saving and Economic Performance*, Chicago: University of Chicago Press for the National Bureau of Economic Research, 221–6.

Feldstein, Martin and Charles Horioka (1980), 'Domestic saving and international capital flows', *Economic Journal*, **90**, (358), June, 311–29.

Feldstein, Martin and Philippe Bacchetta (1991), 'National saving and international investment' in B. Douglas Bernheim and John B. Shoven (eds), *National Saving and Economic Performance*, Chicago: University of Chicago Press for the National Bureau of Economic Research, 201–20.

Frankel, Jeffrey A. (1991), 'Quantifying international capital mobility in the 1980s', in B. Douglas Bernheim and John B. Shoven (eds), *National Saving and Economic Performance*, Chicago: University of Chicago Press for the National Bureau of Economic Research, 227–68.

Fry, Maxwell J. (1988), *Money, Interest, and Banking in Economic Development,* Baltimore: Johns Hopkins University Press.

Fry, Maxwell J. and Andrew Mason (1982), 'The variable rate-of-growth effect in the life cycle saving model: children, capital inflows, interest and growth in a new specification of the life-cycle model applied to seven Asian developing countries', *Economic Inquiry*, **20**, (3), July, 426–42.

Hausman, Jerry A. (1978), 'Specification tests in econometrics', *Econometrica,* **46**, (6), November, 1251–71.

Hill, Hal (1990), 'Foreign investment and East Asian economic development', *Asian–Pacific Economic Literature*, **4**, (2), September, 21–58.

Kharas, Homi J. (1989), 'Malaysian saving in the 1990s: problems and prospects', Kuala Lumpur: Persatuan Ekonomi Malaysia Tenth Economic Convention, 7–9 August.

Metzler, Lloyd A. (1968), 'The process of international adjustment under conditions of full employment: a Keynesian view', in Richard E. Caves and Harry G. Johnson (eds), *Readings in International Economics*, Homewood, Ill.: Richard D. Irwin for the American Economic Association, 465–86.

Parry, Thomas G. (1988), 'The role of foreign capital in East Asian industrialization, growth and development', in Helen Hughes (ed.), *Achieving Industrialization in East Asia*, Cambridge: Cambridge University Press, 95–128.

Persson, Torsten and Lars E.O. Svensson (1985), 'Current account dynamics and the terms of trade: Harberger–Laursen–Metzler two generations later', *Journal of Political Economy*, **93**, (1), February, 43–65.

World Bank (1991), *World Development Report 1991,* New York: Oxford University Press for the World Bank.

Index